First World War
and Army of Occupation
War Diary
France, Belgium and Germany

2 DIVISION
99 Infantry Brigade
Princess Charlotte of Wales's (Royal Berkshire Regiment)
1st Battalion
11 February 1915 - 31 December 1918

WO95/1371/1

The Naval & Military Press Ltd
www.nmarchive.com
Published in association with The National Archives

Published by

The Naval & Military Press Ltd

Unit 10 Ridgewood Industrial Park,

Uckfield, East Sussex,

TN22 5QE England

Tel: +44 (0) 1825 749494

www.naval-military-press.com

www.nmarchive.com

This diary has been reprinted in facsimile from the original. Any imperfections are inevitably reproduced and the quality may fall short of modern type and cartographic standards.

Contents

Document type	Place/Title	Date From	Date To
Heading	99 Infantry Brigade. 1 Battalion Royal Berkshire Regiment. 1916 Jan To 1919 Apr. 1bn Kings Royal Rifle Corps 1915 Dec To 1919 Apr.		
Heading	99 Infantry Brigade. 1 Battalion Royal Berkshire Regiment. 1916 Jan To 1919 Apr. 1 Bn Kings Royal Rifle Corps. 1915 Dec To 1919 Apr.		
Heading	WO95/1371/1		
Heading	2nd Division 99 Brigade 1st Battn. Royal Berkshire Reg. January To December 1916		
Heading	99th Brigade. 2nd Division. 1st Battalion Royal Berkshire Regiment January 1916		
War Diary	Bellerive	01/01/1916	15/01/1916
War Diary	Hingille	16/01/1916	16/01/1916
War Diary	Hrineetie-Letouret	17/01/1916	17/01/1916
War Diary	Le Touret and C2 Subsection	18/01/1916	18/01/1916
War Diary	C 2 Subsection	18/01/1916	18/01/1916
War Diary	C 2	18/01/1916	22/01/1916
War Diary	Le Touret	23/01/1916	26/01/1916
War Diary	Bellerive	27/01/1916	30/01/1916
War Diary	Essars	31/01/1916	31/01/1916
Heading	99th Brigade. 2nd Division. 1st Battalion Royal Berkshire Regiment February 1916:		
War Diary	Essars	01/02/1916	02/02/1916
War Diary	Givenchy B2 Sub Sec.	03/02/1916	06/02/1916
War Diary	Lequesnoy	07/02/1916	10/02/1916
War Diary	Lequesnoy and B3	11/02/1915	11/02/1915
War Diary	B3	12/02/1915	15/02/1915
War Diary	Village Line	16/02/1916	17/02/1916
War Diary	Hingette	18/02/1916	18/02/1916
War Diary	Hingette-Bourecq (Hazebrouck Sheet)	19/02/1916	20/02/1916
War Diary	Bourecq	21/02/1916	26/02/1916
War Diary	Barlin	26/02/1916	27/02/1916
War Diary	Pt Sains	28/02/1916	28/02/1916
War Diary	Pt Sains-Souchez Right	29/02/1916	29/02/1916
Heading	99th Brigade 2nd Division. 1st Battalion Royal Berkshire Regiment March 1916		
War Diary	Souchez Right	01/03/1916	04/03/1916
War Diary	Souchez Right and Bois de Noulettc	05/03/1916	05/03/1916
War Diary	Bois de Noulette	06/03/1916	08/03/1916
War Diary	Souchez Right	09/03/1916	13/03/1916
War Diary	Bouvigny	14/03/1916	17/03/1916
War Diary	Bouvigny & Souchez Right	17/03/1916	17/03/1916
War Diary	Souchez Right	18/03/1916	21/03/1916
War Diary	Hersin	22/03/1916	28/03/1916
War Diary	Divion	29/03/1916	31/03/1916
Heading	99th Brigade. 2nd Division. 1st Battalion Royal Berkshire Regiment April 1916		
War Diary	Divion	01/04/1916	08/04/1916
War Diary	Divion-Bomy	09/04/1916	11/04/1916
War Diary	Bomy	11/04/1916	12/04/1916

War Diary	Bomy-Divion	13/04/1916	13/04/1916
War Diary	Divion	14/04/1916	16/04/1916
War Diary	Divion Bouvigny	17/04/1916	17/04/1916
War Diary	Bouvigny	18/04/1916	20/04/1916
War Diary	Souchezi	21/04/1916	25/04/1916
War Diary	Bois De Noulette	26/04/1916	28/04/1916
War Diary	Souchezi	29/04/1916	30/04/1916
Heading	99th Brigade. 2nd Division. 1st Battalion Royal Berkshire Regiment May 1916		
War Diary	Souchezi	01/05/1916	03/05/1916
War Diary	Bouvigny	04/05/1916	07/05/1916
War Diary	Souchezi	08/05/1916	10/05/1916
War Diary	Bruay	11/05/1916	11/05/1916
War Diary	Calonne Ricouart	12/05/1916	16/05/1916
War Diary	Divion	17/05/1916	20/05/1916
War Diary	Divion-Hersin	21/05/1916	21/05/1916
War Diary	Hersin-Gouyservins	21/05/1916	22/05/1916
War Diary	Berthonval Sector	23/05/1916	23/05/1916
War Diary	Berthonval	23/05/1916	26/05/1916
War Diary	Camblain L'Abbe	27/05/1916	28/05/1916
War Diary	Berthonval Sector	29/05/1916	30/05/1916
Heading	99th Brigade. 2nd Division. 1st Battalion Royal Berkshire Regiment June 1916		
War Diary	Berthonval Sector	01/06/1916	05/06/1916
War Diary	Gouy Servins	06/06/1916	10/06/1916
War Diary	Carency Sector (Support)	11/06/1916	15/06/1916
War Diary	Carency	16/06/1916	18/06/1916
War Diary	Villers au Bois	19/06/1916	24/06/1916
War Diary	Carency	24/06/1916	27/06/1916
War Diary	Gouy Servins	28/06/1916	30/06/1916
Operation(al) Order(s)	1st Royal Berkshire Regt Order No. 23	24/06/1916	24/06/1916
Miscellaneous	1st Royal Berkshire Regt.	26/06/1916	26/06/1916
Diagram etc	Approx Scale		
Heading	99th Inf. Bde. 2nd Div. War Diary 1st Battn. The Royal Berkshire Regiment July 1916		
War Diary	Gouy Servins	01/07/1916	05/07/1916
War Diary	Cabaret Rouge	06/07/1916	08/07/1916
War Diary	Berthonval North	09/07/1916	13/07/1916
War Diary	Camblain L'Abbe	14/07/1916	15/07/1916
War Diary	Estree Cauchie	15/07/1916	16/07/1916
War Diary	Frevillers	17/07/1916	19/07/1916
War Diary	Frevillers Dieval Morlancourt	20/07/1916	20/07/1916
War Diary	Morlancourt	21/07/1916	22/07/1916
War Diary	Morlancourt-Sandpit Valley	23/07/1916	23/07/1916
War Diary	Sandpit Valley	24/07/1916	24/07/1916
War Diary	Longueval Reference Montauban Trench Map 1/20.000	25/07/1916	25/07/1916
War Diary	Bernafay Wood	26/07/1916	26/07/1916
War Diary	Delville Wood	27/07/1916	28/07/1916
War Diary	Mine Support	29/07/1916	29/07/1916
War Diary	Trench	30/07/1916	30/07/1916
War Diary	Bernafay Wood	31/07/1916	31/07/1916
Heading	99th Brigade 2nd Division 1st Battalion Royal Berkshire Regiment August 1916		
War Diary	Bernafay Wood Mine	01/08/1916	01/08/1916
War Diary	Support Trench	02/08/1916	05/08/1916
War Diary	Mansel Copse	05/08/1916	08/08/1916

War Diary	Sandpit Valley	09/08/1916	11/08/1916
War Diary	Mericourt L'Abbe	12/08/1916	13/08/1916
War Diary	St Sauveur	13/08/1916	15/08/1916
War Diary	Naours	16/08/1916	16/08/1916
War Diary	Autheux	17/08/1916	17/08/1916
War Diary	Authie	18/08/1916	19/08/1916
War Diary	Busles Artois	20/08/1916	20/08/1916
War Diary	Couin	21/08/1916	24/08/1916
War Diary	Hebuterne Sector	25/08/1916	27/08/1916
War Diary	Hebuterne	28/08/1916	28/08/1916
War Diary	J. 23 A. 7.6	29/08/1916	31/08/1916
Heading	99th Brigade. 2nd Division. 1st Battalion Royal Berkshire Regiment September 1916		
Miscellaneous	To HQ 99th Bde	02/10/1916	02/10/1916
War Diary	J. 23 A.7.6	01/09/1916	03/09/1916
War Diary	Hebuterne	04/09/1916	06/09/1916
War Diary	Hebuterne North	08/09/1916	09/09/1916
War Diary	Couin	10/09/1916	15/09/1916
War Diary	Hebuterne North	16/09/1916	19/09/1916
War Diary	Couin	20/09/1916	29/09/1916
War Diary	Serre	30/09/1916	30/09/1916
Heading	99th Brigade. 2nd Division. 1st Battalion Royal Berkshire Regiment October 1916		
War Diary	Serre Sector	01/10/1916	06/10/1916
War Diary	Mailly-Maillet	07/10/1916	07/10/1916
War Diary	Arqueues	08/10/1916	16/10/1916
War Diary	Maillymaillet Wood East	17/10/1916	19/10/1916
War Diary	Serre Section	20/10/1916	21/10/1916
War Diary	Serre Bertrancourt	22/10/1916	22/10/1916
War Diary	Bertrancourt	23/10/1916	29/10/1916
War Diary	Mailly Maillet	30/10/1916	31/10/1916
Heading	99th Brigade. 2nd Division 1st Battalion Royal Berkshire Regiment November 1916		
War Diary	Mailly Maillet	01/11/1916	01/11/1916
War Diary	Serre	02/11/1916	04/11/1916
War Diary	Mailly-Maillet	05/11/1916	06/11/1916
War Diary	Arqueves	07/11/1916	10/11/1916
War Diary	Bertrancourt	11/11/1916	11/11/1916
War Diary	Serre	12/11/1916	16/11/1916
War Diary	Serre in Captured Enemy Pesehin	16/11/1916	17/11/1916
War Diary	Mailly-Maillet	17/11/1916	17/11/1916
War Diary	Terramesnils	18/11/1916	20/11/1916
War Diary	Gezaincourt	20/11/1916	20/11/1916
War Diary	Fienvillers	21/11/1916	22/11/1916
War Diary	Domquer	23/11/1916	24/11/1916
War Diary	Le Plessiel	25/11/1916	26/11/1916
War Diary	Colilonvillers	27/11/1916	29/11/1916
War Diary	Conteville & Bernatre	30/11/1916	30/11/1916
Heading	99th Brigade. 2nd Division. 1st Battalion Royal Berkshire Regiment December 1916		
War Diary	Conteville & Bernatre	01/12/1916	16/12/1916
War Diary	Oneux	17/12/1916	02/01/1917
Heading	2nd Division 99th Infy Bde 1st Battalion Royal Berkshire Regt. Jan-Dec 1917		
Heading	99th Brigade/2nd Division. 1st Battalion Royal Berkshire Regiment January 1917		

War Diary	Oneux	01/01/1917	09/01/1917
War Diary	Fienvillers	10/01/1917	11/01/1917
War Diary	Sarton	12/01/1917	12/01/1917
War Diary	Raincheval	13/01/1917	13/01/1917
War Diary	Bouzincourt	14/01/1917	20/01/1917
War Diary	Ovillers	21/01/1917	31/01/1917
Heading	99th Brigade/2nd Division. 1st Battalion Royal Berkshire Regiment February 1917		
War Diary	Coorcelette	01/02/1917	05/02/1917
War Diary	Aveluy	06/02/1917	14/02/1917
War Diary	Ovillers Huts	15/02/1917	15/02/1917
War Diary	Courcelette	16/02/1917	18/02/1917
War Diary	Bruce Huts Aveluy	19/02/1917	19/02/1917
Miscellaneous	5th Infantry Brigade	07/02/1917	07/02/1917
War Diary	Bruce Huts Aveluy	20/02/1917	24/02/1917
War Diary	Ovillers Huts	25/02/1917	27/02/1917
War Diary	Pozieres Camp	28/02/1917	28/02/1917
Miscellaneous	Artillery Programme For Raid. On 4th/5th February.		
Miscellaneous	Stretcher Bearers. Appendix II		
Operation(al) Order(s)	1st. Royal Berks. Order No. 52		
Miscellaneous	Report On Raid On Enemy Salient In ?. 13. By 1/R. Berks Regt. 99th Infantry Brigade At 3 A.M. On 5th February 1917		
Map	Trench Map		
Heading	99th Brigade/2nd Division. 1st Battalion Royal Berkshire Regiment March 1917		
War Diary	Pozieres Camp	01/03/1917	03/03/1917
War Diary	Front Line B HQ. Aque Duct Rd N Pys	04/03/1917	05/03/1917
War Diary	O.B.L Nr Pys	06/03/1917	09/03/1917
War Diary	Front Line Nr Irles	10/03/1917	11/03/1917
War Diary	Albert	12/03/1917	15/03/1917
War Diary	Ovillers Huts	16/03/1917	19/03/1917
War Diary	Albert	20/03/1917	25/03/1917
War Diary	Harponville	26/03/1917	26/03/1917
War Diary	Amplier	27/03/1917	27/03/1917
War Diary	Bonnieres	28/03/1917	30/03/1917
War Diary	Tangry	31/03/1917	31/03/1917
Heading	99th Brigade/2nd Division. 1st Battalion Royal Berkshire Regiment April 1917		
War Diary	Tangry	01/04/1917	07/04/1917
War Diary	Orlencourt	08/04/1917	10/04/1917
War Diary	Etrun Huts	11/04/1917	11/04/1917
War Diary	Roclincourt Trenches	12/04/1917	14/04/1917
War Diary	Bailleul Trenches	15/04/1917	16/04/1917
War Diary	Roclincourt Trenches	17/04/1917	18/04/1917
War Diary	Maroeuil Huts	19/04/1917	23/04/1917
War Diary	Roclincourt	24/04/1917	24/04/1917
War Diary	Front Line Bailleul	25/04/1917	26/04/1917
War Diary	Roclincourt Trenches	27/04/1917	28/04/1917
War Diary	Front Line E of Bailleul	29/04/1917	29/04/1917
War Diary	Roclincourt Trenches	30/04/1917	30/04/1917
Heading	99th Brigade/2nd Division. 1st Battalion Royal Berkshire Regiment May 1917		
War Diary	Roclincourt Trenches	01/05/1917	01/05/1917
War Diary	Ecurie	02/05/1917	03/05/1917
War Diary	Ecoivres	04/05/1917	06/05/1917

War Diary	La Comte	07/05/1917	10/05/1917
War Diary	Bray	11/05/1917	11/05/1917
War Diary	St Nicholas	12/05/1917	23/05/1917
War Diary	Reserve Trenches Behind Arleux	24/05/1917	29/05/1917
War Diary	St Aubin	30/05/1917	31/05/1917
Miscellaneous			
Miscellaneous	Attached To War Diary Sheet No. 312		
Heading	99th Brigade/2nd Division. 1st Battalion Royal Berkshire Regiment June 1917		
War Diary	Close Support Trenches Arleux Oppy	01/06/1917	04/06/1917
War Diary	Front Line Between Arleux and Oppy	05/06/1917	08/06/1917
War Diary	Reserve Line In Front of Roclincourt	09/06/1917	11/06/1917
War Diary	St. Aubin	12/06/1917	13/06/1917
War Diary	Leeds Camp	14/06/1917	19/06/1917
War Diary	A C Q	20/06/1917	20/06/1917
War Diary	Bethune	21/06/1917	21/06/1917
War Diary	Noyelles	22/06/1917	27/06/1917
War Diary	Front Line Cambrin Right	28/06/1917	30/06/1917
Heading	99th Brigade/2nd Division. 1st Battalion Royal Berkshire Regiment July 1917		
War Diary	Front Line Trenches Cambrin Right	01/07/1917	03/07/1917
War Diary	Annequin	04/07/1917	09/07/1917
War Diary	Front Line Trenches Canbin Right	10/07/1917	16/07/1917
War Diary	Annequin	16/07/1917	21/07/1917
War Diary	Front Line Trenches Cambrin Right	22/07/1917	27/07/1917
War Diary	Annequin	28/07/1917	31/07/1917
Heading	99th Brigade/2nd Division.1st Battalion Royal Berkshire Regiment August 1917		
War Diary	Annequin	01/08/1917	02/08/1917
War Diary	Front Line Trenches Cambrin Right	03/08/1917	08/08/1917
War Diary	Reserve Billets Annequin	09/08/1917	14/08/1917
War Diary	Front Line Trenches Cambrin Right	15/08/1917	20/08/1917
War Diary	Support Annequin	21/08/1917	26/08/1917
War Diary	Billets Beuvry	27/08/1917	31/08/1917
War Diary		21/06/1917	31/08/1917
Map	Reference Sheets Square		
Heading	99 Brigade/2nd Division. 1st Battalion Royal Berkshire Regiment September 1917		
War Diary	Billets Beuvry	01/09/1917	07/09/1917
War Diary	Front Line Givenchy Right	07/09/1917	13/09/1917
War Diary	Givenchy Right	13/09/1917	13/09/1917
War Diary	Billets Gorre Chateau	14/09/1917	18/09/1917
War Diary	Billets Beuvry	19/09/1917	20/09/1917
War Diary	Front Line Cambrin Right	21/09/1917	26/09/1917
War Diary	Support Annequin	26/09/1917	30/09/1917
Heading	99th Brigade/2nd Division. 1st Battalion Royal Berkshire Regiment October 1917		
War Diary	Cambrin Right (Support)	01/10/1917	02/10/1917
War Diary	Front Line Cambrin Right	03/10/1917	05/10/1917
War Diary	Bethune	06/10/1917	06/10/1917
War Diary	Billets Auchel	07/10/1917	31/10/1917
Heading	99th Brigade/2nd Division. 1st Battalion Royal Berkshire Regiment November 1917		
War Diary	Billets Auchel	01/11/1917	04/11/1917
War Diary	Robecq	05/11/1917	05/11/1917
War Diary	Neuf Berquin	06/11/1917	06/11/1917

War Diary	Eecke	07/11/1917	07/11/1917
War Diary	Herzeele	08/11/1917	08/11/1917
War Diary	Billets Herzeele	09/11/1917	24/11/1917
War Diary	Barastre & Beaumetz Les Cambrai	25/11/1917	25/11/1917
War Diary	Beumetz Les Cambrai	26/11/1917	26/11/1917
War Diary	Support Line W of Bourlon Wood	27/11/1917	28/11/1917
War Diary	Front Line W of Bourlon Wood	29/11/1917	30/11/1917
Heading	99th Brigade/2nd Division. 1st Battalion Royal Berkshire Regiment December 1917		
War Diary	Front Line Near Bourlon	01/12/1917	05/12/1917
War Diary	Billets Hermies	05/12/1917	11/12/1917
War Diary	Front Line Trenches Canal	12/12/1917	13/12/1917
War Diary	Front Line Canal	13/12/1917	13/12/1917
War Diary	Reserve Hermies	14/12/1917	17/12/1917
War Diary	Front Line Canal	17/12/1917	20/12/1917
War Diary	O'Shea Camp Lebucquiere	21/12/1917	24/12/1917
Miscellaneous	99 Infantry Brigade		
War Diary	O'Shea Camp Lebucquiere	24/12/1917	26/12/1917
War Diary	Support Line Canal	27/12/1917	29/12/1917
War Diary	Support Line Canal & Front Line	30/12/1917	31/12/1917
War Diary	Front Line Canal	31/12/1917	31/12/1917
Heading	2nd Division 99th Infantry Bde. War Diaries 1st Royal Bends January To December 1918		
War Diary	Front Line Canal Du Nord	01/01/1918	03/01/1918
War Diary	Billets Barastre	04/01/1918	23/01/1918
War Diary	Billets Metz-En-Couture	24/01/1918	25/01/1918
War Diary	Front Line Lavacquerie Right	26/01/1918	31/01/1918
War Diary	Support Villers Plouich	01/02/1918	01/02/1918
War Diary	Front Line-La Vacquerie	02/02/1918	03/02/1918
War Diary	Billets Manancourt	04/02/1918	09/02/1918
War Diary	Brigade Reserve Havrincourt Wood And Villers Plouich	10/02/1918	12/02/1918
War Diary	Brigade Reserve	13/02/1918	15/02/1918
War Diary	Front Line	15/02/1918	22/02/1918
War Diary	Divnl Reserve Metz	22/02/1918	22/02/1918
War Diary	Metz	23/02/1918	28/02/1918
Heading	99th Brigade. 2nd Division. 1st Battalion Royal Berkshire Regiment March 1918		
War Diary	Brigade Support Villers Plouich	01/03/1918	05/03/1918
War Diary	Front Line-La Vacquerie Right	06/03/1918	12/03/1918
War Diary	Divisional Reserve Metz	13/03/1918	18/03/1918
War Diary	In Support Highland Line	19/03/1918	19/03/1918
War Diary	Corps Reserve Manancourt	20/03/1918	23/03/1918
War Diary	In Constant Movement	23/03/1918	26/03/1918
War Diary	Mailly-Maillet & Forceville	27/03/1918	27/03/1918
War Diary	Forceville	27/03/1918	28/03/1918
War Diary	Lealvillers	29/03/1918	31/03/1918
Miscellaneous	1st Battn Royal Berkshire Regt. Report On Operation From 21-31/3/18		
War Diary	Front Line (Left) Boiry St Martin	01/05/1918	05/05/1918
War Diary	Brigade Reserve Purple Line	06/05/1918	08/05/1918
War Diary	Front Line (Right) Boiry-St-Martin	09/05/1918	12/05/1918
War Diary	Laherliere Corps Reserve	13/05/1918	31/05/1918
War Diary	Synopis	13/05/1918	31/05/1918
War Diary	Laherliere Corps Reserve	31/05/1918	31/05/1918
War Diary	Laherliere	01/06/1918	01/06/1918

War Diary	La Bazeque	02/06/1918	08/06/1918
War Diary	In The Line	08/06/1918	30/06/1918
War Diary	Brigade Reserve Near Monchy	01/07/1918	05/07/1918
War Diary	In The Line Left Sector Near Douchy	06/07/1918	15/07/1918
War Diary	Brigade Reserve Near Monchy	16/07/1918	19/07/1918
War Diary	Front Line	20/07/1918	20/07/1918
War Diary	Right Sub Sector	21/07/1918	30/07/1918
War Diary	Brigade Reserve Near Monchy	31/07/1918	31/07/1918
War Diary	Monchy	01/08/1918	04/08/1918
War Diary	Front Line and Ayette	05/08/1918	12/08/1918
War Diary	Support Position Behind Douchy	13/08/1918	16/08/1918
War Diary	St Amand	17/08/1918	20/08/1918
War Diary	Near Ayette	21/08/1918	21/08/1918
War Diary	Quesnoy Farm	22/08/1918	23/08/1918
War Diary	Ervillers	24/08/1918	24/08/1918
War Diary	Near Ayette	25/08/1918	25/08/1918
War Diary	Calverley Copse Near Ayette	26/08/1918	02/09/1918
War Diary	Near Mory	03/09/1918	03/09/1918
War Diary	Near Lagnicourt	04/09/1918	04/09/1918
War Diary	In The Line Demcourt Hermies	05/09/1918	08/09/1918
War Diary	Near Beaumetz	09/09/1918	15/09/1918
War Diary	Reserve Mory	16/09/1918	16/09/1918
War Diary	Reserve Near Mory	17/09/1918	27/09/1918
War Diary	Beaumetz	27/09/1918	27/09/1918
War Diary	Trenches in J10 C & D	27/09/1918	27/09/1918
War Diary	W of Canal Du Nord in Trenches in K 8 C	27/09/1918	27/09/1918
War Diary	E of Canal in K Q G	27/09/1918	27/09/1918
War Diary	Trenches in K 17 B & D	27/09/1918	28/09/1918
War Diary	Noyelles	28/09/1918	29/09/1918
War Diary	Marcoing Support East of Canal De St Quentin	29/09/1918	30/09/1918
War Diary	Positions East of Canal De St Quentin	30/09/1918	30/09/1918
Miscellaneous	War Diary		
Miscellaneous	To Headquarters 99th Inf. Bde.	15/09/1918	15/09/1918
Miscellaneous	A Form Messages And Signals		
Heading	99th Brigade 2nd Division. 1st Battalion Royal Berkshire Regiment April 1918		
War Diary	Engelbelmer & Hedauville	01/04/1918	02/04/1918
War Diary	Marderoute To Beauval	02/04/1918	03/04/1918
War Diary	Beauval To Houvin Houvigneul	03/04/1918	03/04/1918
War Diary	Houvin Houvigneul	03/04/1918	08/04/1918
War Diary	Ivergny	09/04/1918	10/04/1918
War Diary	Ivergny To Sombrin	11/04/1918	12/04/1918
War Diary	Laherliere	12/04/1918	14/04/1918
War Diary	Front Line Boiry-St Martin	15/04/1918	18/04/1918
War Diary	To Reserve Blaireville	18/04/1918	20/04/1918
War Diary	Front Line (Right) Boiry-St-Martin	21/04/1918	26/04/1918
War Diary	Brigade Reserve Purple Line	26/04/1918	29/04/1918
War Diary	Front Line (Left) Boiry-St-Martin	29/04/1918	30/04/1918
Miscellaneous	1st Bn Royal Berkshire Regt. Narration of Events 1/9/18., To 9/9/18	03/09/1918	03/09/1918
War Diary	W of Nine Wood	01/10/1918	07/10/1918
War Diary	Near Rumilly	08/10/1918	09/10/1918
War Diary	Flesquieres	09/10/1918	12/10/1918
War Diary	Wambaix	13/10/1918	19/10/1918
War Diary	Wambaix Carnieres	20/10/1918	21/10/1918
War Diary	Carnieres St. Hilaire	22/10/1918	22/10/1918

War Diary	Factori St. Hilaire	23/10/1918	23/10/1918
War Diary	St. Python	23/10/1918	23/10/1918
War Diary	Near Bermerain	24/10/1918	24/10/1918
War Diary	Near Ruesnes	24/10/1918	26/10/1918
War Diary	Bermerain	26/10/1918	27/10/1918
War Diary	Solesmes	28/10/1918	29/10/1918
War Diary	Escarmain	30/10/1918	31/10/1918
Miscellaneous	Sheet No 463		
War Diary	Escarmain	01/11/1918	02/11/1918
War Diary	St. Hilaire	03/11/1918	08/11/1918
War Diary	Escarmain	09/11/1918	16/11/1918
War Diary	Villers Pol	17/11/1918	18/11/1918
War Diary	Lalongueville	19/11/1918	20/11/1918
War Diary	Villers-Sire-Nicole	21/11/1918	24/11/1918
War Diary	Binche	25/11/1918	25/11/1918
War Diary	Marchienne au Pont	26/11/1918	28/11/1918
War Diary	Chatelet	29/11/1918	29/11/1918
War Diary	Fosse	30/11/1918	30/11/1918
Miscellaneous	Sheet No 469		
War Diary	Fosse	01/12/1918	03/12/1918
War Diary	Fosse Beez	04/12/1918	04/12/1918
War Diary	Beez Andenne	05/12/1918	05/12/1918
War Diary	Andenne Vierset Barse	06/12/1918	06/12/1918
War Diary	Vierset Barse Comblain La Tour	07/12/1918	07/12/1918
War Diary	Comblain La Tour	08/12/1918	09/12/1918
War Diary	Basse Desnie	09/12/1918	11/12/1918
War Diary	Burnenville	11/12/1918	11/12/1918
War Diary	Lager Elsenborn	12/12/1918	13/12/1918
War Diary	Imgen Broich	14/12/1918	14/12/1918
War Diary	Nideggen	15/12/1918	19/12/1918
War Diary	Arnolds Weiler	20/12/1918	31/12/1918

99 INFANTRY BRIGADE.

1 BATTALION ROYAL BERKSHIRE REGIMENT.
1916 JAN TO 1919 APR.

1 BN KINGS ROYAL RIFLE CORPS
1915 DEC TO 1919 APR.

1371

99 INFANTRY BRIGADE.

1 BATTALION ROYAL BERKSHIRE REGIMENT.
1916 JAN TO 1919 APR.

1 BN KINGS ROYAL RIFLE CORPS.
1915 DEC TO 1919 APR.

2nd Division

99 Brigade

1st Battn Royal Berkshire Reg

JANUARY to December

1916

FROM 6 BDE 2 DIV

99th Brigade.

2nd Division.

1st BATTALION ROYAL BERKSHIRE REGIMENT

JANUARY 1 9 1 6:

Instructions regarding War Diaries and Intelligence Summaries are contained in F. S. Regs., Part II. and the Staff Manual respectively. Title pages will be prepared in manuscript.

Confidential

WAR DIARY
or
~~INTELLIGENCE SUMMARY.~~
(Erase heading not required.)

Army Form C. 2118.

Sheet 216

1st Bn Royal Berkshire Regt

Place	Date	Hour	Summary of Events and Information	Remarks and references to Appendices
BELLERIVE	1.1.16		New Years Day 1st Day of Work according to Divisional programme. Company training including Arm Drill, squad drill, physical training and bayonet fighting. Musketry (Care of arms, firing exercises and rapid loading. Short lectures by Company Commanders. In addition the Brigadier ordered that the march past be practised daily, during the preliminary stages of training. Hours of parade were 8.30–9.30. 9.45–10.45. 11–12.15. 12.15–12.45. as ordered by the Brigade. Owing to the weather and state of the country, the greatest difficulty was experienced in getting ground suitable for training. A & C companies managed to get [illegible] but B & D were forced, so far as parts of the companies were concerned, to do most of their work on the road.	[illegible] 2/Lt Pugh rejoined from [illegible]
"	2.1.16		Programme of Work in accordance with Divisional Programme 2nd Day, which was the same as the 2nd Day. Captain Dennis rejoined from attachment to 2nd Div Staff. He had commenced his attachment 26.12.15.	[illegible]
	3.1.16		Same as preceding days except Platoon Drill was substituted for Squad Drill. A Draft of 86 N.C.O's and men arrived about 7 p.m. The men were all of good physique, ~~and~~ were well equipped and of an average age of 25. Captain Gregson Ellis proceeded to 2nd Div for attachment to [illegible] Div Hqrs.	[illegible]

2353 Wt. W2514/1454 700,000 5/15 D. D. & L. A.D.S.S./Forms/C. 2118.

Instructions regarding War Diaries and Intelligence Summaries are contained in F. S. Regs., Part II. and the Staff Manual respectively. Title pages will be prepared in manuscript.

WAR DIARY
or
~~INTELLIGENCE SUMMARY.~~

(Erase heading not required.)

Army Form C. 2118.

Confidential

Sht 1217

Place	Date	Hour	Summary of Events and Information	Remarks and references to Appendices
BELLERIVE	4.1.6		Programme as per Divisional Programme 6th Day which was the same as the three preceding days except "Company Drill" instead of Platoon Drill. It was again impossible to carry this out owing to the state of the country. Weather still very bad continual rain. 2nd Lieuts Dodd & Dobson and 32 other ranks proceeded to join 8th Brigade Machine Gun Coy and were struck off the strength.	Jcr[illegible]
	5.1.6		Programme of work 7th Day of Divisional Programme is Company training framed on offensive lines. The usual difficulty of ground prevented this being carried out with any success, and companies were confined to doing the greater part of their work by platoons. Protection and Outposts were the chief subjects of instruction. Weather still bad. The 1st hour of work 8.30 - 9.30 was devoted to Physical Exercises.	Jcr[illegible]
	6.1.6		Programme same as previous day. Except Commanding Officer's lecture to the Officers from 9.15 to 9.45 on work to be done. Weather bad but not so much rain.	Jcr[illegible]
	7.1.6		Programme same as previous days commencing with Physical Training. High Wind blowing.	Jcr[illegible]
	8.1.6		This was to be allotted for Battalion training but any attempt to carry this out was impossible. Lt Izard proceeded to the Divisional Bomb School at FOUQUEREIL on a course of instruction relieving Lt [illegible] who returned the day	

Army Form C. 2118.

WAR DIARY
or
INTELLIGENCE SUMMARY.

(*Erase heading not required.*)

Instructions regarding War Diaries and Intelligence Summaries are contained in F. S. Regs., Part II. and the Staff Manual respectively. Title pages will be prepared in manuscript.

Confidential

Sheet 218

Place	Date	Hour	Summary of Events and Information	Remarks and references to Appendices
	8.1.16		Programme of Work was issued to Coys. This included simple outposts schemes and the training of Section & Platoon Leaders. Great stress was laid by the Division and Brigade on the training of men to work with their tube helmets on, we had about 80 issued for instructional purposes, these were allotted to different Coys each day, the Medical Officer attending each parade. The helmets were kept on for about half an hour at a time, and the men were exercised in doubling and marching. It was found that with practice the inconvenience of wearing these helmets was lessened considerably. A Class for Instruction in the LEWIS Gun which had formed on the 1st of January was dispersed and fresh one formed as the Commanding Officer considered it advisable to have as large number of men as possible trained in the use of the Gun. Lieut Jenwood the late Machine Gun Officer was in charge of this class.	[illegible]

Instructions regarding War Diaries and Intelligence Summaries are contained in F. S. Regs., Part II. and the Staff Manual respectively. Title pages will be prepared in manuscript.

WAR DIARY
or
~~INTELLIGENCE SUMMARY.~~

(Erase heading not required.)

Army Form C. 2118.

Confidential

Sheet 2 19

Place	Date	Hour	Summary of Events and Information	Remarks and references to Appendices
9.1.16 BELLERIVE	9.1.16		Sunday. The battalion with the Drums went to Church at CONNEHEM. Parading at 10.30 in time for 11am Service. The Drums had just started organizing properly, we had applied for Sgt [illegible] to come out from the 3rd Battalion and he had arrived with the last reinforcement. Up to this time we had only had scratch bands made up from men employed all over the Battalion but the Commanding Officer agreed to have these men selected & struck off all other duties. Weather windy but not much rain.	[initials]
	10.1.16		This day ~~was~~ and every other day have been devoted to battalion training until the end of Divisional Rest Period. ~~[illegible]~~ But the programme carried out was the same as the days before with special stress on the training of Platoon and Section leaders. Weather better.	2/Lt Strong to Officers School BETHUNE [initials]
	11.1.16		The Battalion paraded for inspection by Coys in full marching order. Owing the absence of Col May at a lecture the inspection was conducted by Captain Sharpe. After A Coy's inspection was over the G.O.C 99th Brigade arrived and inspected C D & B in turn. He ~~was~~ expressed himself in turn extremely gratified at their turn out and spoke most highly of the battalion saying he	

2353 Wt. W2544/1454 700,000 5/15 D. D. & L. A.D.S.S./Forms/C. 2118.

Army Form C. 2118.

WAR DIARY
or
INTELLIGENCE SUMMARY.
(Erase heading not required.)

Instructions regarding War Diaries and Intelligence Summaries are contained in F. S. Regs., Part II. and the Staff Manual respectively. Title pages will be prepared in manuscript.

Confidential

Sheet 220

Place	Date	Hour	Summary of Events and Information	Remarks and references to Appendices
BELLERIVE	11/1/16		he considered it an honour to have such a fine Battalion in his Brigade. The interval between inspections were taken up by Coy and Platoon training	[illegible]
	12/1/16		Brigade Route March. Battalion paraded at 9.10 and passed brigade starting point at 9.43, three minutes late. We were the leading battalion, the only unit in front of us being the Brigade Headquarters. The route lay through the outskirts of BETHUNE along the RUE D'AIRE to CHOCQUES and GONNEHEM where units dispersed to their billeting areas. The Brigadier complimented the Commanding Officer on our turn out. The following units took part in the march in the following order: 1 KRRC (advanced guard) 1st R Berks 22nd Royal Fusiliers 23rd Royal Fusiliers 162 Bde RFA. 5th Field Coy R.E. 15 T.M.B. 2/3 T.M.B. D/167 Bde. RFA (Hows) 34 [illegible] BAC. 6th Field Ambulance. The battalion arrived back at BELLERIVE at 12.35. Captain Shipp and [illegible] attended a lecture on Co-operation between Artillery and Infantry at AIRE, to officers (CO's, 2nd in Commands, + Coy Commanders) of the Division. ~~The~~ The afternoon was devoted to football refl competitions. Cases of bad feet however and in fact any kind of sickness were very few during this rest period. The general condition and health of the men was very good.	[illegible]

2353 Wt. W2544/1454 700,000 5/15 D. D. & L. A.D.S.S./Forms/C. 2118.

Instructions regarding War Diaries and Intelligence Summaries are contained in F. S. Regs., Part II. and the Staff Manual respectively. Title pages will be prepared in manuscript.

Confidential

WAR DIARY
or
~~INTELLIGENCE SUMMARY.~~

(*Erase heading not required.*)

Army Form C. 2118.

Sheet #21

Place	Date	Hour	Summary of Events and Information	Remarks and references to Appendices
[illegible]	13.1.16		Coys paraded for Physical Training from 8.30 – 9.30. 10 – 12.45 was taken up with Coy and Platoon training on offensive lines. Also the latest reinforcements received special instruction in Trench Warfare i.e. Gas attacks, Tube Helmets, Digging, Trenching, building of parapets, signals for gas and Trench Motor [illegible]. Weather very cold but dry.	[illegible] M.C. by the King [illegible] [illegible]
	14.1.16		Baths at [illegible] allotted to the Battalion. C + D bathed at 10.15 & 11.30. A + B at 2 + 3.15. In the morning the Medical Officer inspected the Tube Helmets. Intervals between bathing and inspections were occupied by Coy and Platoon training. 2nd Lieut Legard returned from Divisional Bombing School. Weather cold but fine.	[illegible]
	15.1.16		Physical Training 8.30 – 9.30. Lecture to Officers and N.C.O's by C.O. remainder of morning devoted to Company training in the Attack. The ground was very passable owing to the dry weather. Orders received from 95th Bde to move the next day to Hinguette. In the afternoon the M.O. inspected all Coys for Scabies which seems to have become prevalent in certain formations. The few cases, about 4 or 5 were sent to Hospital. [illegible]	[illegible]
Hinguette	16.1.16		The Battalion paraded at 9.10 AM and ~~[illegible]~~ marched to HINGETTE. Arrived HINGETTE 10.45 AM and came under orders of 12th Div. On arrival the Medical Officer held a [illegible] inspection and again cases numbering 4 or 5 were sent to Hospital. This being Sunday no parades were held. [illegible]	[illegible] Honours [illegible] D.S.O. Captain Bond M.C. Captain [illegible] D.C.M. C.S.M. [illegible] L/Cpl Brennan C.S.M. Burley Cpl. Adams Cpl. Bates L/Cpl Best

2353 Wt. W2544/1454 700,000 5/15 D. D. & L. A.D.S.S./Forms/C. 2118.

Instructions regarding War Diaries and Intelligence Summaries are contained in F. S. Regs., Part II. and the Staff Manual respectively. Title pages will be prepared in manuscript.

WAR DIARY
or
~~INTELLIGENCE SUMMARY.~~ Sheet 222

(*Erase heading not required.*)

Confidential

Army Form C. 2118.

Place	Date	Hour	Summary of Events and Information	Remarks and references to Appendices
HINGETTE – LETOURET	17.1.16		The Batn paraded at 10.15 and marched to LE TOURET and took over the billets vacated same morning by 6th Buffs. Arrived LE TOURET 12.15 pm and came under orders of 37th Bde 12th DIV. Weather was dry. The billets were not bad. The Medical Officer again inspected boys for cases of Scabies this time only two men were sent to Hospital. The 6th Queens, the regiment we were to relieve in the trenches next day, sent guides at dusk to conduct the Commanding Officer and the four company commanders to view the line. The[y] returned about 11 p m.	
LE TOURET and C2 Subsection	18.1.16		As the Battalion was going into the trenches the same to night, boys did not do much training during the morning, after 1 hours Physical Training the men were allowed to rest. The first Coy (B) paraded at X24.a.8.6 (Bethune Combined Sheet) at 4.15 where gum boots were issued, they then proceeded to relieve the Reserve Coy of the ~~[illegible]~~ 6th Queens in OLD BRITISH LINE. The remaining coys paraded at the Gum Boot Store at the following hours: D 4.30 pm A 5 pm C 5.30 pm and proceeded independently to the relief of the Coys of the Queens. C Coy occupied RICHMOND TRENCH in Support line. D took over the right front company's line. A the left. The front line trenches in this sector (C2 Subsection) differed considerably from any we had occupied before. The actual front line was an old trench flooded, and dotted about at regular intervals were posts built in the trench each garrisoned	[illegible]

Instructions regarding War Diaries and Intelligence Summaries are contained in F. S. Regs., Part II. and the Staff Manual respectively. Title pages will be prepared in manuscript.

WAR DIARY
or
~~INTELLIGENCE SUMMARY.~~
(Erase heading not required.)

Army Form C. 2118.

Confidential   Sheet 223

Place	Date	Hour	Summary of Events and Information	Remarks and references to Appendices
C? Subsection	18.1.16		by 6 men with an NCO in charge. These posts were known officially as "Islands". The Left Company had twelve of these in their line, the right Coy seven. Immediately in rear (about 50 yards) there was a cover trench ~~also occupied~~, where the ~~remainder~~ surplus men of the bays in the front line took up their positions and where two men from the garrison of each island came back to rest during the day. The wire in front of the islands and cover trench lines was continuous but not nearly thick enough. RICHMOND TRENCH was flooded completely and a track of trench boards had been laid down in rear of the parados, and a few dugouts constructed, or rather shelters, as it was not possible to dig down on account of the water. The support Coy lent a platoon to A Coy (Left Front) for the night, as A Coy was weak and had a longer line than usual to hold. This platoon returned each morning to RICHMOND TRENCH. The OLD BRITISH LINE held by the Reserve Coy (B) had been worked on a lot both by other units and the R.E. It was really a continuous breastwork with traverses built of sandbags and other revetments. The whole country in this sector was very wet. The original trench was used in most cases as a drain and on the whole successfully. Trench boards had been laid down everywhere, so that walking was easy so long as one kept to the track. Communication	

2353 Wt. W2544/1454 700,000 5/15 D. D. & L. A.D.S.S./Forms/C. 2118.

Instructions regarding War Diaries and Intelligence Summaries are contained in F. S. Regs., Part II. and the Staff Manual respectively. Title pages will be prepared in manuscript.

WAR DIARY
or
INTELLIGENCE SUMMARY.
(Erase heading not required.)

Army Form C. 2118.

Confidential Sheet 224

Place	Date	Hour	Summary of Events and Information	Remarks and references to Appendices
C	13.1.16		to the front line was good but very exposed. PIONEER ROAD was used by the Front Line and Support Coy for carrying Stores etc, this was an old communication trench running from the BREWERY on the RUE DE CAILLOUX through the OLD BRITISH LINE to the right of RICHMOND TRENCH, a good wooden floor raised three feet off the original bottom of the trench had been constructed, the sides were also boarded, it was not possible to use this during the day as a man was exposed from the shoulders upwards. We were supported by the Artillery of the 13th Division for this night. Reliefs were carried out quickly and completed by 7 p.m. The Battalion on our left was the 4th Kings Liverpools (Extra Special Reserve). On our right we had the 23rd Royal Fusiliers. Weather dry and fine. Bright Moon nearly full.	
	14.1.16		The enemy were very quiet during the night with the exception of a little high indirect Machine Gun Fire, there was no display at all on the part of the Germans. We had at this time no Machine Guns with the Battalion, and emplacements were held by LEWIS GUNS for which purpose all men trained in this gun had been detached the day before going into the line, and came under the orders of the Brigade Machine Gun Officer. Hostile aircraft were active during the morning	[illegible]

2353 Wt. W2544/1454 700,000 5/15 D. D. & L. A.D.S.S./Forms/C. 2118.

Army Form C. 2118.

Instructions regarding War Diaries and Intelligence Summaries are contained in F. S. Regs., Part II. and the Staff Manual respectively. Title pages will be prepared in manuscript.

WAR DIARY
or
~~INTELLIGENCE SUMMARY.~~ Sheet 225

Confidential (*Erase heading not required.*)

Place	Date	Hour	Summary of Events and Information	Remarks and references to Appendices
C?	19.1.16		between the hours of 10 AM and 12 noon, They did not attempt to cross our lines owing to the fact that our own aircraft were also active. No fights took place. Work was carried on all parts of the line held by the Battn. The right Coy put out about ~~#~~ 450 feet of barbed wire and also strengthened 70 yards of French wire by interspersing with barbed wire. Much work was required, in all the islands and cover trench, on the parapets, these required heightening and thickening everywhere. All work had to be done at night. In Richmond Trench pumping was continued day and night. The pumps in this part of the line were good and worked very well. The Reserve Coy continued the work of building traverses in Old British Line, here it was quite possible to work by day. Weather was cold but fine.	
"	20.1.16		Quiet night. More wire was laid out by the Regt Front Coy (D). Work of on all parapets continued. The Left Coy (A) worked at reclaiming Orchard trench. Pumping and baling operations continued. Reserve Coy continued work on Old British Line. The 2nd Div Artillery (9th 16th and 56th Battys) relieved 12th Division Art in this sector. Between 8 AM and 10 AM the Left Coy was shelled by 4.2 Howitzer. No damage was done. About 7 30 AM two groups of Germans each about 50 strong were observed on a ridge 1700 yards to the front of the centre of our right Coy. The Artillery were warned but could	[illegible]

2353 Wt. W2544/1454 700,000 5/15 D. D. & L. A.D.S.S./Forms/C. 2118.

Instructions regarding War Diaries and Intelligence Summaries are contained in F. S. Regs., Part II. and the Staff Manual respectively. Title pages will be prepared in manuscript.

WAR DIARY
or
INTELLIGENCE SUMMARY. Sheet 226

(Erase heading not required.)

Confidential

Army Form C. 2118.

Place	Date	Hour	Summary of Events and Information	Remarks and references to Appendices
C²	20.1.16		pick up the mark. Wire entanglements were seen where these groups were, it was therefore presumed that they were working on a new defensive line.	
	21.1.16		Quiet night. About 12 noon three enemy shells (4.2 hows) ~~exploded~~ burst on the OLD BRI. LINE on right of RUE DE CAILLOUX, uncomfortably close to a working party of ours, but no casualties occurred. Orchard Trench was again shelled between 10 AM and 12 noon. Opposite our Left bay (A) the Germans displayed two flags (colour etc not ascertained) for what purpose we could not guess. Right bay continued wiring and building parapets. Left bay continued reclaiming Orchard Trench. Seven bodies were found by the Support bay and buried close behind Richmond Trench. A working party of 400 men from 23rd Royal Fusiliers ~~[illegible]~~ 10th was ordered to report to us in two reliefs of 200 each at 8 p.m. and 12 midnight. These parties were specially detailed for work on the Old British Line. ~~[illegible]~~ This made a great difference to the line. About 40 yards of parapet were built up and made bullet proof. ~~[illegible]~~ They also carried on with the building of traverses. The second relief left at 4 AM ~~[illegible]~~	Lieut. Duff & 5 Other ranks arrived from England. All signallers
	22.1.16		A similar working party to the previous day reported at same times and carried on with the work on Old British Line. 100 yards of Parapet was built up and made bullet proof, and several yards of fire step constructed. The Left and Right Front bays carried on with wiring and draining. They reported that parapets were all bullet proof and sufficiently high for protective purposes. During the night enemy snipers were quite active	

2353 Wt. W2544/1454 700,000 5/15 D. D. & L. A.D.S.S./Forms/C. 2118.

Army Form C. 2118.

Instructions regarding War Diaries and Intelligence Summaries are contained in F. S. Regs., Part II. and the Staff Manual respectively. Title pages will be prepared in manuscript.

WAR DIARY
or
~~INTELLIGENCE SUMMARY.~~
(Erase heading not required.)

Confidential Sheet 227

Place	Date	Hour	Summary of Events and Information	Remarks and references to Appendices
C?	22.1.16		About 7.30 AM the parties of Germans similar to those mentioned in this diary on the 20th inst. were again seen in the same place. The Artillery fired but shots dropped short. Our left bay heard the Germans working on their line during the night, also about 9 p.m. on the 21st. Three of the enemy were observed coming towards Island no 30 but on being fired on they at once retired. The Battalion was relieved by the 23rd Royal Fusiliers. Relief completed about 7 p.m. Coys marched independently to billets in LE. TOURET. During the whole of our tour we only sustained one casualty, this was the man mentioned in remarks column (this page). He was shot through the head, but is reported doing well. The man was one of the reinforcements who joined us on the 21st inst.	1 casualty head wound
LE. TOURET	23.1.16		Sunday. Voluntary Church Parade. Baths allotted to the Battalion all day. A & B bathed in the morning C and D in the afternoon. We had to supply fatigue parties for work on OLD BRITISH. LINE, numbering in all 380. These worked in two reliefs and carried on the same work as the 23rd R.F. parties had done when we were in the line. The first relief left at 6.30 p.m., the second at 10.30 p.m. The men of the second party did not arrive back in billets until 4.30 AM on the next morning 24th inst.	[illegible signature]

8353 Wt. W2544/1454 700,000 5/15 D. D. & L. A.D.S.S./Forms/C. 2118.

Instructions regarding War Diaries and Intelligence Summaries are contained in F. S. Regs., Part II. and the Staff Manual respectively. Title pages will be prepared in manuscript.

WAR DIARY
or
~~INTELLIGENCE SUMMARY.~~

Confidential (*Erase heading not required.*) Sheet 228

Army Form C. 2118.

Place	Date	Hour	Summary of Events and Information	Remarks and references to Appendices
?? LE TOURET	24.1.16		Owing to the men being on fatigue all night, no work was done in the morning except an inspection by the M.O. for itch, one case was sent to hospital. The Armourer Sergeant inspected the rifles of A + B Coys. More fatigues asked for, for the night in parties as follows 4 Officers 200 men (divided into two reliefs) for work on OLD. BRITISH. LINE. 2 Officers 100 men for carrying R.E. material. 1 NCO and 25 men also for R.E. fatigues. These were sent, the last returning about 4 AM	
"	25.1.16		The G.O.C. 2nd Division came through our area but although preparations were made for him, he did not go over any of the billets. Orders received to move on the 26th to ~~new~~ our old billets in BELLERIVE. Same fatigues were again asked for, and in addition A Coy was detailed to remain behind on the 28th to carry out fatigues for the R.E. Weather was nice, and in consequence hostile and our own aircraft were very active, over our billets and elsewhere	
"	26.1.16		Brigade left the line to-day & became Divisional Reserve. Batt handed over to 2nd HLI (5th Brigade) Batt paraded at 1 pm & marched into former billets at Bellerive where they arrived at 4.30 pm	

2353 Wt. W2544/1454 700,000 5/15 D. D. & L. A.D.S.S./Forms/C. 2118.

Instructions regarding War Diaries and Intelligence Summaries are contained in F. S. Regs., Part II. and the Staff Manual respectively. Title pages will be prepared in manuscript.

WAR DIARY
or
~~INTELLIGENCE SUMMARY.~~
(Erase heading not required.)

Army Form C. 2118.

Confidential

Sheet 229

Place	Date	Hour	Summary of Events and Information	Remarks and references to Appendices
Bellewarde	Jan 27 1916		The day was spent cleaning up & repairing equipment. Rifles, ammunition, feet etc were inspected by O/C Companies. Weather very mild & fine.	
	28		Coys paraded at 9 am – 10 for physical training; from 10·15 – 11·15 Company & platoon drill; from 11·30 – 12·00 musketry with special regard to recognition of targets. All Coys bathed during the day at [illegible] and smoke helmets were inspected by the M/O. From 5·45 pm the Batt was put on "short notice" to be ready to march immediately.	
	29		From 9 am the Batt was put on 1½ hours notice. Coys at the disposal of Coy Commanders. Weather still mild & fine.	[illegible]
	30		[illegible] proceeded to [illegible] as Assistant Instructor at the Grenade School. Batt vacated billets at 2 pm & marched to [illegible] where they arrived at 4 pm. A voluntary church service was held in the morning.	[illegible]
[illegible]	31		Coys at disposal of O/C Coys for physical training, platoon & company drill & musketry. A & B Coys were [illegible] MONTE & SORBE ROAD respectively. They [illegible] the [illegible] of defence.	[illegible]

2353 Wt. W2544/1454 700,000 5/15 D. D. & L. A.D.S.S./Forms/C. 2118.

99th Brigade.

2nd Division.

1st BATTALION ROYAL BERKSHIRE REGIMENT

FEBRUARY 1 9 1 6:

Army Form C. 2118.

WAR DIARY
or
~~INTELLIGENCE SUMMARY.~~
(Erase heading not required.)

Instructions regarding War Diaries and Intelligence Summaries are contained in F. S. Regs., Part II. and the Staff Manual respectively. Title pages will be prepared in manuscript.

Sheet 229

Place	Date	Hour	Summary of Events and Information	Remarks and references to Appendices
Essars	1.2.16		Coys at disposal of O.C. Coys for physical training, platoon & company drill & musketry. A part of the drill was carried out in smoke helmets. Weather still fine but rather colder. D & C Coys being in the [illegible] relief working at LA MOTTE & GORRE WOOD respectively. They strengthened the auxiliary line of defence.	Jcm
	2.2.16		Programme as for the first except that A & B relieve D & C respectively in the auxiliary line of defence.	Jcm
GIVENCHY B2 Subsec.	3.2.16		The Battalion relieved ~~[illegible] in B2 Subsection~~ the 1st Herts in B2 Subsector. The trenches were in fair condition most of them being boarded. As at FESTUBERT the left of the line ~~was~~ consisted of GROUSE BUTTS. About 10 p.m. it was thought that enemy mining was going on between J and K saps (right front bay). Enemy working parties were heard during the night. Work by all companies consisted of building parados and parapets. Trench mortars and rifle grenades were active against the saps held by the Batt. Bombers in the right bay's (B) line.	Jcm
"	4.2.16		Day was very quiet except for rifle ~~and~~ grenades against our saps. Little or no damage was effected by these. About 11 p.m. 3 patrols were sent out from left of ROSE TRENCH & DEADMANS TRENCH. These patrols reported enemy wire good. They also heard sounds of hammering timbers and metal behind LEFT CRATER. Work done during the day was same as 3rd i.e. rebuilding and building parados and parapets	Jcm

2353 Wt. W2544/1454 700,000 5/15 D. D. & L. A.D.S.S./Forms/C. 2118.

Army Form C. 2118.

WAR DIARY
or
INTELLIGENCE SUMMARY.
(*Erase heading not required.*)

Instructions regarding War Diaries and Intelligence Summaries are contained in F. S. Regs., Part II. and the Staff Manual respectively. Title pages will be prepared in manuscript.

CONFIDENTIAL

Sheet 230

Place	Date	Hour	Summary of Events and Information	Remarks and references to Appendices
(B2) (B2a)	Feb 5th		Conditions much the same as preceding days. enemy grenades again annoyed our saps. About 3.30 PM LE PLANTIN was lightly shelled by the enemy. Minenwerfer were active from 5 p.m. to 10 p.m. against our Right bay. From PRINCES ISLAND enemy could be heard working. Work on parapets continued. The supply of rifle grenades was inadequate and we were not able to retaliate in the way we should have liked. Weather fine	Two men wounded by rifle grenades
"	Feb 6th		A patrol was again sent out to examine DEADMANS TRENCH. This patrol went all the length of the TRENCH but found no signs of recent occupation by enemy. Rifle and hand grenades were again active against our saps. Enemy snipers opposite PRINCES ISLAND were active. The enemy commenced wiring on their front. Fire along the battalion front was only fair. Observation was kept on the FORT during the day and it was thought that some kind of work was going on there. Work on parapets again continued. Weather fine on the whole. slight showers	[?] 6 men wounded by rifle grenade. Capt Lambert [?] returned from leave and resumed duties of Adjt
(B2) LE QUESNOY	Feb 7th		During the day all was quiet. The Battn was relieved at 7.45 p.m. by the 23rd R.F. and marched to billets in LE QUESNOY, arriving there about 9 p.m.	[?]
LE QUESNOY	Feb 8th		Battalion bathed. Interval was devoted to cleaning up and rest. The billets were all good. Two coys in huts (C.D.) A&B were in farms. Weather fine	[?]

Instructions regarding War Diaries and Intelligence Summaries are contained in F. S. Regs., Part II. and the Staff Manual respectively. Title pages will be prepared in manuscript.

WAR DIARY
or
~~INTELLIGENCE SUMMARY.~~
(Erase heading not required.)

Army Form C. 2118.

Sheet 231

Place	Date	Hour	Summary of Events and Information	Remarks and references to Appendices
LE QUESNOY	9.2.15	..	Companies paraded for inspection by Commanding Officer on their respective parade grounds. The general turn out was very satisfactory. The armourer inspected the rifles of the Battn. Weather fine.	
"	10.2.15	..	Battalion went for a route march from 10 to 12 noon. CO and 2 coy commanders went up to B3 Subsection to view line etc. Weather fine.	
" and B3	11.2.15	..	As the Battalion was going into the trenches in the evening no programme of work was issued. Battn paraded at 5.30 and companies marched independently to B3. Relief was complete about 7.45 p.m. Night was quiet up to midnight.	[illegible]
B3	12.2.15	..	Battn H.Q. was shelled from 2.30 to 4.15 p.m. no damage was done but many of the shells were very close. 14 failed to explode. Wiring was carried out by the front line coys. as the G.O.C. 2nd Divn had laid special stress on the necessity of the wire being good. Enemy were generally quiet except for rifle grenades opposite the saps.	[illegible]
"	13.2.15		A German bombing party advanced towards J. Sap, throwing bombs, shouting "Come on Tommy, Hoch! Hoch!". Our bombers retaliated and drove them back. Work of wiring continued. Also made progress on the parados in NEW ROSE ST., as this trench was really only a breastwork it was necessary to construct the parados entirely of built up material. Enemy on the whole were very quiet	[illegible]

Instructions regarding War Diaries and Intelligence Summaries are contained in F. S. Regs., Part II. and the Staff Manual respectively. Title pages will be prepared in manuscript.

WAR DIARY

or

~~INTELLIGENCE SUMMARY~~.

(*Erase heading not required.*)

Army Form C. 2118.

Confidential

Sheet 232

Place	Date	Hour	Summary of Events and Information	Remarks and references to Appendices
B3.	14th		Bath Hq was again shelled about 9.30 AM. this time lightly. About dusk 6 to 8 Germans approached sunken road with ~~appa~~ the apparent intention of bombing. Sec. Lieut Chace and one bomber crept out and bombed them, they retired at once. Work of wiring and building parados continued.	[illegible]
"	15th		Bath Hqs lightly shelled about 10.30 AM. Between 6 AM and 7 AM the RLEPLANTIN ROAD was ~~lightly~~ swept with M.Gs. During the time the Bath was in the trenches this tour. RE working parties were supplied nightly. Bath relieved about 8 pm by 23rd R.F. and occupied supports billets in VILLAGE LINE vacated by them. Billets were quite good. Very wet day	[illegible]
VILLAGE LINE.	16th		The battalion (support) area was scattered and held mostly by a system of keeps. Enemy were quiet. Casualties during tour 4 killed 3 wounded	[illegible]
"	17th		Bath was relieved by 13th RWF about 7.45 pm and marched on to billets in HINGETTE, where they arrived about 10.45. The night was very clear and fine	[illegible]
HINGETTE	18th		Morning devoted to cleaning up. Billets were very scattered but good on the whole.	[illegible]

Instructions regarding War Diaries and Intelligence Summaries are contained in F. S. Regs., Part II. and the Staff Manual respectively. Title pages will be prepared in manuscript.

WAR DIARY
or
~~INTELLIGENCE SUMMARY.~~
(Erase heading not required.)

Army Form C. 2118.

Confidential

Sheet 233.

Place	Date	Hour	Summary of Events and Information	Remarks and references to Appendices
HINGETTE – BOURECQ (Hazebrouck Sheet)	19/2/16		Batn paraded at 10.30 AM and marched to BOURECQ where we arrived about 2.30 p.m. The new billets were very good. We were able to get a general officers mess here and dispense with coy messes. Weather fine but cold.	
	20/2/16		Sunday. Church parade.	
BOURECQ	21/2/16		Companies bathed and held kit inspections. Day fine but cold.	Jen
"	22/2/16		Company training. Wiring instruction and bayonet fight. Snowing all day.	Jen
"	23/2/16		Company training. Rifle shooting on range. Wiring. Drill etc. Orders received from Brigade to hold ourselves in readiness to move at short notice. Snowing heavily	Jen
"	24/2/16		On short notice but training carried on as usual. About 11.30 p.m. brigade wired to say the battalion was no longer on short notice move probably postponed to 29th inst. Snowing	Jen
"	25/2/16		Coy training wiring and rifle shooting. Thawing and weather unpleasant	Jen
"	26/2/16		Ordered to entrain from LILLERS at 4.31. The Batn marched to LILLERS STA: and were conveyed to NOEUX LES MINES where we arrived about 5.30 p.m. The Batn then proceeded by road to billets in BARLIN arriving there about 8 p.m. A slight hitch occurred as regards billets and it was 10 o'clock before we finally settled down. This was the first time English troops had occupied this sector. On the whole	

2353 Wt. W2544/1454 700,000 5/15 D. D. & L. A.D.S.S./Forms/C. 2118.

Instructions regarding War Diaries and Intelligence Summaries are contained in F. S. Regs., Part II. and the Staff Manual respectively. Title pages will be prepared in manuscript.

Confidential

WAR DIARY
or
~~INTELLIGENCE~~ SUMMARY.
(Erase heading not required.)

Army Form C. 2118.

Sheet 234

Place	Date	Hour	Summary of Events and Information	Remarks and references to Appendices
~~27.2.16~~ BARLIN	26.2.16		billets were comfortable although scattered. The C.O. and 2 coy commanders went up this day to see the part of the line to taken over from the French	Sen
	27.2.16		Remained in same billets.	
PISAINS	28.2.16		Received orders to move from BARLIN to billets in PISAINS preparatory to going in to the line. We moved independently by coys commencing at 6.30 the whole Battalion arrived by 1 p.m. Billets were not very good.	Sen
PISAINS - SOUCHEZ RIGHT	29.2.16		About 3 p.m. a shell burst on the main road by Battn Hq. and wounded 2 men. The Battn moved at dusk to the trenches. Coys marching at intervals of 15 mins. We reported at Brigade Hqrs in AIX NOULETTE (36ème Brigade French) and found guides awaiting us. It was a long march from PISAINS to the trenches, and the roads extremely bad on account of the thaw and numerous shell holes. The leading coy arrived at the new line about 9 p.m. the whole relief being complete by 10.45. The French regiment from which we took over was the 77th. ~~The~~ The trenches were on the whole bad and dug out accomodation scanty. Sanitary arrangements were non-existent	Sen Casualties 2.

2353 Wt. W2544/1454 700,000 5/15 D. D. & L. A.D.S.S./Forms/C. 2118.

7/3/16 — [illegible] Lt Col Commdg 1st R Berks Regt

99th Brigade

2nd Division.

1st BATTALION ROYAL BERKSHIRE REGIMENT

MARCH 1 9 1 6::::::

Instructions regarding War Diaries and Intelligence Summaries are contained in F. S. Regs., Part II. and the Staff Manual respectively. Title pages will be prepared in manuscript.

Army Form C. 2118.

WAR DIARY
or
~~INTELLIGENCE SUMMARY.~~
(Erase heading not required.)

Confidential

Sheet 235

Place	Date	Hour	Summary of Events and Information	Remarks and references to Appendices
SOUCHEZ RIGHT	1/3/16		The enemy were very quiet indeed so far as rifle and MG fire was concerned. Artillery on both sides were fairly active. In this subsection the front line was held by 2 companies. 1 coy in support and 1 in reserve. Communication with the front line & support coys was not possible ~~[illegible]~~ in the day time except by telephone. also part of the reserve coy was isolated. At night fatigue parties had to go over the top, the communication trenches were waterlogged. This was a most interesting part of the line to hold from certain parts of the line one could see ~~for several miles~~ the country for several miles. The town of LENS on our left front was wholly visible and the opposing lines of trenches around it ~~[illegible]~~ were clearly distinguishable. On the other hand from a tactical point of view the position was not good, the front line ran in diverse directions towards the enemy and could be enfiladed from all sides, similarly we could of course enfilade the enemy. The regt on our left was the 23rd R F on our right across the SOUCHEZ RIVER were the French (17th Division French)	[illegible]
"	2/3/16		Quiet night. We managed to get some work done on the trenches and improve the sanitary arrangements. Much labour was required to make the position in a proper state of defence. In the meantime we ~~[illegible]~~ [illegible]	

2353 Wt. W2544/1454 700,000 5/15 D. D. & L. A.D.S.S./Forms/C. 2118.

Instructions regarding War Diaries and Intelligence Summaries are contained in F. S. Regs., Part II. and the Staff Manual respectively. Title pages will be prepared in manuscript.

Confidential

WAR DIARY
or
~~INTELLIGENCE SUMMARY.~~
(Erase heading not required.)

Sheet 236

Army Form C. 2118.

Place	Date	Hour	Summary of Events and Information	Remarks and references to Appendices
SOUCHEZ RIGHT.	2/3/16.		(ctd) not annoy the Germans any more than we could help, and they left us alone	[illegible]
"	3/3/16		Nothing of importance occurred. The enemy artillery fired several salvos of shrapnel during the night. Work on parapets continued. Snowing	[illegible]
"	4/3/16		Nothing of importance occurred. Snowing hard	
SOUCHEZ RIGHT and BOIS de NOULETTE	5/3/16		Relieved by 22nd R. Fusiliers. One of the slowest reliefs experienced. Their 1st coy entered the reserve trench at 8.15 but relief was not finally complete until 11.45. On relief ~~the~~ 3 coys marched to billets in hutments in the BOIS DE NOULETTE the other coy was detached and lay about a mile nearer the line than the remainder of the Bn. Billets were quite good. Casualties during tour 6	[illegible]
Bois de Noulette	6/3/16		260 men on fatigue at night. ~~[illegible]~~ Bn rested during the day. Snowing	[illegible]
"	7/3/16		200 men on fatigue at night. Snowing	[illegible]
"	8/3/16		260 men on fatigue. Cold	[illegible]
SOUCHEZ RIGHT	9/3/16		Relieved 22nd R.F. in the trenches relief complete by 9.45 pm. Quiet night. The battalion on our right was the 9th West Riding	[illegible]
"	10/3/16		Enemy Artillery were active with Fizz bangs on most parts of our line during the day. Hostile aircraft were active. Large working parties of the 23rd London Regt and RE worked on our Reserve and Front Line. We sent two	

Instructions regarding War Diaries and Intelligence Summaries are contained in F. S. Regs., Part II. and the Staff Manual respectively. Title pages will be prepared in manuscript.

Confidential

WAR DIARY
or
~~INTELLIGENCE SUMMARY~~.
(Erase heading not required.)

Sheet 237

Army Form C. 2118.

Place	Date	Hour	Summary of Events and Information	Remarks and references to Appendices
SOUCHEZ RIGHT ~~10/3/16~~	10/3/16		working parties to the R.E. for work on the COMPANY ROAD. The general directed that this trench was to be cleared with all possible speed so as to open communication by day.	[illegible]
~~11/3/16~~	11/3/16		Nothing of importance occurred. The usual shelling with fizz bangs continued day and night. There was *no* rifle fire. ~~He~~ Although the situation in this sector was always more or less normal, it was extremely interesting from many points of view both on account of the proximity of the Germans to our front line and from the fact that one could observe for many miles the lines of trenches of both sides. In our front line the enemy freely exposed himself at dusk and dawn, and on many occasions endeavoured to open friendly conversation. We were not in a position to alter this state of affairs owing partly to the badly constructed parapets and partly to the fact that we were enfiladed (as were the enemy) from all sides. The wire in front of our own and enemy trenches was better than we ever had before	[illegible]
~~12/3~~	12/3/16		Nothing to record. Situation the same as yesterday. A lovely spring day	[illegible]
	13/3/16		Nothing to record during the day. Relieved by 22nd R.F. (code name PRAWN) about 10.30 pm and marched independently to Billets in BOUVIGNY and	

T2134. Wt. W708—776. 500000. 4/15. Sir J. C. & S.

Instructions regarding War Diaries and Intelligence Summaries are contained in F. S. Regs., Part II. and the Staff Manual respectively. Title pages will be prepared in manuscript.

Confidential

WAR DIARY
or
~~INTELLIGENCE SUMMARY.~~
(Erase heading not required.)

Sheet - 238

Army Form C. 2118.

Place	Date	Hour	Summary of Events and Information	Remarks and references to Appendices
S SOUCHEZ RIGHT	13/3/16		being the Battalion in reserve. Two Companies and H.Q being at BOUVIGNY one Company at BOIS DE NOULETTE and one Company at BOIS SIX. Enemy very quiet during relief.	[illegible]
BOUVIGNY	14/3/16		Village shelled during the day. Very fine day. 200 men were required for working parties.	[illegible]
"	15/3/16		Shelling again commenced about 10 a.m. and was continued intermittently during the morning. Very fine day.- Two parties of 50 each were required for carrying parties and were taken from B & D Coy.	[illegible]
"	16/3/16		Quiet day - very little shelling. Companies at disposal of Company Commanders in the morning - Two parties of 50 each were required for carrying parties and were taken from A & C Company - Fine day.	CARLHEVEN admitted Hospital.
"	17/3/16		Quiet day - Relieved the 22nd ROYAL FUSILIERS in SOUCHEZ RIGHT - Relief commenced from Battn H.Q. at 6.30 pm and was completed by 10.15 pm. Lovely night - relief very satisfactory, no shelling or machine gun fire during relief - Dispositions of Companies as follows:- C Co right front line Company, A Co left front line	

T2134. Wt. W708-776. 500000. 4/15. Sir J. C. & S.

Instructions regarding War Diaries and Intelligence Summaries are contained in F. S. Regs., Part II. and the Staff Manual respectively. Title pages will be prepared in manuscript.

Confidential

WAR DIARY or INTELLIGENCE SUMMARY.

(Erase heading not required.)

Sheet 239

Army Form C. 2118.

Place	Date	Hour	Summary of Events and Information	Remarks and references to Appendices
BOUVIGNY & SOUCHEZ RIGHT	17/3/16		line Company – D Co Support Company and B Co Reserve Company. – 23rd R. FUSILIERS were on our left and 47th Division on our right – Since our last tour the trenches were much improved and drier. –	2 Lt JACKSON to Trench Mortar Div. School. 2Lt PUGH to Div. Bombing School. [illegible]
SOUCHEZ RIGHT	18/3/16		Nothing of importance occurred – both our aircraft and hostile aircraft were very active – hostile artillery normal – our left front company was slightly shelled with light field guns between 5.30 p.m. and 6.30 p.m. – no damage done – Excellent weather and consequently much work done in front trenches and Headquarter Trench – Company Road is still worked at under R.E. supervision and two working parties are found by us nightly for that – Enemy still very quiet and exposes themselves frequently during day, but until our trenches are much improved it is essential for us to remain quiet also – Enemy are doing a considerable amount of work on their lines. –	Casualties One Wounded [illegible]
SOUCHEZ RIGHT	19/3/16		Everything normal – hostile aircraft very active – Headquarter Trench shelled with light field guns between 8.0 a.m. and 9.0 a.m. – no damage done. Thankful day – trenches drying up well – Enemy machine guns were active at night. G.O.C. 23rd Division and B.G.G.S. IVth Corps went round our front line after dark	[illegible] to Gymnastic Course.

T2134. Wt. W708–776. 500000. 4/15. Sir J. C. & S.

Army Form C. 2118.

Instructions regarding War Diaries and Intelligence Summaries are contained in F. S. Regs., Part II. and the Staff Manual respectively. Title pages will be prepared in manuscript.

Confidential

WAR DIARY
or
INTELLIGENCE SUMMARY.
(Erase heading not required.)

Sheet 2010

Place	Date	Hour	Summary of Events and Information	Remarks and references to Appendices
SOUCHEZ RIGHT	20/3/16		Everything normal - Intermittent shelling by light field guns all day - Headquarters trench shelled by 6" Howitzers at 1.0 p.m. (6 shells) and again at 3.30 p.m. (4 shells). Officers of 1st WORCESTERS, 24th Brigade, 23rd Division, came up to Headquarters in the afternoon with a view to taking over the line from us to-morrow night. Thankful day.	Casualties one wounded. [initials]
" "	21/3/16.		Very quiet day - rather hazy and consequently no aircraft activity - were relieved by 1st WORCESTERS - Relief commenced at 6.30 p.m. and was completed by 12.0 p.m. - Everything went satisfactorily - On relief battalion marched to billets at HERSIN which were reached about 1.15 a.m. - Lovely night.	Casualties 2 wounded [initials]
HERSIN.	22/3/16		Billets at HERSIN quite good - the whole battalion is in a large building and the men very comfortable - the day spent in cleaning up and washing - Boshell arranged very excellent baths - we had to send 300 men for a working party on the 2nd line trenches - they were out from 7.0 p.m. - 2.0 a.m. - dull day. TORREKDON - men from 2nd Battalion + Captain REDSTONE	LIEUT. HILLIARD went on leave. [initials]
"	23/3/16		Companies at disposal of Company Commanders - nasty day, heavy fall of snow - Battalion found working party of 200 men to-night -	[initials]

T2134. Wt. W708—776. 500000. 4/15. Sir J. C. & S.

Army Form C. 2118.

Instructions regarding War Diaries and Intelligence Summaries are contained in F. S. Regs., Part II. and the Staff Manual respectively. Title pages will be prepared in manuscript.

Confidential

WAR DIARY
or
INTELLIGENCE SUMMARY.
(Erase heading not required.)

Sheet 241

Place	Date	Hour	Summary of Events and Information	Remarks and references to Appendices
HERSIN	24.3.16	-	Companies at disposal of Company Commanders. Battalion found working parties of 200 men. Very wet day.	[illegible]
"	25.3.16		Companies at disposal of Company Commanders - Battalion found working parties of 200 men. Showery day.	[illegible]
"	26.3.16		Church parade in the morning at 11.0 a.m. 200 men for working parties - fine day.	CAPTAIN ELLIS + W.G.GREEN went on leave. [illegible]
"	27.3.16		Companies at disposal of Company Commanders - 250 men were warned for working parties, but this was cancelled at the last minute owing to the weather.	[illegible]
"	28.3.16		Battalion moved by rail from HERSIN to HOUDAIN - train left at 11.15 - from HOUDAIN we marched to DIVION where we took over the billets from 52nd Light Infantry - Whole Brigade moved back into Reserve area - 1st K.R.R. Corps are also billeted at DIVION - billets fair but not as good as HERSIN - fine day but very windy.	[illegible]
DIVION	29.3.16		Companies at disposal of Company Commanders - Lt. HANNEY commenced a class of instruction to 4 officers and 32 N.C.O's in Physical Training and Bayonet Fighting. Cloudy day.	

Army Form C. 2118.

WAR DIARY
or
INTELLIGENCE SUMMARY.
(*Erase heading not required.*)

Instructions regarding War Diaries and Intelligence Summaries are contained in F. S. Regs., Part II. and the Staff Manual respectively. Title pages will be prepared in manuscript.

Confidential

Sheet 243

Place	Date	Hour	Summary of Events and Information	Remarks and references to Appendices
DIVION	30/3/16.		Companies at disposal of Company Commanders – classes as usual – Fine cold day.	Capt. BOSWELL on leave. [illegible]
	31/3/16.		Companies at disposal of Company Commanders – classes as usual – Cloudy day –	[illegible]
			Fighting strength of the Battalion 31st March 1916 – 880 [illegible]	
			[illegible] Lieut Colonel Comdg 1/ Royal Berkshire Regt	

T2134. Wt. W708–776. 500000. 4/15. Sir J. C. & S.

99th Brigade.

2nd Division.

1st BATTALION ROYAL BERKSHIRE REGIMENT

APRIL 1 9 1 6::::::

Instructions regarding War Diaries and Intelligence Summaries are contained in F. S. Regs., Part II. and the Staff Manual respectively. Title pages will be prepared in manuscript.

Confidential

WAR DIARY
or
~~INTELLIGENCE SUMMARY.~~
(Erase heading not required.)

243

Army Form C. 2118.

Place	Date	Hour	Summary of Events and Information	Remarks and references to Appendices
DIVION	1/4/16		The Corps Commander (Lieut Gen Sir H H Wilson) having announced the fact that he would inspect the 99th Brigade on the 3rd April, a practice parade was held. The Battn marched to the place of parade and formed up in Quarter column. We then practised the General Salute and marched past in fours. and returned to billets about noon. The baths at BRUAY were allotted to the Battn in the afternoon. Weather very fine	[illegible]
	2/4/16		Sunday. Church Parade in the Cinema. Weather very fine	Lieuts Cook and Inwood on leave
	3/4/16		The Brigade was inspected by the Corps Commander. Battalions were drawn up in quarter column. After the inspection the Brigade marched past in fours. General Wilson remarked that our men (1st R Berks) looked very fit and strong. Weather fine.	[illegible]
	4/4/16		In the morning Coys were at disposal of O C Coys for musketry classes as usual. In the afternoon the G.O.C. 1st Army (General Sir Charles Munro) inspected the battalion at musketry and saw one company firing on the range. Day showery	

Instructions regarding War Diaries and Intelligence Summaries are contained in F. S. Regs., Part II. and the Staff Manual respectively. Title pages will be prepared in manuscript.

Confidential

WAR DIARY
or
~~INTELLIGENCE SUMMARY.~~

(Erase heading not required.)

244

Army Form C. 2118.

Place	Date	Hour	Summary of Events and Information	Remarks and references to Appendices
DIVION.	5/4/16		Practically whole Battalion on fatigue digging trenches. Weather fine	[illegible]
~~5/4/16~~	6/4/16		Route March lasting about 3 hours in the morning. Weather fine	
	7/4/16		Coys at Disposal of O.C. Coys for training. Bayonet Fighting and Bombing Classes. A regrettable incident occurred with the Bombing Class owing to the premature explosion of a bomb. Sec Lieut Dropley and 4 men were wounded none fatally, but 3 of the men were serious cases.	[illegible]
	8/4/16		Whole Battalion on fatigue digging trenches. (~~successfully~~).	[illegible]
DIVION – BOMY.	9/4/16		Battalion moved to 1st Army Training Area. Entrained at CALONNE RICOUART, 12.45 AM and were taken to AIRE by rail. Marched from AIRE to BOMY a distance of 15 kilometres, arriving about 7 p.m. Companies were very scattered. 1 being at RUPIGNY. 1 at FREUPPE. and 2 in BOMY. Billets were fair.	Ref Hazebrouck Sheet V 1/100,000 [illegible]
	10/4/16		Battalion training. 2 Coys under Major Shanks. 2 under the Commanding Officer. The facilities as regards ground were very good. The subject of training was "the attack". Weather very fine	[illegible]
	11/4/16		Brigade Training. The scheme laid down was intended for a continuous 2 days work. The Battalion marched to BEAUMETZ – LEZ – AIRE ~~arriving at~~ at 9.30 AM. The 23rd R. F. and ourselves were in reserve	

Instructions regarding War Diaries and Intelligence Summaries are contained in F. S. Regs., Part II. and the Staff Manual respectively. Title pages will be prepared in manuscript.

Confidential

WAR DIARY
or
~~INTELLIGENCE SUMMARY.~~
(Erase heading not required.)

245

Army Form C. 2118.

Place	Date	Hour	Summary of Events and Information	Remarks and references to Appendices
BOMY	11/4/16		did not move until 11 A.M. We then advanced across country to Hill 179 and returned to billets about 3.15 P.M. Raining heavily.	Ref Hazebrouck. Sheet 1/100.000
	12/4/16		We marched out to Hill 179 and formed up in mass with the rest of the Brigade prepared to continue the advance begun yesterday. But the weather was so bad that the Brigade Commander ordered units to return to their billets. Weather very wet	[initials]
BOMY—DIVION	13/4/16		The Battn paraded at 9.50 AM and marched to AIRE where we entrained and were conveyed to CALONNE. STA from whence we returned to our former billets in DIVION. A wire was received from Bde this day informing us that all leave was stopped and that all ranks were to be recalled so as to rejoin their units by the 18th. Weather dry strong wind blowing	Major Sharpe & Lt. [illegible] went on leave; [initials]
DIVION	14/4/16		Coys at disposal of OC Coys for musketry etc. A small rifle range was available. Two coys bathed in the afternoon. Weather ~~[illegible]~~ fair	[initials]
	17/4/16		Every available man of on fatigue (400). For work on reserve and support trenches. Parties were conveyed in motor buses. Conference for all mounted Officers at Bde HQ in the afternoon.	[initials]

T2134. Wt. W708—776. 500000. 4/15. Sir J. C. & S.

Instructions regarding War Diaries and Intelligence Summaries are contained in F. S. Regs., Part II. and the Staff Manual respectively. Title pages will be prepared in manuscript.

Confidential

WAR DIARY
or
~~INTELLIGENCE SUMMARY.~~
(Erase heading not required.)

Army Form C. 2118.

246

Place	Date	Hour	Summary of Events and Information	Remarks and references to Appendices
			Ref Sheet 36 A SE 1/40000	
DIVION	16/4/16		Sunday. Church Parade in the Cinema at 10 o'clock. day free	Captain & QrMr Roskell struck off strength
DIVION — BOUVIGNY	17/4/16		Batt entrained at CALONNE RICOUART STA. at 2 p.m. and was conveyed to HERSIN arriving ~~about~~ at 5 p.m. The train was a tactical one. The distance from DIVION to HERSIN by road was about 4 miles whereas by rail the distance was something like 20 miles. From HERSIN we marched to BOUVIGNY halting for half an hour in order not to clash with the 1st KRRC who were leaving BOUVIGNY at 7 p.m. We discovered that during our absence ~~[illegible]~~ the place had been shelled fairly heavily. The KRRC having sustained numerous casualties. Weather very wet.	[initials]
BOUVIGNY	18/4/16		All quiet. Weather very wet. Supplied carrying parties totalling 200. They were used for carrying R.E. Material to the 176th Tunnelling Coy in SOUCHEZ SECTOR	[initials]
	19/4/16		All quiet & Weather unsettled but brighter. Supplied working parties same as previous day	Maj Sharpe 2nd Lt Green from leave
	20/4/16		All quiet Weather brighter. Same working parties	
SOUCHEZ I	21/4/16		Relieved 23rd R.F. in SOUCHEZ I. Relief complete at 12.15 A.M. Night very wet. All quiet	— [initials]
	22/4/16		During the day all was quiet. About 5 p.m. COMPANY ROAD was	

Instructions regarding War Diaries and Intelligence Summaries are contained in F. S. Regs., Part II. and the Staff Manual respectively. Title pages will be prepared in manuscript.

Confidential

WAR DIARY
or
~~INTELLIGENCE SUMMARY~~.
(Erase heading not required.)

247

Place	Date	Hour	Summary of Events and Information	Remarks and references to Appendices
SOUCHEZ	C[illegible] 22/4/16		Shelled with light field guns, and ~~continuously~~ intermittently throughout the night. We had three casualties 2 killed and 1 wounded. Weather very wet. Working parties from the 23rd Division were employed on digging new trench in front of HEADQUARTER trench, also parties were at work on SAP 8 and COMPANY RD the two communication trenches to the front line, neither of which were usable.	[illegible]
	23/4/16		Weather fine. Day quiet until 5 p.m when a machine gun commenced to traverse along HEADQUARTER TRENCH, also there was a fair amount of shelling with light field guns in same places as on the 22nd. About 11 p.m the Right Front bay was shelled with shrapnel resulting in 6 yards of trench being blown in. Working parties were employed again as on previous night. ~~On~~ In the right front coy, the RE were working at a new drainage scheme, also in the same part of the line the wire in front of the trenches was thin and we had men employed all the time putting out French and barbed wire.	[illegible]
	24/4/16		Weather fine. The Brigade sent up three English Newspapers with orders that these were to be thrown into the German trenches. This was done	

Instructions regarding War Diaries and Intelligence Summaries are contained in F. S. Regs., Part II. and the Staff Manual respectively. Title pages will be prepared in manuscript.

Confidential

WAR DIARY
or
~~INTELLIGENCE SUMMARY.~~
(Erase heading not required.)

248

Army Form C. 2118.

Place	Date	Hour	Summary of Events and Information	Remarks and references to Appendices
SOUCHEZ	24/4/16		by Pte Barnes who threw them on to the enemy parapet and retired. A German crawled out & took the papers acknowledging them with a salute. The same working parties were employed as on previous nights. Hostile Artillery not quite so active at night, but during the day HEADrs TRENCH was shelled with Fizzbangs. Weather fine.	[illegible]
"	25/4/16		Day Quiet except for Machine Gun playing in the evening. Relieved by 22nd R.F. Relief complete 12.15 AM. Delay was caused by working parties for the R.E. being mixed up with companies coming in gang out. The relief being marched to the hutments in the BOIS DE NOULETTE. The last coy arriving at 3.30 AM about which time a heavy bombardment could be heard on the right of SOUCHEZ.	[illegible]
BOIS DE NOULETTE	26/4/16		The Battn rested during the day. Fatigue parties numbering in all 200 were required, mostly for carrying R.E. material to the Battns in the trenches. Weather warm.	[illegible]
"	27/4/16		Fatigue parties of 200 again required. Weather very fine	
	28/4/16		Fatigue of 200. Weather very fine	[illegible]

T2134. Wt. W708–776. 500000. 4/15. Sir J. C. & S.

Instructions regarding War Diaries and Intelligence Summaries are contained in F. S. Regs., Part II. and the Staff Manual respectively. Title pages will be prepared in manuscript.

Confidential

WAR DIARY
or
~~INTELLIGENCE SUMMARY.~~
(Erase heading not required.)

Army Form C. 2118.

249

Place	Date	Hour	Summary of Events and Information	Remarks and references to Appendices
SOUCHEZ I.	29/4/16	–	Battn relieved 22nd R.F. in SOUCHEZ I. parading about 9.30 p.m. at the BOIS DE NOULETTE relief was complete by 12.30 AM. The night on the whole was quiet.	
	30/4/16	–	All quiet until about 5 p.m. in the afternoon when the Germans exploded a mine on our right and followed it up with a very heavy bombardment, which was not however followed by any infantry attack. HEADQUARTER TRENCH was lightly shelled with fizzbangs. Coys in the front line were busily employed in cleaning the trenches. The Right front coy was employed in drainage ~~work~~ of the line under R.E. The German infantry opposite to us were still inactive. By order of the Brigade we sent over several English newspapers and were given 3 copies of the "Hamburger Fremdenblatt".	Major Sharpe Lieut Peake on leave [illegible]
			Total number with Battn 21 Officers 690 other ranks	

[illegible] Lt Col
Commdg 1st Royal Berks Regt

99th Brigade.

2nd Division.

1st BATTALION

ROYAL BERKSHIRE REGIMENT

M A Y   1 9 1 6

Summaries are contained in F. S. Regs., Part II. and the Staff Manual respectively. Title pages will be prepared in manuscript.

Confidential

INTELLIGENCE SUMMARY.

(Erase heading not required.)

Vol 19

Place	Date	Hour	Summary of Events and Information	Remarks and references to Appendices
SOUCHEZ	1/5/16		HEADQrs TRENCH shelled by 4.2 Howitzer about 8 AM. Machine Gun active in the evening about 5 pm traversing HQ trench. Work of draining and wiring continued in front line. Large fatigue party found by the Battn for work on COMPY. RD. Every night large working parties from the 23rd Divn were employed in building a new Support Line. Weather very fine	Encl. map
	2/5/16		HEADQrs TRENCH again shelled in the morning. Same working parties as on previous days. About 12 midnight the front line was heavily shelled with Pizzbangs. Also Sap 8 had a few high explosive [illegible] about the same time. A Sniper on the hill of GIVENCHY was somewhat troublesome during this tour and caused several casualties. Weather fine	Encl. map
	3/5/16		We were warned by Bde that the Divn of the right would explode a mine at 4.45 pm, this happened and was followed by a heavy bombardment of the enemy trenches lasting until dark (8 pm). We were relieved by 22nd R.F. about 12.45 AM and marched to billets in BOUVIGNY arriving there about 3.30 AM. A Coy was billeted in the dug outs in BOIS 6. Weather fine. Total casualties during tour 1 killed 16 wounded, one of the heaviest casualty lists the battalion has had in the trenches	Encl. map

T2134. Wt. W708—776. 500000. 4/15. Sir J. C. & S.

Instructions regarding War Diaries and Intelligence Summaries are contained in F. S. Regs., Part II. and the Staff Manual respectively. Title pages will be prepared in manuscript.

Confidential

WAR DIARY
or
INTELLIGENCE SUMMARY.

(Erase heading not required.)

Sheet No 251

Army Form C. 2118.

Place	Date	Hour	Summary of Events and Information	Remarks and references to Appendices
4/5/16 BOUVIGNY	4/5/16		The Battn rested during the day. Baths were good and used by everyone. At night fatigues numbering 250 were required. Some of these were used for carrying for 176th Tunnelling Coy and others for work on Support line in Souchez I.	Sec Lieut A.A.G. Hamilton joined the Bn for duty.
	5/5/16		Little work could be done. Most of the men on fatigue did not get back to billets before daylight. Fatigues of same strength as on day previous were required at night	Genl Major
	6/5/16		Same fatigues were required as on previous nights. During the day the farm yards were cleared out, and the manure carted on to the land. This work was done in conjunction with the K.R.R's.	Capt My Pow? Lieut Shaw on leave. Genl Major
	7/5/16		Work of clearing yards was carried on during the day. The Battn relieved the 22nd R Fusiliers in SOUCHEZ I. Relief complete 11.35 P.M. Night was quiet.	Genl Major
SOUCHEZ I	8/5/16		Everything very quiet with the exception of a few Minenwerfer sent over on the extreme left of our sector about 12 MN. Cleared up trenches and straightened wire in front line. Working party supplied to RE's	Genl Major

T2134. Wt. W708—776. 500000. 4/15. Sir J. C. & S.

Instructions regarding War Diaries and Intelligence Summaries are contained in F. S. Regs., Part II. and the Staff Manual respectively. Title pages will be prepared in manuscript.

WAR DIARY
or
INTELLIGENCE SUMMARY.
(Erase heading not required.)

Sheet no 252

Army Form C. 2118.

Confidential

Place	Date	Hour	Summary of Events and Information	Remarks and references to Appendices
SOUCHEZ I	8/5/16	Cont	for work on dug outs in Company R. Party supplied at night to R.E.'s for drainage in RIGHT FRONT line. Also to Sapping Coy for work on Company R & SAPS.	Sec Lieut Powell joined Bn for duty. [illegible] Major
"	9/5/16		Minenwerfers were sent over on our extreme left about 9 AM. The position of the battery was observed and our Artillery fired on it during the morning. We were not troubled with it again. Everything quiet. On our right a mine was exploded at 7 PM, and heavy bombardment ensued. Same working parties were supplied as previous night. Cleaning trenches and wiring continued. A very wet night.	[illegible] Major
"	10/5/16		Night again very quiet. About 10.30 PM there was a bombing attack on our right, which was followed by a bombardment lasting about 1½ hours, after which everything was quiet. The Battn was relieved by the 1st Worcesters and completed by 11.55 PM. A very quiet relief. On completion of relief the Battn marched to billets at HERSIN for one night.	[illegible] on leave. [illegible] Major
BRUAY	11/5/16		The Battn moved off from HERSIN at 12.30 PM and marched to billets at BRUAY for one night.	[illegible] on leave [illegible] Major.

T2134. Wt. W708—776. 500000. 4/15. Sir J. C. & S.

WAR DIARY
or
INTELLIGENCE SUMMARY.
(Erase heading not required.)

Sheet no 253

Army Form C. 2118.

Instructions regarding War Diaries and Intelligence Summaries are contained in F. S. Regs., Part II. and the Staff Manual respectively. Title pages will be prepared in manuscript.

Confidential

Place	Date	Hour	Summary of Events and Information	Remarks and references to Appendices
CALONNE RICOUART	11/5/16		Battⁿ moved off from BRUAY en route for CALONNE RICOUART at 10 A.M. and arrived in billets at 11-30 AM. Billets fair but very scattered. Rest of the day was given up to cleaning.	Genl Map
	13/5/16		Very wet day. Commanding Officers inspection had to be postponed and Coys held a kit inspection. One platoon had to be isolated on account of German Measles. Medical Officer in communication with ADMS re the same.	Genl Map
	14/5/16		Working parties sent by Motor Lorries for work at Bouvigny &. Strength 325.	2nd Lt Tizard & 2nd Lt Parsons on leave. Genl Map
	15/5/16		Battⁿ was to have moved to BEUGIN for training, but no billeting accommodation could be found, and it was subsequently changed to DIVION which was reached by a circuitous route at 3 15 PM. Billets very scattered. A very wet morning and the March was postponed 1 hour, afterwards cleared up.	Genl Map
	16/5/16		Battalion Training. 2 Coys musketry on range at BOIS.LOUIS. Training consisted of Companies working in the Attack. Dinners were eaten in the field. Battalion returned to billets about 4.p.m. One company bathed	Captain Matthews from leave. Genl Map

Instructions regarding War Diaries and Intelligence Summaries are contained in F. S. Regs., Part II. and the Staff Manual respectively. Title pages will be prepared in manuscript.

WAR DIARY
or
~~INTELLIGENCE~~ SUMMARY.
(Erase heading not required.)

Army Form C. 2118.

Sheet No 254

Confidential

Place	Date	Hour	Summary of Events and Information	Remarks and references to Appendices
DIVION	17/5/16		325. Men on fatigue digging new reserve line in the BOUVIGNY area. During the morning the C.O and Coy commanders went out to examine ground at J. 31 where a complete set of German and English trenches on a front of 500 yards had been dug with a view to their being used for practice attacks and other schemes.	Sec Lieut Sharp + Powell on leave. Gen'l Major
	18/5/16		Battalion training at the instructional trenches J. 31. During the morning coys worked independently, training for the attack. In the afternoon the Battn worked as a whole. The Corps Commander and the Divn General were both present and saw the Battn at work. This days work was in preparation for a brigade scheme for the 20th	Gen'l Major
	19/5/16		Battalion training. A rifle range at BOIS LOUIS was used by two coys, the other two coys training on the high ground above HOUDAIN (J. 20). The ground here was good and suitable for carrying out attacks in open country. Battn returned to billets about 4 p.m. Weather warm	Gen'l Major
	20/5/16		Brigade training at J 31. (attached to this sheet is the Battn + Bde Operation orders) The Brigade formed up & carried out a preliminary attack at 9.15 A.M.	

T2134. Wt. W708—776. 500000. 4/15. Sir J. C. & S.

Instructions regarding War Diaries and Intelligence Summaries are contained in F. S. Regs., Part II. and the Staff Manual respectively. Title pages will be prepared in manuscript.

Confidential

WAR DIARY
or
~~INTELLIGENCE~~ SUMMARY.
(Erase heading not required.)

Sheet No 255

Army Form C. 2118.

Place	Date	Hour	Summary of Events and Information	Remarks and references to Appendices
DIVION.	20/5/16		which went off successfully. At 11.6 AM this was repeated. The Corps Commander ~~and~~ Divisional General and the other Brigade and Artillery Staffs of the Division were present. After the assault there was a short conference at which the Divn Commander expressed himself as being satisfied with the way in which the morning's work had been done. Btn returned to billets about 1 PM Weather Warm	Gen l. Maj
DIVION—HERSIN	21/5/16		The Battalion proceeded to HERSIN by line of march. Parading at 9 AM we arrived at HERSIN at 1 p.m. and billeted in the Orphanage. About 3 p.m. the Germans commenced to shell the town causing considerable damage and several casualties. About half an hour after the bombardment had commenced we were warned that the enemy had turned on gas, but although the gas cloud could be observed from the high ground on the outskirts of the town, no effects were felt. Hersin is from 4 to 5 miles from the present firing line. The shelling lasted about ~~[illegible]~~ 2 hours ceasing at 5 p.m. The Brigade was ordered to be in readiness to move at 2 hours notice from 7.0 p.m. At 9 p.m. orders to stand to in readiness to embark on motor buses were issued. The Battalion stood to on the alarm post outside the	See Lieut Pughe Men on leave Gen l. Maj

T2134. Wt. W708–776. 500000. 4/15. Sir J. C. & S.

Instructions regarding War Diaries and Intelligence Summaries are contained in F. S. Regs., Part II. and the Staff Manual respectively. Title pages will be prepared in manuscript.

WAR DIARY
or
~~INTELLIGENCE SUMMARY.~~
(Erase heading not required.)

Confidential

Sheet No 256

Army Form C. 2118.

Place	Date	Hour	Summary of Events and Information	Remarks and references to Appendices
			Ref Sheet 36B	
HERSIN	21/22nd		Orphanage. The Commanding Officer appointed Captain West 2nd in command.	
GOUY SERVINS	22nd		A & B Coys left HERSIN in motor buses about 11.30 P.M. en route for GOUY SERVINS. No more buses were available so the other half battalion commenced to march to their destination, but were met about 2 miles out by motor buses which picked them up and completed the journey, arriving in bivouacs in a wood at Q.35 c about 4 A.M. On arrival the Battn found the 22nd R. Fus in occupation of the wood, but they were replaced by the 1st K.R.R.C at 8 AM. As the weather was very fine, the men were able to get well rested. The C O was sent for to Bde HQrs at VILLERS AU BOIS at 12.30 p.m. and was informed by the Brigade Commander that the Brigade would make a counter attack that night on two lines of trenches which the Germans had captured from the 47th Div on the 20th May. The time of assault was to be 1.30AM. Battalion Commanders then went up to view the line. The CO returned about 5.30 p.m. At 6.15 p.m. after the Battalion had paraded in readiness to move orders were received from Brigade cancelling the attack for that night, but instructing us to relieve the 7th LONDON Regt in the trenches from which the attack would have been made. Relief was completed about 2.15 AM	Ppl W.O.P. #7th LONDON RGT.

T2134. Wt. W708—776. 500000. 4/15. Sir J. C. & S.

Instructions regarding War Diaries and Intelligence Summaries are contained in F. S. Regs., Part II. and the Staff Manual respectively. Title pages will be prepared in manuscript.

Confidential

WAR DIARY
or
~~INTELLIGENCE SUMMARY.~~
(Erase heading not required.)

25/a

Army Form C. 2118.

Place	Date	Hour	Summary of Events and Information	Remarks and references to Appendices
BERTHONVAL SECTOR	23rd		The remaining half of B Coy + the remaining LEWIS GUN were to remain in OLD BOOTS TRENCH, their original position. About noon the enemy opened heavy shell fire on the TALUS des ZOUAVES and Headquarters trench which was continued without cessation until 7.45 p.m. when the bombardment developed into a ~~barrage~~ dense barrage which was continued until 9.30 p.m. Companies received orders to be in their assembly trenches by 7.55 p.m. but this was rendered impossible by the barrage. C and D Coys ~~[illegible]~~ each made an attempt to get into position but both were checked by the heavy fire. About 8 p.m. the Commanding Officer ordered Coys ~~[illegible]~~ not to attempt to get into their assembly trenches but to stand fast and await orders. The assembly trenches were very shallow and afforded no cover. A wireless message (a station had been established in the morning at Bn. H.Q. but it could not receive messages) was sent to Brigade about 8.10 p.m. informing the Staff that it was impossible to carry out the attack. The Brigade Commander ~~came~~ came up to the trenches and ordered	Gwd hour

T2134. Wt. W708—776. 500000. 4/15. Sir J. C. & S.

Instructions regarding War Diaries and Intelligence Summaries are contained in F. S. Regs., Part II. and the Staff Manual respectively. Title pages will be prepared in manuscript.

Confidential

WAR DIARY
or
INTELLIGENCE SUMMARY.
(Erase heading not required.)

Sheet No 257

Army Form C. 2118.

Place	Date	Hour	Summary of Events and Information	Remarks and references to Appendices
BERTHONVAL SECTOR	23rd	—	About 5 A.M. the right of our line held by B Coy was heavily shelled causing them 18 casualties. In the morning about 11 A.M. a German Prisoner belonging to the 86th Prussian Regt was captured and sent to Brigade H.Qrs. Fresh orders were received at 6.30 pm from the Brigade ordering the attack to take place on that night at 8.25 p.m.	
			Dispositions made by Commanding Officer. The assault was to be carried out in six lines as follows	
			1st Line 2 Platoons of C Coy	Gmd
			2nd Line 2 " C Coy + 2 Lewis Guns	
			3rd Line 2 " D Coy (with orders to consolidate captured trenches. these carried picks + shovels	maps
			Followed by 2 Platoons of B Coy carrying S.A.A	
			4th Line 2 Platoons D Coy + 1 Lewis Gun	
			5th Line 2 " A Coy (with orders to consolidate. these carried picks and shovel	
			6th Line 2 " A Coy	
			The 1st three lines had as their objective the old British Support line. The 4th 5th + 6th were to occupy a trench in rear of that captured by the 1st three lines	

T2134. Wt. W708—776. 500000. 4/15. Sir J. C. & S.

Instructions regarding War Diaries and Intelligence Summaries are contained in F. S. Regs., Part II. and the Staff Manual respectively. Title pages will be prepared in manuscript.

Confidential

WAR DIARY
or
~~INTELLIGENCE SUMMARY.~~
(Erase heading not required.)

Sheet No 258

Army Form C. 2118.

Place	Date	Hour	Summary of Events and Information	Remarks and references to Appendices
	May			
BERTHONVAL	23/24th	—	the 1st KRRC to relieve the Battn and carry out the attack at 1.30AM. but this order was cancelled and it was finally decided that no attack would take place that night. On relief the Battalion moved over to relieve the 22nd R.F.	Genl map
	24th		On taking over from the 22nd R.F. the Battn was ordered to commence work on a new line. about 250 yards in front of the TALUS des ZOUAVES which at that time only consisted of very shallow trenches. Work was commenced at once and considerable progress made. On the whole the day was quiet, ~~with the~~ and with the exception of occasional shelling of the communication trenches the enemy showed no activity	Genl map
	25th		Work was continued on the new line and progress made. Enemy were very quiet. Day was showery.	Genl map
	26th		Work on new line continued. Relieved by 22nd R.F. about 12 midnight and returned to billets at CAMBLAIN L'ABBE about 3 AM on 27th.	Total casualties during tour. OR killed wounded; Genl map
CAMBLAIN L'ABBE	27th		Men rested during the day. MAJOR A.E.F. HARRIS. DSO arrived and assumed command of the Battn. during the absence of Col May DSO	Genl map

Instructions regarding War Diaries and Intelligence Summaries are contained in F. S. Regs., Part II. and the Staff Manual respectively. Title pages will be prepared in manuscript.

Confidential

WAR DIARY
or
~~INTELLIGENCE~~ SUMMARY.
(Erase heading not required.)

Sheet no. 259

Army Form C. 2118.

Place	Date	Hour	Summary of Events and Information	Remarks and references to Appendices
CAMBLAIN L'ABBE	27th		on leave. Weather fine. The Battalion was billeted in huts in a wood on the outskirts of the village, accomodation was very good	Capt Fazell Ammy
..	28th		Companies at disposal of O.C Coys for training. ~~[illegible]~~ Ground available was not extensive. Weather fine	rejoined for duty Ammy
BERTHONVAL SECTOR.	29th		Battn relieved the 22nd Royal Fusiliers in left subsection. Relief complete about 1 AM. A considerable amount of work had been done on the new line, but it was by no means in a sound state for defensive purposes. Very little wire had been put out. Work was begun straight away and considerable progress made, both in digging and wiring. Enemy artillery was not very active except against the communication trenches WORTLEY and CENTRAL AVENUES. Little or no M Gun or rifle fire. Weather was fine. — Orders re Telephones. Before going into the trenches the tour orders were issued forbidding the use of telephones between front line companies and battalion H.Qrs, except for conversations ~~[illegible]~~ then between Officers and these were to be limited as far as possible. This order was framed on account of the German listening apparatus which apparently enabled them to hear both speech and buzzing.	Ammy

T2134. Wt. W708—776. 500000. 4/15. Sir J. C. & S.

Instructions regarding War Diaries and Intelligence Summaries are contained in F. S. Regs., Part II. and the Staff Manual respectively. Title pages will be prepared in manuscript.

Confidential

WAR DIARY
or
~~INTELLIGENCE~~ ~~SUMMARY~~.
(Erase heading not required.)

Sheet No. 260

Army Form C. 2118.

Place	Date	Hour	Summary of Events and Information	Remarks and references to Appendices
BERTHONVAL SECTOR	30th	–	Work on trenches and wire continued and considerable progress made. ~~assisted~~ The Battn was assisted by 2 sections of the 226th Coy. R.E. Enemy were quiet on the whole. Day was showery. Total Casualties during tour. 1 Offr 12 Other Ranks (all wounded.) ~~B~~ Ration strength of Battalion. 705 all ranks. [signature] Lt Col Commdg 1st Royal Berks Regt	[illegible]

T2134. Wt. W708–776. 500000. 4/15. Sir J. C. & S.

99th Brigade.

2nd Division.

1st BATTALION ROYAL BERKSHIRE REGIMENT

JUNE 1916

2

Instructions regarding War Diaries and Intelligence Summaries are contained in F. S. Regs., Part II. and the Staff Manual respectively. Title pages will be prepared in manuscript.

Confidential

WAR DIARY
or
~~INTELLIGENCE SUMMARY~~.
(Erase heading not required.)

1 R. Berks Regt Sheet 261. Vol 20

Army Form C. 2118.

Place	Date	Hour	Summary of Events and Information	Remarks and references to Appendices
BERTHONVAL SECTOR.	1/6/16		A certain amount of work was done during the day but as an attack on the German trenches had been arranged by the Brigade on our left, work had to be suspended owing to the enemy's bombardment which was very severe from 4.30 p.m. and took the form of a barrage on the TALUS des ZOUAVES from about 8 until 9 p.m. From that time until daylight the shelling was heavy and prevented work on the trenches being continued. Weather showery.	[illegible]
	2/6/16		Nothing of importance occurred throughout the day after 2.15 AM (daylight).	[illegible]
	3/6/16		Battalion was relieved by the 2nd Oxford & Bucks L.I. (5th Brigade) about 1 AM and marched independently by companies to billets in GOUY SERVINS, the last coy arriving about 4.30 A.M. Billets were fairly, the whole Battalion being in the CHATEAU. The men rested and cleaned up during the day.	[illegible] Lieuts Freeman & Dempsey joined.
	4/6/16		Sunday. The Commanding Officer inspected two companies in the morning. Voluntary Church Parade at 2 p.m. Weather showery.	[illegible]
	5/6/16		Only short parades were held in the morning as one Company was on fatigue and the remainder of the Battalion had been warned for work in the evening. The Battn supplied 300 men for work on the BAJOLLE LINE. Parties left billets at 6 p.m. and returned about 2 AM.	[illegible]

T2134. Wt. W708—776. 500000. 4/15. Sir J. C. & S.

Instructions regarding War Diaries and Intelligence Summaries are contained in F. S. Regs., Part II. and the Staff Manual respectively. Title pages will be prepared in manuscript.

Confidential

WAR DIARY
or
~~INTELLIGENCE SUMMARY.~~
(Erase heading not required.)

Sheet no 26

Army Form C. 2118.

Place	Date	Hour	Summary of Events and Information	Remarks and references to Appendices
BOUY SERVINS	6.6.16		As the greater part of the Battalion had been on fatigue most of the previous night, no programme of work was laid down. The Commanding Officer inspected 1 Company at 11.30 AM. Two companies played football in the afternoon. No fatigues. Day wet.	AHHC Capt
	7.6.16		Adjutant's parade ~~9-9.45~~ 9–9.45 AM. Company training 10. to 11.45 AM. At night the Battn supplied 300 men for fatigue. During the day 1 Coy had been on fatigue in addition. Weather wet.	Sec Lieut Glass on leave. AHHC Capt
	8.6.16		Very little training was done as the fatigue parties did not return until 2.45 AM. Sergeant Major's parade 2 p.m to 3 p.m. Weather Wet.	AHHC Capt
	9.6.16		One company on fatigue during the day. Remainder of the Battalion did 3 hours training in the morning and went on fatigue at night. During the whole of this period of rest a certain amount of training of bombers and Lewis Gunners was carried out daily but owing to the Battalion being so weak, this was greatly interfered with by the fatigue	AHHC Capt.

T2134. Wt. W708–776. 500000. 4/15. Sir J. C. & S.

Instructions regarding War Diaries and Intelligence Summaries are contained in F. S. Regs., Part II. and the Staff Manual respectively. Title pages will be prepared in manuscript.

Confidential

WAR DIARY
or
~~INTELLIGENCE SUMMARY.~~
(Erase heading not required.)

Sheet 263

Army Form C. 2118.

Place	Date	Hour	Summary of Events and Information	Remarks and references to Appendices
BOUY SERVINS	10.1.16		Short parades in the morning as the Battn was going into the trenches that night. First coy left BOUY at 7.30 p.m.	[illegible]
CARENCY SECTOR (SUPPORT)	11.6.16		Relieved 2nd South Staffords about 1 AM. The Battn was in support, and was split up in various places as follows. HQrs and two coys in the ZOUAVE VALLEY, one at CABARET ROUGE and the other at CARENCY	[illegible]
	12.6.16		Battn was warned by the Brigade that every available man would be required for carrying fatigues at night during the time it was on support. Total trench strength of Bn was 420. Number on fatigue 385. Weather very wet and cold. Day very quiet, no hostile shelling	[illegible]
	13.6.16		Carrying fatigues. Situation quiet. Weather wet and cold.	[illegible]
	14.6.16		Carrying fatigues. Situation quiet. Weather wet and cold	[illegible]
	14.6.16		Daylight Savings Bill came into force. The 23rd R. Fusiliers commenced to relieve the Battn about 11 p.m. Weather wet.	
	15.6.16		Relief completed 2 A.M. The Battn then relieved the 22nd R. Fusiliers in the Right subsection, completing by 3 AM. Night was very quiet. A very great deal of mining was in process in this subsector on the part of the enemy and ourselves. Each company formed a dug out platoon in accordance with the 10th Corp. [illegible]. This consisted of 1/9 all ranks and was used exclusively for making deep dug outs	[illegible]

Instructions regarding War Diaries and Intelligence Summaries are contained in F. S. Regs., Part II. and the Staff Manual respectively. Title pages will be prepared in manuscript.

Confidential

WAR DIARY
or
~~INTELLIGENCE SUMMARY.~~
(Erase heading not required.)

Sheet 264

Army Form C. 2118.

Place	Date	Hour	Summary of Events and Information	Remarks and references to Appendices
CARENCY	16.6.16		At 10 p.m a mine was exploded by us on the right of the Battn front, between the two craters MOMBER and LOVE, about 10 minutes after the explosion a heavy bombing fight commenced in which the Germans were repulsed. Sec Lieut LANE was seriously wounded, in the chest head and arms, by a bomb. Sec Lieut HANNAY was slightly wounded in the face and leg. The bombing continued until 11 p.m. Remainder of night quiet. Contrary to their usual custom the enemy did not open any artillery fire when the mine was exploded, and afterwards fired only a very few rounds of "whizzbangs". It was popularly supposed at the time that the Germans had withdrawn most of their heavy guns to another part of the line. Weather better	Total casualties 14 [illegible]
	17.6.16		About 8 AM Enemy trench mortars were very active against all parts of our line. Our artillery retaliated but failed to silence them. The trenches were knocked about a good deal and much work had to be done at night to put them in state of defence. Night Quiet Weather better	[illegible]
	18.6.16		Enemy trench mortars again active, but this time very little damage was done to the trenches. Battn. The 22nd R. Fus commenced to relieve	

T2134. Wt. W708—776. 500000. 4/15. Sir J. C. & S.

Instructions regarding War Diaries and Intelligence Summaries are contained in F. S. Regs., Part II. and the Staff Manual respectively. Title pages will be prepared in manuscript.

Confidential

WAR DIARY
or
~~INTELLIGENCE SUMMARY~~.
(Erase heading not required.)

Sheet 265.

Army Form C. 2118.

Place	Date	Hour	Summary of Events and Information	Remarks and references to Appendices
CARENCY.	18.6.16		the Battn.	[illegible]
VILLERS au BOIS.	19.6.16		Relief completed 12.30 AM. Coys marched to billets in VILLERS au BOIS. The last company getting in by 3.30 AM. The men rested and cleaned up during the day. Billets were good on the whole, and baths available. 100 men were detached for training in "Raiding" and billeted in CHATEAU de LA HAIE, the party was under the command of Captain West	[illegible] Sec Lieuts CHILDS + LAVERS joined [illegible]
	20.9.16		300 men on carrying fatigues. The DRAKE Battn R.N.D arrived at VILLERS	
	21.9.16		Coys at disposal of O.C. Coys for training. No fatigues. Weather fine	[illegible]
	22.9.16		Coys at disposal of O.C. Coys. Day fine. The Officers played the rest of the Battn at cricket and won by 1 run. Detachment from CHATEAU de LA HAIE rejoined	[illegible]
	23.9.16		Battn left VILLERS at 9 p.m. for the trenches, to relieve 22nd R.F. in right Subsector	[illegible]
	24.9.16		Relief complete 12.30 AM. Day was quiet until 3 p.m. when the enemy commenced to bombard our line with trench mortars, and damaged our trenches	
	[illegible] 6		Our Trench Mortars and artillery were very active, against the enemy	

T2134. Wt. W708—776. 500000. 4/15. Sir J. C. & S.

Instructions regarding War Diaries and Intelligence Summaries are contained in F. S. Regs., Part II. and the Staff Manual respectively. Title pages will be prepared in manuscript.

Confidential

WAR DIARY
or
~~INTELLIGENCE~~ SUMMARY.
(Erase heading not required.)

Sheet 266.

Army Form C. 2118.

Place	Date	Hour	Summary of Events and Information	Remarks and references to Appendices
CARENCY	(contd) 24.6.16		wire. Our bombardment was effective and many gaps were made in the enemy wire Night quiet. Weather fine	Attach-col
"	25.6.16		Trench mortar activity on both sides throughout the day. Enemy wire again cut in many places. Night quiet	Attach-col
"	26.6.16		The party of 100 under Captain WEST which had been withdrawn from the line on the 24th returned at 5 p.m. This party was to make a raid on the German front line at 11.30 p.m. (Battn orders and instructions are attached) The plan being to make a frontal attack in two waves with 2 officers and 56 other ranks simultaneously with bombing attacks on both flanks along the communication trenches which led into the enemy line. The cutting of their wire had apparently put the Germans on the alert, for on the signal being given to advance, a very heavy trench mortar bombing and machine gun fire was opened and prevented any of our parties reaching their objectives. Casualties in the raiding party were Lieut THORNE missing Sec Lieut JACKSON wounded 4 ORs killed 1 missing and 21 wounded. Total casualties in the Battn during raid 2 Officers 43 ORs wounded killed and missing.	Attach-col

T2134. Wt. W708—776. 500000. 4/15. Sir J. C. & S.

Instructions regarding War Diaries and Intelligence Summaries are contained in F. S. Regs., Part II. and the Staff Manual respectively. Title pages will be prepared in manuscript.

Confidential

WAR DIARY
or
~~INTELLIGENCE~~ ~~SUMMARY.~~
(Erase heading not required.)

Sheet 267

Army Form C. 2118.

Place	Date	Hour	Summary of Events and Information	Remarks and references to Appendices
CARENCY	27.6.16		The raiding party were withdrawn to billets in VILLERS au BOIS as soon as the situation became quieter, which was about 1 A.M. their place being taken by a company of the 22nd R.F. Day Quiet. Weather fine. Relieved by 2nd H.L.I. about midnight	Casualties during tour 2 Offs 56 O.Rs [illegible initials]
BOUY SERVINS	28.6.16		Billeted in BOUY SERVINS. Men rested during the day. Weather fine	[illegible initials]
	29.6.16		Large fatigue parties	[illegible initials]
	30.6.16		Companies at disposal of O.C. Coys for training. Battn played 22nd R.F at cricket and lost by 3 wickets	[illegible initials]
			Numbers with Battn 27 Offrs 641 O.Rs	

[illegible signature] Lt Col
Commdg 1st Royal Berks Regt

T2134. Wt. W708—776. 500000. 4/15. Sir J. C. & S.

Secret:

1st Royal Berkshire Regt.
Order No 23.

Ref Plans A 24.6.16

Intention 1. 'C' & 'D' will raid enemy trench XY on night of 26/27th June 1916.

Object 2. (A) To rush XY with the bayonet, kill or capture the garrison there, damage any mine shafts and obtain information regarding any preparations for gas attack.

(B) To bring back enemy badges, identity discs, papers found on enemy, gas helmets & automatic rifles.

Method of Carrying out. 3. (A) On a given signal strong bombing attacks will be made up ERBATZ, HARTUNG, & S of MEMBER CRATER whilst a bombing party moving round the N side of LOVE CRATER will attack the enemy bombing sap there. The parties will establish themselves respectively at points marked K. L. M.

(B) Simultaneously with above signal a raiding party strength 2 officers & 56 other ranks will rush enemy trench XY from line C.D at all costs & will act as in para 2

(C) On a given signal from Strombus horn,

(1) Raiding party will move back the shortest way to our trench marked bringing with them articles mentioned in para 2 (b)

(2) All bombing parties will be withdrawn silently.

Garrison 4. The normal garrison & dispositions of front line will be maintained. Sentries and bombing posts will simply stand aside to give attacking parties free access to trenches & will immediately resume their positions on the advance of attacking parties. They will thenceforth remain in their positions at all times, and all attacking parties will retire behind them. The vigilance of the normal garrison will in no way be relaxed during the operations. The bombing post at COBRON will act under special instructions from Capt West.

Time of Advance. 5. All advances will take place simultaneously at "ZERO" This time will be notified to all officers concerned on 26th inst.

Watches will be synchronised at 5 p.m. on 26th inst, and again at 10 p.m. on same date.

Method of (6) Method of timing different parties is laid down in special Timing. instructions issued with these orders.

Officers (7.) The following officers are detailed for timing attacks:-

ERSATZ 2/Lieut Strong. Raiding Party Capt West.

HARTUNG 2/Lieut Cook. MOMBER 2/Lieut Parsons.

Instructions will be issued to them at CHATEAU DE LA HAIE on 26th inst.

Ammunition 8. Reserves of ammunition will be established at head of URBAN and TANCHOT under Regt arrangements.

Bombs 9. The bombing officer will establish the following reserves of bombs in addition to the normal supply for garrisons:-

30 boxes in ERSATZ, 30 in HARTUNG, 150 boxes in TANCHOT.

Equipment of 10. The raiding party will have their faces blackened.

Raiding Party. They will wear drill order & carry 100 rds of S.A.A. & 3 grenades.

Bayonets will be fixed & blackened & scabbards will not be carried.

Wire cutters will be carried by the leading wave.

Men with wire cutters will have a small white band tied round the right shoulder strap.

Caps will not be worn.

All ranks will leave behind all badges, identity discs & paper.

Aid Post 11. The M.O. will establish an Aid Post in main Battn H.Q.

Wounded 12. Wounded will be evacuated via GOODMAN.

Prisoners. 13.(A) O.C. 'C' Coy will detail a party of 2 N.C.O's & 6 men to receive prisoners at E and conduct them to Advance Battn H.Q. This party will report to Advance Battn H.Q. at 10 p.m. on 26th inst.

(B) Escorts will consist of 2 men with one or two prisoners and one extra man for every two prisoners.

Escorts will carry loaded rifles and fixed bayonets.

and on any attempt to escape will be fired on or killed.
O.C. 'C' Coy will detail further escorts as required.

Reports 14. Reports to Advanced Battn H.Q at Junction of TANCHOT and LIME ST.

1st Royal Berkshire Regt.

Secret. Special Instructions for attacking party 26.6.16.

Composition. 1. The attacking party will consist of O.C. Capt West.

(A) Special Parties { No 1 Bombing party strenght 12 attack up ERSATZ.
No 2. Bombing party strenght 12 attack up HARTUNG.
No 3. Bombing party strenght 16 attack round South of MEMBER CRATER & block approaches to captured enemy trench from N & E. }

(B) Raiding party { No 4. Bombing party 12 to advance with raiding party and protect their right flank on entering enemy trench.
No 5. Bombing party 8 at disposal of Lt Thorne as reserve to accompany him in the attack.
No 6. Bombing party to advance with raiding party & protect their left flank on entering enemy trench.
Bayonet men 2 Officers & 99 men, (including 4 orderlies & 4 bayonet men as escort R.E.) To rush enemy trench K.Y. with bayonet }

(C) Other details Clearing party 1 N.C.O. 4 men, To follow immediately behind R.E., & clear wire obstacles out of GORDON.
Stretcher bearers 6, to follow behind 2nd wave & remove wounded.
R.E. To follow behind 2nd wave under direction of R.E. Officer.

Formation 2. The raiding party will attack in two waves on a front of 60 yards, 30 paces between each wave as follows

P.T.O.

		CENTRE.	RIGHT	LEFT.
(A.)	1st wave	2/Lieut Jackson	6 bombers	6 bombers
		3 bombers	of	of
		16 bayonet men	No 4 Party	No. 6 Party
B.	2nd wave	Lt Thorne	6 bombers of	6 bombers of
		19. bayonet men	No 4 Party	No. 6. Party

C. R.E. Party in rear of 2nd wave under orders of R.E. Officer. Four bayonet men will accompany this party as escort.

D. Clearing party immediately in rear of R.E. and escort.

E. Stretcher parties will follow under orders of the M.O. Lt Bailey.

Programme. 3. The programme on night of attack will be as follows:—

Time 5 p.m., Arrive trenches and move up UHLAN into LINE ST

5.5 p.m., Watches synchronised at main Battn H.Q.

5.30 p.m., Reserve of bombs & ammunition placed in position

2 hours before Zero } Raiding parties dress, blacken faces & bayonets. Advance Battn H.Q. established.

1 hour before Zero } All bombing parties move to immediate rear of barricades (from whence they attack)

1 hour before Zero. } Raiding party file into starting off trench. R.E., Stretcher party & clearing party take up positions.

10. p.m., Watches again synchronised at Advanced Battn H.Q.

10.30 p.m. Our wire cut. Patrol sent out

½ hour before Zero } Raiding party deploys.

½ hour before Zero } No's 1, 2, & 3 bombing parties crawl out and prepare to throw.

Signal for Start. (4) At Zero a Very Pistol will be fired by Capt West from E end of COBRON and by 2/Lt Cook simultaneously from E end of HARTUNG and immediately:—

(A.) Starting officers at ERSATZ, HARTUNG, MOMBER & LOVE will start their attack by word of command.

(B.) Bombers detailed by Capt West will throw into enemy barricade at COBRON, and of explosion of those bombs the raiding party will rush the enemy trench.

5. On arrival in enemy trench:-

(A) Bombing parties on the flanks will move rapidly outwards, bombing all dug-outs on the way and will hold enemy in check.

(B) The remainder of raiding party will kill or capture all enemy in trench & bomb dug-outs.

A proportion of men (detailed before hand) will watch the front whilst others enter the dug-outs under N.C.O's and seize any papers or prisoners that can be found there. All bodies will be stripped of badges, shoulder straps, & caps, identity discs & papers. Any officer taken prisoner will be immediately searched. Prisoners will be sent back to starting off trench under direction of the senior officer or N.C.O on the spot.

Withdrawal (6). The signal for withdrawal will be a blast from a Strombus horn from Advanced Battn H.Q sounded at fifteen minutes past zero by Capt West. Parties will then act in accordance with instructions (previously) issued by O.C. Raiding party (Capt West)

Equipment (7.) (A) Bayonet men, Drill Order, 100 rds of S.A.A., bayonets fixed, 3 Mills grenades, wire cutters, hedging gloves. Men with wire cutters will have a small white band on right shoulder strap.

(B) Bombers, one third will carry rifle & bayonet with 10 rds in magazine, one third knobkerries.

All will carry a bucket with 20 grenades.

All faces will be blackened & bayonets smoked.

Method of Bombing Party (8) The action of all bombing parties will be as follows:-

PRIOR TO ZERO. They will crawl forward outside their trenches until close to enemy bombing posts.

AT ZERO. They will throw grenades & then jump into trench & rapidly follow enemy as far as but not farther than their assigned objectives.

PARTY No 3. will work round S lip of MOMBER CRATER and after bombing enemy bombing post will establish themselves at S.E. end of enemy C.T. running round E foot of MOMBER CRATER and prevent enemy counter-attacking our raiding party from the N.

Patrol. 9. An Officer's patrol will be sent out by Capt West at 10.30 p.m to report on state of enemy wire.

10. The raiding party & each bombing party will be given a separate password, namely, the name of officer and N.C.O in charge of that party.

11. All men will be warned to take no notice of orders to "retire" other than the Strombus horn.

12. All will be personally warned by Capt West that prisoners of war must give their correct Regt No & names, but under no circumstances any further information of any sort or kind especially concerning position or movement of troops.

13. On return from enemy's lines attacking party will file into LIME ST.

* The objectives are as follows:-

No. 1. Party point K.

No 2. — — L.

No 3. — — M.

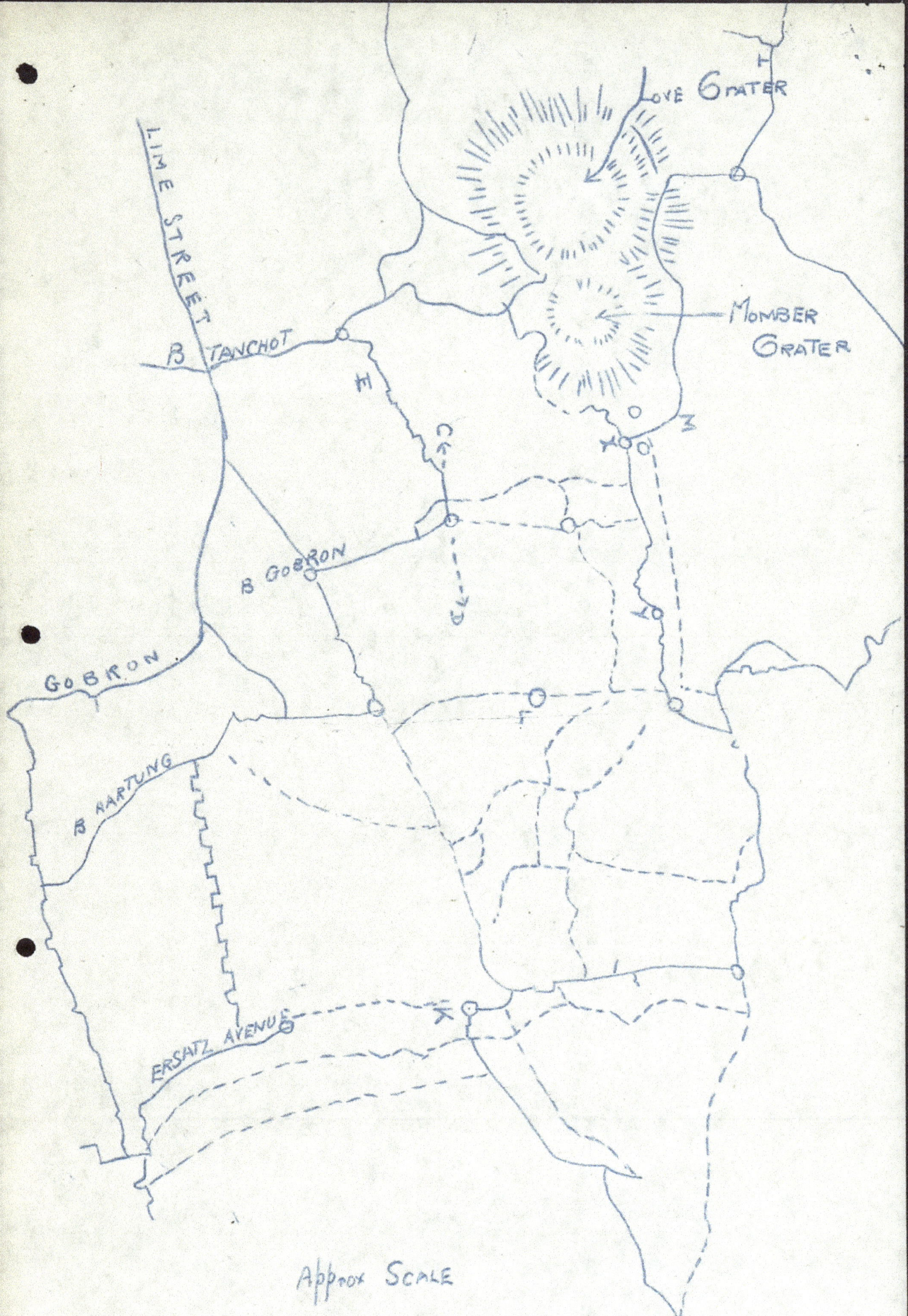

LOVE CRATER

LIME STREET

MOMBER CRATER

B TANCHOT

B GOBRON

GOBRON

B HARTUNG

ERSATZ AVENUE

Approx SCALE

100 0 200 YDS

99th Inf.Bde.
2nd Div.

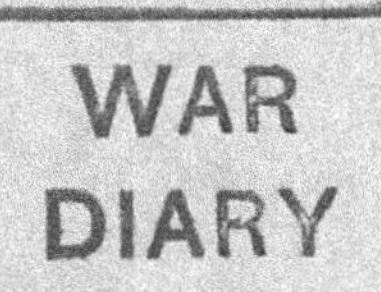

1st BATTN. THE ROYAL BERKSHIRE REGIMENT.

J U L Y

1 9 1 6

Instructions regarding War Diaries and Intelligence Summaries are contained in F. S. Regs., Part II. and the Staff Manual respectively. Title pages will be prepared in manuscript.

Confidential

~~WAR DIARY~~ or ~~INTELLIGENCE SUMMARY.~~

(Erase heading not required.)

Sheet 268

Vol 21

99/2

Place	Date	Hour	Summary of Events and Information	Remarks and references to Appendices
BOUY SERVINS	1.7.16		Coys at disposal of O.C Coys for training. News received that the 3rd and 4th Armies in conjunction with the French had assumed the offensive. A summary of official wires relating to these operations is attached to this page. Weather fine	[initials]
"	2.7.16		Sunday. Church Parade in the morning at 9.30 AM. 400 men on fatigue at night. Weather fine. News received 2nd Lt LANE "died from wounds"	[initials]
	3.7.16		Men rested during the morning. Adjutants parade in the afternoon. An inter platoon football competition was started.	[initials]
	4.7.16		Coys at disposal of O.C. Coys for training. A rifle range allotted to the Battn was used by two companies. 400 men on fatigue at night.	[initials]
	5.7.16		As the Battn was going into the trenches the same night only a short parade was held in the morning. Leading company left billets at 10. p m	[initials]
CABARET ROUGE	6.7.16		Relieved 2nd S. Staffs in support about 2 AM. In this position the Battalion was used for fatigues both day and night. Weather fine. Our aircraft were very active	[initials]
	7.7.16		Weather fine. Every available man on fatigue	2nd Lt Strong left Bn for Special Works Park. R.E. [initials]

T2134. Wt. W708–776. 500000. 4/15. Sir J. C. & S.

Instructions regarding War Diaries and Intelligence Summaries are contained in F. S. Regs., Part II. and the Staff Manual respectively. Title pages will be prepared in manuscript.

Confiden[tial]

or

~~INTELLIGENCE SUMMARY~~.

(Erase heading not required.)

Sheet 269

Place	Date	Hour	Summary of Events and Information	Remarks and references to Appendices
CABARET ROUGE	8.7.16		Every available man on fatigue. Our aircraft were very active. [illegible]	[illegible]
BERTHONVAL NORTH	9.7.16		Relieved 22 Royal Fusiliers in BERTHONVAL NORTH at 10.30 p.m. Dispositions in this subsection were – 3 Coys Front line 1 Coy in Reserve. Since the last tour of the Battalion in this subsection a great deal of work had been done in the front line system of trenches and a very good line constructed. The night was quiet save for occasional Machine Gun activity on the part of the enemy. Weather fair.	[illegible]
"	10.7.16		Day very quiet. Weather fine	[illegible]
"	11.7.16		Considerable enemy T.M activity against our positions in the TALUS des ZOUAVES, otherwise day quiet	[illegible]
"	12.7.16		Enemy trench mortars active between 8AM and 9AM. Night quiet except for occasional sniping and M.G. Fire.	[illegible]
"	13.7.16		Enemy Artillery fairly active against our communication trenches during the morning. Relieved by the 22nd Royal Fusiliers at 11.30 PM	[illegible]

T2134. Wt. W708—776. 500000. 4/15. Sir J. C. & S.

Instructions regarding War Diaries and Intelligence Summaries are contained in F. S. Regs., Part II. and the Staff Manual respectively. Title pages will be prepared in manuscript.

Confidential

~~WAR DIARY~~ or ~~INTELLIGENCE~~ SUMMARY. (Erase heading not required.)

Sheet 270

Place	Date	Hour	Summary of Events and Information	Remarks and references to Appendices
			Ref. Sheet 36 B	
CAMBLAIN L'ABBÉ	14/7/16		Last company arrived at CAMBLAIN L'ABBE about 3 AM. The battalion was billeted in huts and accomodation was good.	
CAMLAIN L'ABBÉ — ESTRÉE CAUCHIE	15/7/16		Orders were received to move to ESTRÉE-CAUCHEE. Battn paraded 5.15 p.m. and arrived in new billets about 6.30 p.m. 200 men were sent on fatigue at night carrying for Tunnelling Coys. Weather fine	Appx Captain Frizzell rejoined from 5th Bde
ESTRÉE CAUCHIE — FREVILLERS	16/7/16		Battn paraded 2 p.m. and marched to FREVILLERS. arriving about 5.30 p.m. New billets were good. Weather very wet	Appx Sec Lieut Stoh rejoined from Div School
FREVILLERS	17/7/16		Company training for which fairly good ground was available. Billets inspected by B.G. 99 Inf Bde. Weather wet and ground heavy.	Appx
"	18/7/16		Battalion training. Weather fine	Appx
	19/7/16		Short parades in the morning remainder of day was spent in preparing for a move. Weather fine	Appx
FREVILLERS DIEVAL MORLANCOURT	20/7/16	Ref. Amiens	Battalion with 1st Line Transport paraded 9 AM and marched to DIÈVAL where it entrained and was conveyed by rail to LONGEAU near AMIENS arriving at 6.30 p.m. and proceeded by road to MORLANCOURT, a distance of 11 miles. The Battn arrived about 2.45. New billets were good on the whole.	2nd Div transferred to 13th Corps Appx

T2134. Wt. W708—776. 500000. 4/15. Sir J. C. & S.

Instructions regarding War Diaries and Intelligence Summaries are contained in F. S. Regs., Part II. and the Staff Manual respectively. Title pages will be prepared in manuscript.

Confidential

WAR DIARY
or
~~INTELLIGENCE SUMMARY.~~
(Erase heading not required.)

Sheet 271.

Army Form [illegible]. 2118.

Place	Date	Hour	Summary of Events and Information	Remarks and references to Appendices
			Reference AMIENS Sheet	
MORLANCOURT	21/7/16		Men rested and cleaned up. Weather very warm.	[illegible]
	22/7/16		Battalion training: good ground was available. Ordered to be in readiness to move at short notice. B.G. 99th Brigade addressed the Battalion. Weather warm.	[illegible]
MORLANCOURT – SANDPIT VALLEY	23/7/16		Moved at 10 AM to bivouacs in SANDPIT VALLEY arriving there about mid-day. Weather warm.	2nd Lt H.V. STIDWELL and 2nd Lt C.V. WILSON joined for duty. [illegible]
SANDPIT VALLEY	24/7/16		Battalion training in the "Attack" in the morning. Moved at 6 pm and marched via FRICOURT and MONTAUBAN and relieved 1st R. SCOTS FUSILIERS in LONGUEVAL VILLAGE and western portion of DELVILLE WOOD.	[illegible]
LONGUEVAL	25/7/16		Relief complete 6.30 AM. Battalion on left 1st GORDON HIGHLANDERS – on right 1st K.O.S.L.I. Shelling in the neighbourhood of the village was very heavy and rendered movement difficult. Dispositions of Companies were as follows. – Three companies front line, one in support. The village was shelled intermittently throughout the day. At 8 pm orders were received to withdraw the right and left front companies the relief by a company of the DURHAMS and a company of the SHROPSHIRES respectively. The front centre company and the support	
Reference MONTAUBAN Trench Map 1/20.000				

T2134. Wt. W708–776. 500000. 4/15. Sir J. C. & S.

Instructions regarding War Diaries and Intelligence Summaries are contained in F. S. Regs., Part II. and the Staff Manual respectively. Title pages will be prepared in manuscript.

or

INTELLIGENCE ~~SUMMARY~~.

(*Erase heading not required.*)

Sheet 272

Place	Date	Hour	Reference MONTAUBAN Trench Map 1/20 000 — Summary of Events and Information	Remarks and references to Appendices
LONGUEVAL (continued)	25/7/16		support company were to remain in position.	Abbr
BERNAFAY WOOD	26/7/16	~~10 AM~~	B and C Companies on relief proceeded to dug-outs in western edge of BERNAFAY WOOD. &	Abbr
		10 AM	C.Os conference at Brigade Hdqs. where it was announced that the Brigade would attack DELVILLE WOOD on the morning of the 27th the Bn to be in support.	
		5 pm	Company commanders and the C.O went up to view the ground over which the attack was to be carried out. A Company was detached under orders of O.C. 23rd R.F.	
		8.45 pm	C.O and Company Commanders returned. Gas shells commenced to fall in the wood and helmets had to be worn almost continuously until midnight.	Abbr
DELVILLE WOOD	27/7/16	2 AM	Battalion moved to DELVILLE WOOD and took up position on southern edge of	
		4.15 AM	wood, and lay down in "jumping off" formation immediately in front of SOUTH STREET. Companies were disposed as follows. Left. A Company (Capt WESTON) in support to and under orders of 23rd R.F. Left centre, B Company (Capt WEST). Right centre, C Company (Capt GREGSON-ELLIS). Right, D Company (Lieut REID). Right company was detailed for protection of right flank.	

T2134. Wt. W708—776. 500000. 4/15. Sir J. C. & S.

Instructions regarding War Diaries and Intelligence Summaries are contained in F. S. Regs., Part II. and the Staff Manual respectively. Title pages will be prepared in manuscript.

or

INTELLIGENCE SUMMARY.

(Erase heading not required.)

Sheet 273

Place	Date	Hour	Reference HONTAUBAN Trench Map 1/20 000 — Summary of Events and Information	Remarks and references to Appendices
DELVILLE	27/7/16	5.10 AM	Our Bombardment of LONGUEVAL VILLAGE commenced.	
WOOD		6.10 AM	Our bombardment of DELVILLE WOOD commenced.	
(continued)		7.10 AM	Leading waves of 1st K.R.R.C and 23rd RF moved forward from their assembly trenches	
		7.12 AM	Battalion less A Company advanced in two waves in support: Btn. Hdqs in centre of leading wave. After advancing 270 yards the leading battalions halted. The Battalion halted and dug in at this point. Our bombardment had lengthened by this time to the northern ~~edge~~ portion of the wood.	Attached
		8.10 AM	Advance continued. The Battalion finally halted and dug in on the PRINCES STREET line [illegible] (Map attached). During the advance from SOUTH STREET enemy's rifle fire was considerable but extremely inaccurate. Enemy machine-gun, apparently fired from vicinity of LONGUEVAL VILLAGE, enfiladed the advance and consolidating parties. Another machine-gun was traversing opposite the centre of the advance. These two guns ceased firing, having apparently been silenced just before the Battalion reached ~~SOUTH~~ PRINCES STREET	
		9 AM	By this time the Battalion was dug in. Enemy opened extremely accurate ~~enfil~~ H.E fire, enfilading the position from right to left.	

T2134. Wt. W708—776. 500000. 4/15. Sir J. C. & S.

Instructions regarding War Diaries and Intelligence Summaries are contained in F. S. Regs., Part II. and the Staff Manual respectively. Title pages will be prepared in manuscript.

or

INTELLIGENCE SUMMARY.

(Erase heading not required.)

Sheet 274

Reference MONTAUBAN Trench Map 1/20.000

Place	Date	Hour	Summary of Events and Information	Remarks and references to Appendices
DELVILLE WOOD (continued)	27/7/16	9 AM	Consolidation of the line was continued throughout the remainder of the day, and a very fair line was made. Weather throughout the day was very warm and no water supply was available, other than that carried in the bottles. The line was continually shelled from 9 AM to 8 pm	
		10.40 AM	Officer from 1st KRRC support trench came back and stated that the enemy were bombing along right flank of his battalion, and that the position there was being retained with difficulty. Orders were immediately issued for bombs to be collected (each man was carrying two bombs). This was done with very little delay, and the bombs were sent up with 12 bombers from the two centre companies. A pigeon message to Brigade was sent off "Send up bombs: very urgently needed".	"
		10.50 AM	An old dump containing 30 boxes SAA and about 100 boxes of bombs was discovered about 50 yards in rear of PRINCESS STREET line: this having been evidently left there in a previous advance, and overlooked by the enemy. Parties were detailed to take quantities of bombs and SAA to the KRR support trench.	
		11.30 AM	Another officer from KRR arrived at Btn Hdqs. and asked for further reinforcements	Abbs[illegible]

T2134. Wt. W708–776. 500000. 4/15. Sir J. C. & S.

Instructions regarding War Diaries and Intelligence Summaries are contained in F. S. Regs., Part II. and the Staff Manual respectively. Title pages will be prepared in manuscript.

~~INTELLIGENCE SUMMARY.~~
(Erase heading not required.)

Sheet 275

Place	Date	Hour	Reference MONTAUBAN Trench Map 1/20.000 — Summary of Events and Information	Remarks and references to Appendices
DELVILLE	27/7/16		reinforcements to assist in holding the right flank of his battalion. He	
WOOD		11.30	stated that 12 men and a Lewis Gun and team would be sufficient. ~~These~~ 12 men & L.G. team	
(continued)		AM.	were sent forward immediately together with a further supply of bombs.	
		4 pm	Same officer from KRR returned and stated that the right of the firing line of his Battalion had been slightly pushed back, and the Lewis Guns which we had sent up knocked out. Reinforcements were then sent forward consisting of the remainder of right centre company under 2 Lt CHILDS (who was killed shortly after he had got his party into position) ~~to reinforce~~. The remainder of left centre company was transferred to the position vacated by right centre company in order to be prepared to counter-attack. Pigeon message was then sent to Brigade to the effect that the firing line had been reinforced, and only a small number of men were left in hand for support, and that reinforcements were urgently required. Enemy shelling lessened about 5 pm.	
		9 PM	From this time onwards until dawn the situation was quiet with little or no shelling.	AWH

T2134. Wt. W708—776. 500000. 4/15. Sir J. C. & S.

Instructions regarding War Diaries and Intelligence Summaries are contained in F. S. Regs., Part II. and the Staff Manual respectively. Title pages will be prepared in manuscript.

~~INTELLIGENCE SUMMARY~~.
(Erase heading not required.)

Sheet 276

Place	Date	Hour	Summary of Events and Information (Reference MONTAUBAN French Map 1/20 000)	Remarks and references to Appendices
DELVILLE	28/7/16		It was discovered that the 1st KRRC had been relieved by a Btn of 6th Brigade	
WOOD		6.45am	and that the Battalion was also going to be relieved by the 6th Brigade.	
		9AM.	Enemy commenced to shell with heavy guns, including 8 inch, fire from which became intense for short periods from 2 to 4 pm. but finally subsided at 4.30 pm.	
		5pm	In consequence of instructions received from Brigade, Battalion withdrew to MINE SUPPORT TRENCH (A.8.a); the flank company - D - were unable to withdraw until after dark owing to proximity of the enemy.	
			Total casualties during tour 1 Officer Killed. 2 Lt. CHILDS	
			Other Ranks. Killed 37 — 2 Officers Missing. Lt. REID, 2 Lt STIDWELL	
			Missing 55 — 5 Officers Wounded. Capt GREGSON-ELLIS,	
			Wounded 152 — Lt FREEMAN, 2 Lt MOORE, 2 Lt PARSONS	
			2 Lt WILSON.	
			Battn went into action strength 450	A.W.H. Lt Col
MINE SUPPORT	29/7/16		Battalion rested and cleaned up. Day very warm	A.W.H. Lt Col
TRENCH.	30/7/16		Received orders at 11 pm to take over positions vacated by 2nd H.L.I. in BERNAFAY WOOD. Moved about midnight.	A.W.H. Lt Col

T2134. Wt. W708—776. 500000. 4/15. Sir J. C. & S.

Instructions regarding War Diaries and Intelligence Summaries are contained in F. S. Regs., Part II. and the Staff Manual respectively. Title pages will be prepared in manuscript.

or

INTE~~LLIGENCE SUMMA~~RY.

(Erase heading not required.)

Sheet 277

Place	Date	Hour	Reference MONTAUBAN Trench Map 1/20.000. Summary of Events and Information	Remarks and references to Appendices
BERNAFAY WOOD	31/7/16		Day quiet. Weather warm. Nothing of interest occurred. In this position the Battalion was in support to the 5th Brigade.	[illegible]
			[illegible] Lt Col Comdg [illegible]	
			Numbers actually with Battalion	
			Officers. 16. Other Ranks. 512.	

T2134. Wt. W708—776. 500000. 4/15. Sir J. C. & S.

99th BRIGADE
2ND Division

1st BATTALION

ROYAL BERKSHIRE REGIMENT

AUGUST 1 9 1 6

Confidential

WAR DIARY
or
~~INTELLIGENCE SUMMARY.~~
(Erase heading not required.)

99/2

Sheet 278

1st Royal Berks

Army Form C. 2118.

Instructions regarding War Diaries and Intelligence Summaries are contained in F. S. Regs., Part II. and the Staff Manual respectively. Title pages will be prepared in manuscript.

Vol 22

Place	Date	Hour	Summary of Events and Information (Reference MONTAUBAN Trench Map 1/20.000.)	Remarks and references to Appendices
BERNAFAY WOOD and MINE SUPPORT TRENCH.	1/8/16	6.30 AM	Battalion vacated dug-outs in BERNAFAY WOOD and moved to MINE SUPPORT TRENCH area (A.8.a) Weather very warm. Found Fatigue party of 200 for digging and carrying.	Alh.
	2/8/16		Battalion rested during the day. as the 200 men on fatigue did not get back until 6 AM Weather very warm. 200 men on fatigue at night, carrying and digging	Reinforcement 9 4 2 OR's joined
	3/8/16		Battalion paraded at 7.30 pm and proceeded to relieve 22nd R F in DELVILLE WOOD	Alh.
	4/8/16		Relieved 22nd R.F. 4.15 AM. Battalion at this time was only 280 strong and was in consequence formed into 2 Companies - A and D = A, B and C = B. and to make up this small number 20 men from the Transport and 20 men from the Drums were taken for duty with Companies. Both companies were in the front line: 3 companies of the 1st K.R.R.C. were in support During the relief there was considerable Trench Mortar activity on the part of the enemy. our artillery were warned of this, and fired with Howitzers on the positions where enemy T Ms had been located and apparently put them out of action, as they did not fire again during the day. Enemy artillery were fairly active during the day. Relief ~~???~~ of Battalion by 7th BORDER REGIMENT at 10 pm	Alh
	5/8/16		Relief complete 3.45 AM. On relief the Battalion marched to MANSEL COPSE (F.11.c)	

T2134. Wt. W708—776. 500000. 4/15. Sir J. C. & S.

Instructions regarding War Diaries and Intelligence Summaries are contained in F. S. Regs., Part II. and the Staff Manual respectively. Title pages will be prepared in manuscript.

Confidential

WAR DIARY
or
~~INTELLIGENCE~~ SUMMARY.
(Erase heading not required.)

279

Army Form C. 2118.

Place	Date	Hour	Summary of Events and Information	Remarks and references to Appendices
			Ref. MONTAUBAN. Trench Map and SHEET 62D. N.E.	
MANSEL COPSE.	(Ctd) 5/8/16		200 Men on fatigue at night digging new trench between WATERLOT. FARM and S.E. corner of DELVILLE. WOOD. Captain WEST who was in charge of this party was accidentally wounded by a bayonet and evacuated to hospital	ARH
	6/8/16		Men rested during the day. Weather warm	ARH
	7/8/16		Battalion training. Battn was again organised into 4 coys. Weather warm.	2/Lt WOOD rejoined ARH
	8/8/16		Battalion training in the morning. Battn paraded at 3.40 p.m and marched to new bivouacs in SAND. PIT. VALLEY, arriving there about 4 p.m. Weather warm.	LIEUT. GREEN rejoined ARH
SAND. PIT VALLEY	9/8/16		Battalion training. Physical training, Bombing and Lewis Gun, classes were formed. A reinforcement of 63 OR's joined the Battn including 53 men of the 2/1st HUNTINGDON. CYCLISTS Battn. Weather warm. Voluntary bathing parade in the afternoon	ARH
	10/8/16		Battalion training in the morning. The G.O.C. 2nd Division (Maj Gen Walker V.C) addressed the Brigade in the afternoon and congratulated it on the capture of DELVILLE. WOOD	ARH

T2134. Wt. W708—776. 500000. 4/15. Sir J. C. & S.

Army Form C. 2118.

Instructions regarding War Diaries and Intelligence Summaries are contained in F. S. Regs., Part II. and the Staff Manual respectively. Title pages will be prepared in manuscript.

Confidential

WAR DIARY
or
~~INTELLIGENCE~~ SUMMARY.
(Erase heading not required.)

Sheet 280

Place	Date	Hour	Summary of Events and Information	Remarks and references to Appendices
			Ref AMIENS Sheet 1/100.000	
SAND. PIT VALLEY	11.8.16		Battn paraded at 1.30 p.m and marched to bivouacs at MERICOURT L'ABBE arriving there at 4.30 p.m. Weather warm.	AEH
MERICOURT L'ABBE	12.8.16		Battalion training. Bathing parades in the river ANCRE. Lt JACKSON rejoined	AEH
"	13.8.16		Battalion entrained at 8 AM from MERICOURT STA and moved by train to SALEUX arriving there at 3 p.m and marched to billets in ST. SAUVEUR	AEH
ST SAUVEUR			arriving about 6.30 p.m. Billets were very good. Lt Col A E HARRIS admitted to hospital. Major C.W. FRIZELL assumed command of the Battn.	AEH
"	14/8/16		Battalion training. Bathing parades in the SOMME. Weather warm.	AEH
	15/8/16		Battalion training. A small proportion of the men were taken by motor bus to visit AMIENS. Weather warm. Draft of 67 O.R.s joined including 47 Hunts Cyclists	AEH
NAOURS	16/8/16		Battalion paraded at 1 p.m and marched to NAOURS arriving there about 4.30 p.m.	AEH
AUTHEUX	17/8/16		Battn paraded at 9.45 am and marched to AUTHEUX arriving there about 1.30 p.m. Day fine	AEH
AUTHIE	18/8/16		Battn paraded at 5.20 AM and marched to AUTHIE arriving there at 12 noon.	AEH

T2134. Wt. W708–776. 500000. 4/15. Sir J. C. & S.

Instructions regarding War Diaries and Intelligence Summaries are contained in F. S. Regs., Part II. and the Staff Manual respectively. Title pages will be prepared in manuscript.

Confidential

WAR DIARY
or
~~INTELLIGENCE SUMMARY.~~
(Erase heading not required.)

Sheet 281.

Army Form C. 2118.

Place	Date	Hour	Summary of Events and Information	Remarks and references to Appendices
			Ref Sheets 57d NE	
AUTHIE	19.8.16		Battalion training and kit inspections. Men bathed. Day showery. Maj. P.W. North joined for duty	AEU
BUS LES ARTOIS	20.8.16		Paraded at 2 p.m. and marched to BUS. LES ARTOIS arriving there 3 p.m.	AEU
COUIN	21.8.16		Lt Col Harris rejoined from hospital. Paraded at 7.30 AM and marched to COUIN arriving there 8.45 AM. Training carried on in the morning. Men bathed in the afternoon	AEU
	22.8.16		Battalion Training. Bombing & Lewis Gun classes. Weather fine	AEU
	23.8.16		Training. Capt. West rejoined from the Base	AEU
	24.8.16		Training. Supplied at night working parties of 4 Off and 170 men for carrying gas cylinders up to the front line (FORE ST)	AEU
HÉBUTERNE SECTOR	25/8.16		Paraded 7.30 AM and marched to HÉBUTERNE and relieved the 22 R.F. in the Left subsection. Relief complete 11 AM. Remainder of day quiet. Enemy MG's were active during the night	AEU
	26.8.16		Day Quiet. Work of deepening trenches and laying trench boards in fire and communication trenches. Weather wet.	AEU
	27.8.16		A German patrol approached our ~~bombing~~ Lewis gun post at POPLAR SAP but was immediately driven back by our few bombers and one their number killed. Work on trenches continued. Weather wet	AEU

T2134. Wt. W708—776. 500000. 4/15. Sir J. C. & S.

Instructions regarding War Diaries and Intelligence Summaries are contained in F. S. Regs., Part II. and the Staff Manual respectively. Title pages will be prepared in manuscript.

Confidential

WAR DIARY
or
~~INTELLIGENCE SUMMARY~~.
(Erase heading not required.)

Army Form C. 2118.

Sheet. 282

Place	Date	Hour	Summary of Events and Information	Remarks and references to Appendices
			Ref Sheet 57 D NE	9/Lk DORBIE and FURLONG joined
HÈBUTERNE	28.8.16		Enemy shelled the village with light field guns from 9 to 11 AM but did very little damage. Work on trenches continued. Weather very wet.	[initials]
J.23A.7.6	29.8.16		Relieved by 22nd R.F 10.30 AM and marched independently by coys to bivouacs near SAILLY au BOIS. Men bathed in the afternoon. Very wet and stormy. Men bathed in the afternoon	[initials]
"	30.8.16		The weather prevented all outside training. Lectures to Officers and N.C.O's	[initials] 3 casualties
"	31.8.16		Weather very wet. Working party of 270 men supplied at night for digging new trench. (FUSILIER. TRENCH)	[initials]
			No of Officers serving with the Battalion 19 O.R.S 677.	

[signature] Lt Col
Commdg 1st Royal Berks Regt

6/9/16.

T2134. Wt. W708—776. 500000. 4/15. Sir J. C. & S.

99th Brigade.

2nd Division.

1st BATTALION ROYAL BERKSHIRE REGIMENT

SEPTEMBER 1 9 1 6 :

CONFIDENTIAL

To HQ
99th Bde

Herewith War Diary Originals for month of September (Sheets Nos 283 to 286)

Please acknowledge receipt ✓

2/10/16

A E Harris Lieut Colonel
Commdg 1st R Berks Regt

Instructions regarding War Diaries and Intelligence Summaries are contained in F. S. Regs., Part II. and the Staff Manual respectively. Title pages will be prepared in manuscript.

Confidential

WAR DIARY
or
~~INTELLIGENCE SUMMARY.~~
(Erase heading not required.)

Sheet 283

1st R. Berks.

Army Form C. 2118.

Vol 23

Place	Date	Hour	Summary of Events and Information	Remarks and references to Appendices
J.23.a.7.6	1.9.16		Whole Battalion on working parties at night	2 Lt Stonehouse for ... ACH
-	2.9.16		Working parties. Weather fair.	ACH
	3.9.16		No training was carried out during the day as the men did not return until 5.A.M. and orders were received to furnish the same working parties as on the previous night, but these were cancelled as it was proposed to discharge gas on the front where the work was to be carried out. Major FRIZELL posted to command 1st Bn Wilts Regt and struck off strength	ACH
HÉBUTERNE	4.9.16		Relieved 22nd R. Fus in HEBUTERNE NORTH about 10 AM. Gas was successfully discharged by the R.E from the Battn front at 8.30 p.m. Enemy retaliation was slight. An officer's patrol was sent out to secure identifications but did not succeed in obtaining any. The night was very dark.	ACH
	5.9.16		Day quiet. Work of floor boarding the trenches proceeded with by day also wiring at night. The same officer patrol mentioned yesterday again went out and found the body of a German belonging to the 170th Regiment.	ACH
	6.9.16		Day Quiet Weather fine	ACH

T2134. Wt. W708—776. 500000. 4/15. Sir J. C. & S.

Instructions regarding War Diaries and Intelligence Summaries are contained in F. S. Regs., Part II. and the Staff Manual respectively. Title pages will be prepared in manuscript.

Confidential

WAR DIARY
or
~~INTELLIGENCE SUMMARY.~~

(Erase heading not required.)

Sheet 284

Army Form C. 2118.

Place	Date	Hour	Summary of Events and Information	Remarks and references to Appendices
			Ref Sheet 57^D	
HÉBUTERNE NORTH	8.9.16		Day quiet. About 11 p.m a party of the enemy attacked with bombs a small covering party of ours. Our casualties were ~~Other~~ Other Ranks 1 wounded 2 missing.	ACH
"	9.9.16		Village of HÉBUTERNE shelled with field guns in the afternoon between 3 p.m & 4 p.m. Major C.W. Frizell rejoined the Battn. Sec Lieut J.W. Johnson joined for duty	ACH
COUIN	10.9.16		Relieved by 22nd R.F. at 11 AM and marched to billets in COUIN where the Battn was in Divisional Reserve. Weather fine.	ACH
"	11.9.16	.	~~Battalion~~. Company training. Range was available for Musketry practice Bombing and Lewis Gun training. Weather fine	ACH
"	12.9.16		Company training. An exercise in communication between infantry and aircraft was carried out in the morning with one of the Corps Liaison aeroplanes, messages sent by the ground panel were successfully received by the aeroplane. Battalion bathed in the afternoon	ACH
	13.9.16		Company training. Weather fine	ACH
	14.9.16		Company training Weather wet	ACH
	15.9.16		Battalion training in the ~~attack~~ new "French Attack"	ACH
HÉBUTERNE NORTH	16.9.16		Relieved 22nd R.F. 11 A.M. Situation quiet. Weather wet	ACH

T2134. Wt. W708—776. 500000. 4/15. Sir J. C. & S.

Army Form C. 2118

Instructions regarding War Diaries and Intelligence Summaries are contained in F. S. Regs., Part II. and the Staff Manual respectively. Title pages will be prepared in manuscript.

Confidential

WAR DIARY
or
~~INTELLIGENCE SUMMARY.~~
(Erase heading not required.)

Sheet 285.

Place	Date	Hour	Summary of Events and Information	Remarks and references to Appendices
HEBUTERNE NORTH	17.9.16		Situation quiet. Owing to the weather the trenches were in a bad state and a great deal of work was required to keep them in repair.	ACH
"	18.9.16		Situation quiet. Weather wet. Continued work of floorboarding trenches. Major C W Frizell posted to command 10th Bn Essex Rgt	ACH
"	19.9.16		Situation quiet Weather wet	ACH
COUIN	20.9.16		Relieved by 17th K.R.R.C (39th Division) 1 p.m. and marched to billets in COUIN. Weather showery	ACH
"	21.9.16		Company training. Batn bathed. All the ground available for training purposes was in a very slippery condition. Instruction of bombers and Lewis Gunners.	ACH
"	22.9.16		Company Training	ACH
	23.9.16		Company Training. Sec Lieut Laver returned from leave. Lieut Massy-Lynch and Sec Lieut Uzielli King's Own Rgt joined for duty.	ACH
	24.9.16		Divine Service parade in the morning with 1st K.R.R.C. Exercise in communication with aircraft in the afternoon.	ACH
	25.9.16		Company Training.	ACH

T2134. Wt. W708–776. 500000. 4/15. Sir J. C. & S.

Instructions regarding War Diaries and Intelligence Summaries are contained in F. S. Regs., Part II. and the Staff Manual respectively. Title pages will be prepared in manuscript.

Army Form C. 2118.

Confidential

WAR DIARY

or

~~INTELLIGENCE SUMMARY~~.

(Erase heading not required.)

Sheet. 286

Place	Date	Hour	Summary of Events and Information	Remarks and references to Appendices
COUIN.	26.9.16		Company Training. Weathr fair	ARH.
	27.9.16		Company Training. Weathr fair	ARH.
	28.9.16		Company Training. Weathr fair	ARH.
	29.9.16		Company Training and C.O's inspection	ARH.
SERRE	30.9.16		Relieved 17th Notts and Derby Rgt in SERRE section at 6.p.m	ARH.

99th Brigade.

2nd Division.

1st BATTALION ROYAL BERKSHIRE REGIMENT

OCTOBER 1 9 1 6

Instructions regarding War Diaries and Intelligence Summaries are contained in F. S. Regs., Part II. and the Staff Manual respectively. Title pages will be prepared in manuscript.

Confidential

WAR DIARY
or
~~INTELLIGENCE SUMMARY.~~
(Erase heading not required.)

1/R Berks

Army Form C. 2118.

Sheet 287

Vol 2

Place	Date	Hour	Summary of Events and Information	Remarks and references to Appendices
			Ref Sheet 57D Sheet 57	
SERRE SECTOR	1.10.16		Situation quiet. Trenches were in a bad state owing to the weather. Wiring parties out at night. Weather wet. Battalion front extended from FLAG to S. AVENUE	ACH
"	2.10.16		Situation quiet. Work. Revetting and traversing trenches	ACH.
"	3.10.16		Situation quiet. Instructions received to put 144 men on work of constructing deep dug outs. Enemy trench mortars active. Weather fair	ACH
"	4.10.16		Enemy trench mortars bombarded our front and support lines but did no serious damage. The enemy's activity was the retaliation for our own T.M. fire. Weather fair. Our 18 pounders cutting wire in front of SERRE Village	ACH
"	5.10.16		Trench mortar activity on both sides. Weather wet	ACH.
"	6.10.16		Considerable Artillery and Trench Mortar activity on both sides. Relieved by 17th Royal Fusiliers (5th Bde) at 5 p.m. Marched to camp in wood South of MAILLY MAILLET (P18B)	ACH.
MAILLY — MAILLET.	7.10.16		300 men on working parties on communication trenches in SERRE + REDAN sections	ACH
ARQUÈVES	8.10.16		Battn paraded 1.40 p.m. and marched to ARQUÈVES arriving there at 5 p.m.	ACH

T2134. Wt. W708—776. 500000. 4/15. Sir J. C. & S.

Instructions regarding War Diaries and Intelligence Summaries are contained in F. S. Regs., Part II. and the Staff Manual respectively. Title pages will be prepared in manuscript.

Confidential

WAR DIARY
or
~~INTELLIGENCE SUMMARY~~.
(Erase heading not required.)

1/R.Berks

Army Form C. 2118.

Sheet 288

Place	Date	Hour	Summary of Events and Information	Remarks and references to Appendices
ARQUÈVES	9.10.16	–	Battalion training in the ~~trench~~ open attack. Weather fine	Aem
"	10.10.16	.	Brigade training in the ~~trench~~ open attack.	Aem
"	11.10.16	.	Brigade training in the ~~trench~~ open attack. Lt. Johnson to hospital.	Aem
"	12.10.16	.	Brigade training in the ~~trench~~ open attack. Lieut. G. P. Jackson struck off strength	Aem
"	13.10.16	.	Divisional practice in the ~~trench~~ open attack. Weather fair	Aem
"	14.10.16	.	Battalion training. Weather fair. 2 coys bathing. Reinforcement of 114 O.R. joined	Aem
"	15.10.16	.	Sunday. Church Parade 10 AM. Weather fair	Aem
"	16.10.16	.	Battalion training.	Aem
MAILLY MAILLET WOOD	17.10.16	.	Battalion paraded at 9 a.m. and moved to bivouacs in MAILLY WOOD.	Aem
			Working parties totalling 290 O.R. at night. Weather wet	Aem
"	18.10.16		Battalion training in the ~~trench~~ open attack. 100 men on carrying fatigue at night	
"	19.10.16		Battalion training. ~~Bivouacs shelled between 4 AM and 6 AM no casualties~~	Aem
SERRE SECTION	20.10.16		~~Relieved 22nd~~ Bivouacs shelled between 4 AM and 6 AM. No casualties.	
			Relieved 22nd Royal Fusiliers in SERRE SECTOR about 5 p.m. Night quiet	Aem
"	21.10.16		Our artillery very active against enemy wire entanglements. Four	
"	22.10.16		officer patrols sent out at night.	Aem

T2134. Wt. W708–776. 500000. 4/15. Sir J. C. & S.

Instructions regarding War Diaries and Intelligence Summaries are contained in F. S. Regs., Part II. and the Staff Manual respectively. Title pages will be prepared in manuscript.

Confidential

WAR DIARY
or
~~INTELLIGENCE SUMMARY.~~
(Erase heading not required.)

1/R Berks

Sheet 289

Army Form C. 2118.

Place	Date	Hour	Summary of Events and Information	Remarks and references to Appendices
SERRE & BERTRANCOURT.	22.10.16	.	Relieved by 17th MIDDLESEX (6th Bde) about 5 p.m. Our artillery very active against German Wire. Weather dry and cold	ACH
BERTRANCOURT	23.10.16	.	Battalion rested and cleaned up. Weather cold.	ACH
"	24.10.16		Weather very wet. No outdoor work possible. 42 men on Fatigue.	ACH
"	25.10.16		Weather very wet. Very little out-door work done – Physical Training & short march	ACH
"	26.10.16		Weather fine & cold. Battalion practice in ~~Trench~~ attack. 219 men on carrying & road cleaning fatigue	ACH
"	27.10.16		Weather wet, no outdoor work possible. 125 men on carrying & road cleaning fatigue	Capt. & Adjt. [illegible] to Hosp.
"	28.10.16		Battalion practice in details of ~~Trench~~ attack. Weather cold & wet. 382 men on road cleaning & carrying fatigue	ACH
"	29.10.16		Owing continual wet weather day spent in cleaning & drying. ~~[illegible]~~ 329 men on road cleaning & carrying.	ACH
MAILLY MAILLET	30.10.16		Batt. practised the attack. Moved to Mailly-Maillet village. Billets good. Weather very wet.	ACH
"	31.10.16		Day spent in cleaning & drying – weather fine. 193 men on road cleaning & carrying fatigues	ACH
"				

99th Brigade.

2nd Division

1st BATTALION ROYAL BERKSHIRE REGIMENT

NOVEMBER 1 9 1 6:

Instructions regarding War Diaries and Intelligence Summaries are contained in F. S. Regs., Part II. and the Staff Manual respectively. Title pages will be prepared in manuscript.

WAR DIARY
or
~~INTELLIGENCE SUMMARY.~~
(Erase heading not required.)

Sheet 290. 99/2

Army Form C. 2118.

1/R Berks

CONFIDENTIAL

Vol 25

Place	Date	Hour	Summary of Events and Information	Remarks and references to Appendices
	1916			
MAILLY-MAILLET	1st Nov.		Weather very wet. Coys Bathing. 180 men on fatigue. Enemy shelled village slightly.	1 O.R. WOUNDED [initials]
SERRE.	2nd Nov.		Relieved 22nd Fusiliers in SERRE-SUB-SECTION, about 5 P.M. Enemy artillery active during night.	
			Our patrols examined enemy wire. Trenches in very bad condition owing to wet weather	[initials]
"	3rd Nov.		Weather fair. Our artillery active cutting enemy's wire. Enemy artillery retaliated. Our	1 O.R. Killed.
			working parties repaired trenches during night	[initials]
"	4th Nov.		Considerable artillery activity on both sides. Weather hazy rendering observation difficult.	[initials]
MAILLY-MAILLET	5th Nov.		Relieved by 22nd Royal Fusiliers. Our artillery continued wire cutting & bombarding	2 O.R. KILLED.
			enemy's rear during the day. Enemy retaliated on our front trenches.	1 O.R. Wounded [initials]
"	6th Nov.		Day devoted to drying & cleaning clothing & equipment. 320 men & NCOs on fatigue.	[initials]
ARQUEVES.	7th Nov.		Ordered to proceed to ACHEUX-WOOD. On arrival there orders cancelled & sent on to	Lt. AVELINE & 26 OR's joined.
			ARQUEVES. weather very wet all day, with high wind. All ranks in billets.	[initials]
"	8th Nov		DAY devoted to drying and cleaning. Company training. Weather fine.	[initials]
"	9th Nov		Weather fine. Company Training.	[initials]
"	10th Nov		Weather fine. Company training.	[initials]
BERTRANCOURT.	11th Nov.		Moved to BERTRANCOURT. Weather wet. C.O. to conference with Bde. Commander, after-	
			wards C.O. interviewed O.C. Coys with regard to forthcoming operations.	[initials]

T2134. Wt. W708-776. 500000. 4/15. Sir J. C. & S.

Instructions regarding War Diaries and Intelligence Summaries are contained in F. S. Regs., Part II. and the Staff Manual respectively. Title pages will be prepared in manuscript.

WAR DIARY
or
~~INTELLIGENCE SUMMARY.~~
(Erase heading not required.)

Army Form C. 2118.

CONFIDENTIAL

Sheet 291

Place	Date	Hour	Summary of Events and Information	Remarks and references to Appendices
SERRE.	12th Nov.	AM 8.30 – NOON 12.00	Battalion moved into trenches in SERRE RIGHT SUB-SECTOR, occupying ELLIS SQUARE EAST. Slight hostile shelling. Condition of trenches very bad owing to wet.	[illegible]
	"	NOON 12 – PM 6.00	Battalion lay in ELLIS SQUARE. Enemy artillery more active. After 6.00 pm until midnight shelling much less in volume. Weather good all day.	[illegible]
	13th Nov	MN 12 – AM 5	Enemy not active. At 2.45 Bn H.Q. moved from ELLIS SQ. to dugout corner of EGG & VALLADE TRENCHES. Battn started to move forward at 5 AM.	Casualties:— 9 ORs KILLED. 23 ORs WOUNDED.
	"	AM 5 – AM 5.30	Battalion moved into forward trenches taking up positions in BORDEN and STIRLING TRENCHES. Our artillery commenced to barrage enemy line. Considerable enemy artillery & Minenwerfer fire. Enemy M.G. active. Morning very misty.	[illegible]
	"	AM 5.30 – 11 am	Battalion remained in new position until 11.00 AM. Enemy active all the time. Weather continued good. Condition of trenches very bad being knee deep or over with liquid mud.	[illegible]
	"	am 11 – am 11.30	Battn moved to VALLADE TRENCH. Remaining there until next morning. Slight enemy shelling with heavies. During afternoon enemy snipers were more active.	
	14th Nov	1.15 AM.	Battn moved forward to captured enemy trenches known as GREEN LINE.	CASUALTIES 2 OFFCRS 14 ORS KILLED. 3 OFFCRS 74 ORS WOUNDED. 1 OFFCR 63 ORS MISSING.
		5.30 AM	Weather very misty. Left half Bn was ordered to form defensive flank facing left. Right half Battn to seize portion of MUNICH TRENCH. Left half Battn were successful but right half battn lost heavily and remainder reached enemy trench too weak in numbers to deal with the garrison. Battn captured 2 officers & 50 other ranks & 1 trench mortar.	

T2134. Wt. W708—776. 500000. 4/15. Sir J. C. & S.

Confidential.

Instructions regarding War Diaries and Intelligence Summaries are contained in F. S. Regs., Part II. and the Staff Manual respectively. Title pages will be prepared in manuscript.

WAR DIARY
or
~~INTELLIGENCE SUMMARY.~~
(Erase heading not required.)

Army Form C. 2118.

Sheet 292

Place	Date	Hour	Summary of Events and Information	Remarks and references to Appendices
			and 1 M.G. & seized 200 yds enemy main trench on left flank. This was handed over to relieving units.	
	14th Nov	AM P.M. 8.30-5.30	Bath occupied in consolidating positions gained. Enemy shelling active but passed over on to the GREEN LINE. Enemy M.G.s & bombers active all day.	Ackhw
		P.M. M.N. 5.30-12	Bath. ~~withdrawn~~ consolidated in ~~[illegible]~~ SERRE TRENCH — ~~MUNICH TRENCH~~. Enemy M.G.s very active. Enemy shelled position with heavy guns, but failed to dislodge Bath. 42 prisoners taken during the day in one dug out. With smaller parties a total of over 60 were sent to the rear.	
	15th		Bath continued in SERRE ~~TRENCH~~. The Bath then made a bombing attack up the SUNKEN ROAD (Part of MUNICH TRENCH) taking ~~twelve~~ prisoners & gaining about 50 yards of trench. The trench was blocked and a picket established. A Lewis Gun was also placed here, and caught enemy retreating across the open when 112th Bde. attacked on our right.	CASUALTIES 2, ORS KILLED. 11, ORS WOUNDED
		5.00 PM	During the day enemy fire was very slight, but at dusk their artillery was very active on the Bath's position. In view of this activity the Bath stood to until 9.30 P.M. Rations were very difficult to bring up owing to hostile shell fire.	
	16th	7 P.M.	MANCHESTER R'G'T. started relief of Bath, but could not complete owing to difficulty of crossing open	
		3 AM	Heavy hostile shelling which lasted until about 7.30 A.M.	

Instructions regarding War Diaries and Intelligence Summaries are contained in F. S. Regs., Part II. and the Staff Manual respectively. Title pages will be prepared in manuscript.

Confidential.

WAR DIARY
or
~~INTELLIGENCE~~ SUMMARY.
(Erase heading not required.)

Army Form C. 2118.

Sheet 293

Place	Date	Hour	Summary of Events and Information	Remarks and references to Appendices
	Novr			
SERRE. In captured Enemy position	16th	9.15 am	Water, which had been short was brought up. Enemy was quiet during the day.	CASUALTIES 2 O.R.S KILLED. 5 O.RS WOUNDED 1 O.R. MISSING
		5-6.30 P.M.	Enemy artillery put barrage on neighbourhood of Bn. Hd. Qrs. This caught the men of the Dorset regiment who were coming up to relieve another unit of the 49th Bde.	
		5 P.M.	The 1st Manchesters ~~started~~ continued to relieve the Battn.	
	16/17th	12 AM	Relief of the Battn completed. Battn moved to billets in MAILLY-MAILLET.	[illegible]
MAILLY-MAILLET	17th		Weather still fine and cold. Morning occupied in resting & cleaning – 45 O.R.S. joined	2 Lts MUSK and [illegible]ANDY joined Bn. 2 Lt & a/Q.M. KING to hospital.
TERRAMESNILS	18th	2.00 pm	Battn moved in Motor lorries to TERRAMESNILS. weather fine. Physical Training, and kit inspections	
TERRAMESNILS	19th		Morning devoted to cleaning & Divine Service.	[illegible]
		2.00 pm	Battn moved to GÉZAINCOURT. weather fine.	
GÉZAINCOURT	20th		Morning devoted to light marching and Physical Training. In the afternoon Battalion inspected by Sir Douglas Haig. C-in-C of the British Armies in France	[illegible]
FIENVILLERS	21st		Battn moved to FIENVILLERS. Weather wet.	[illegible]
	22nd		Kit and arms inspection. Weather cold and fine.	[illegible]
DOMQUER	23rd		Battn moved to DOMQUER.	[illegible]

T2134. Wt. W708—776. 500000. 4/15. Sir J. C. & S.

Instructions regarding War Diaries and Intelligence Summaries are contained in F. S. Regs., Part II. and the Staff Manual respectively. Title pages will be prepared in manuscript.

Army Form C. 2118.

WAR DIARY
or
~~INTELLIGENCE SUMMARY~~.
(Erase heading not required.)

CONFIDENTIAL.

Sheet 294

Place	Date	Hour	Summary of Events and Information	Remarks and references to Appendices
DOMQUER	24th		Light marching physical training and close order drill. weather fine.	Alhtled
LE PLESSIEL	25th		Battn moved to LE PLESSIEL. weather very wet.	Alhtled
"	26th		Divine Service weather misty.	Alhtled
COULONVILLERS	27th		Battn moved to ~~[illegible]~~ COULONVILLERS Weather fine.	Alhtled
"	28th		Company training. close order drill. L.G. & bombing work. weather very misty.	Alhtled
"	29th		Company training. continuing yesterday's work.	Alhtled
CONTEVILLE & BERNATRE	30th		Battn moved to CONTEVILLE and BERNATRE Bn H.Q. A & B coys at the former, C & D coys Q.M. Stores and Transport at the latter.	Alhtled

T2134. Wt. W708—776. 500000. 4/15. Sir J. C. & S.

99th Brigade.

2nd Division.

1st BATTALION ROYAL BERKSHIRE REGIMENT

DECEMBER 1 9 1 6:

Instructions regarding War Diaries and Intelligence Summaries are contained in F. S. Regs., Part II. and the Staff Manual respectively. Title pages will be prepared in manuscript.

WAR DIARY
or
~~INTELLIGENCE SUMMARY.~~
(Erase heading not required.)

CONFIDENTIAL.

SHEET 295.

Army Form C. 2118.

1st Royal Berks Regt

Vol 26

Place	Date	Hour	Summary of Events and Information	Remarks and references to Appendices
	1916			
CONTEVILLE & BERNATRE	1 Dec.		Company training weather fair and cold.	[initials]
do	2 Dec.		Company training. Bath started baths. Canteen opened at Bernatre.	[initials]
do	3 Dec.		Divine service. Weather fine.	[initials]
do	4 Dec		Company training. Division Commander visited the Battn.	[initials]
do	5 Dec		Company training. Weather fine	[initials]
do	6 Dec		Company training weather misty.	[initials]
do	7 Dec.		Company training Lt. Col. Harris proceeded on 30 days leave.	[initials]
do	8 Dec		Company training weather wet, which interfered with out door work.	[initials]
do	9/12/16		Company training	[initials]
do	10/12/16		Sunday Church Parade 2/Lt. R.D. Bacon joined	[initials]
do.	11/12/16		Company training Lieut C. A Pocock and H. F.R Merrick joined	[initials]
do	12/12/16		Company training. Reinforcement 217 other ranks joined	[initials]
do.	13/12/16		Company training Sec Lieut Parsons on leave.	[initials]
do	14/12/16		Company training. Weather wet	[initials]
do	15/12/16		Company training Weather wet	[initials]
do	16/12/16		Moved to new billets in ONEUX (1 coy + HQrs). NEUVILLE (2 coys) & MAISON ROLLAND (1 coy)	[initials]

T2134. Wt. W708—776. 500000. 4/15. Sir J. C. & S.

Instructions regarding War Diaries and Intelligence Summaries are contained in F. S. Regs., Part II. and the Staff Manual respectively. Title pages will be prepared in manuscript.

WAR DIARY
or
~~INTELLIGENCE~~ SUMMARY.
(Erase heading not required.)

Confidential
Sheet 296

Army Form C. 2118.

Place	Date	Hour	Summary of Events and Information	Remarks and references to Appendices
ONEUX	17.12.16		Sunday. Church Parade. Weather showery	SSR
"	18.12.16		Company Training. Sec Lieuts C.M. Archdale and A.A. Gibbons joined for duty. Men bathed	SSR
"	19.12.16		Company Training. Weather wet.	SSR
"	20.12.16		Company Training. Visited by G.O.C 5th Army (Lieut General Gough) Lieuts Lynch, Lavers, Astley and Musk on leave.	SSR
"	21.12.16		Company Training. Weather wet. Capt E.B. Methven rejoined the Battn	SSR
"	22.12.16		Company Training. Weather wet	SSR
"	23.12.16		Company Training. Weather wet.	SSR
"	24.12.16		Sunday. Church Parade. 100 men on loading fatigue at ST. RIQUIER	SSR
"	25.12.16		Christmas day. No parade. Football and sports.	SSR
"	26.12.16		Company Training	SSR
"	27.12.16		Company Training. Very cold	SSR
"	28.12.16		Company Training. Very cold	SSR
"	29.12.16		Company Training. Weather wet	SSR
"	30.12.16		Company Training	SSR
"	31.12.16		Sunday	SSR
"	1.1.17		New Year Day. Company Training. Weather wet	SSR
	2.1.17		Company Training	SSR

SSR Winter
[illegible] Major Commanding 1st R. Berks

A5834 Wt. W4973/M687 750,000 8/16 D. D. & L. Ltd. Forms/C.2118/13.

2ND DIVISION
99TH INFY BDE

1ST BATTALION

ROYAL BERKSHIRE REGT.

JAN-DEC 1917.

99th Brigade / 2nd Division.

1st BATTALION

ROYAL BERKSHIRE REGIMENT

JANUARY 1917.

Army Form C. 2118.

Instructions regarding War Diaries and Intelligence Summaries are contained in F. S. Regs., Part II. and the Staff Manual respectively. Title pages will be prepared in manuscript.

Confidential

WAR DIARY
or
INTELLIGENCE SUMMARY.
(Erase heading not required.)

Sheet 2/97 R Berks Regt

Vol 27

Place	Date	Hour	Summary of Events and Information	Remarks and references to Appendices
ONEUX	1.1.17	—	New Years Day Company Training	[illegible]
"	2.1.17		Company Training. Men issued with new box respirators	[illegible]
"	3.1.17		Battalion Training in the "Attack". Weather fair	[illegible]
	4.1.17		Company Training. Weather wet	[illegible]
	5.1.17		Company Training. Lieut B. F. Bailey RAMC to hospital	[illegible]
	6.1.17		Brigade Training in the "Attack"	[illegible]
"	7.1.17		Sunday	[illegible]
	8.1.17		Company Training	[illegible]
"	9.1.17		Battalion paraded at 11 AM and moved by line of march to FIENVILLERS arriving there at 4.30 pm. LIEUT O J. DOWSON joined Battn. 2/LIEUT W. J. KING rejoined.	CAPT. E. B. METHVEN proceeded on Course [illegible]
FIENVILLERS	10.1.17		Battalion rested. Weather wet.	[illegible]
FIENVILLERS	11.1.17		Battalion paraded at 11.30 AM and moved by line of march to SARTON arriving there at 4.30 pm. Weather wet and snowy.	[illegible]
SARTON	12.1.17		Battalion paraded at 10.50 AM and moved by line of march to RAINCHEVAL arriving there at 12 noon.	[illegible]
RAINCHEVAL	13.1.17		Battalion paraded at 10 AM and moved by line of march to BOUZINCOURT arriving there at 2.30 pm.	[illegible]
BOUZINCOURT	14.1.17		Sunday LIEUT J. W. JEAKES rejoined 2nd LIEUT R. FROST joined Battn.	[illegible]

Army Form C. 2118.

Instructions regarding War Diaries and Intelligence Summaries are contained in F. S. Regs., Part II. and the Staff Manual respectively. Title pages will be prepared in manuscript.

Confidential

WAR DIARY
or
~~INTELLIGENCE~~ SUMMARY.
(Erase heading not required.)

Sheet 298

Place	Date	Hour	Summary of Events and Information	Remarks and references to Appendices
BOUZINCOURT	15.1.17		Company training. Very little ground available. Lieut M.P. PUGH joined	[illegible]
	16.1.17		Company training	[illegible]
	17.1.17		250 men cleaning roads. Weather very cold. Snow lying	[illegible]
	18.1.17		Company Training. Weather cold. Snowing	[illegible]
	19.1.17		350 men on road cleaning. Inspection of billets by G.O.C. 2nd Division. CAPT E.H. BISHOP joined	[illegible]
	20.1.17		At 3.15 the Battalion moved by line of march to OVILLERS and WOLSELEY HUTS. 410 men on working parties. Heavy frost	[illegible]
OVILLERS	21.1.17		Sunday 410 men on working parties. Heavy frost	[illegible]
	22.1.17		160 men on working party	
	23.1.17 24.1.17 25.1.17 26.1.17 27.1.17		440 men on working parties daily Sapping platoon was detached building huts 50 men employed under R.E. Weather very cold	[illegible]
	28.1.17		Relieved ~~[illegible]~~ 9th 13th ESSEX (6th Bde) in COURCELETTE SECTOR. The front line here consisted of a line of posts at intervals of about 200 yards. Only telephone communication was possible by day. The sector was quiet	[illegible]
	29.1.17		Situation quiet	
	30.1.17		Situation quiet	[illegible]
	31.1.17		Situation quiet 1 man killed 1 wounded	[illegible]
	1.2.17			[illegible]

R Barnett Barker Lt Col

A. [illegible] Lt Col
Commdg 1st Royal Berks R.

A5834 Wt. W4973/M687 750,000 8/16 D. D. & L. Ltd. Forms/C.2118/13.

[illegible] 9 17

99th Brigade / 2nd Division.

1st BATTALION

ROYAL BERKSHIRE REGIMENT

FEBRUARY 1917.

Attached :-

Report on Raid 5th February 1917.

Instructions regarding War Diaries and Intelligence Summaries are contained in F. S. Regs., Part II. and the Staff Manual respectively. Title pages will be prepared in manuscript.

Confidential

WAR DIARY
or
INTELLIGENCE SUMMARY.
(Erase heading not required.)

1st Royal Berkshire Regt.

Army Form C. 2118.

Sheet 299

Vol 28

Place	Date	Hour	Summary of Events and Information	Remarks and references to Appendices
COURCELETTE	1/2/17		Relieved by 22nd Royal Fusiliers at 9.30 (pm) and marched to WOLFE HUTS with the exception of 110 other ranks left as garrison to CREIGHTON POST, FRASER'S POST and WINDMILL POST. Weather very cold	[illegible]
"	2/2/17		500 men on working parties	[illegible]
"	3/2/17		500 men on working parties	
"	4/2/17		500 men on working parties. A platoon of 60 other ranks under Lieut BURGESS and AVELINE raided the enemy trenches E of COURCELETTE and took prisoners 2 officers and 50 other ranks. ZERO hour was 3 AM on the 5th.	[illegible]
"	5/2/17		Our casualties were Sec Lieut BURGESS seriously wounded 1 OR killed and 11 wounded. Sec Lieut BURGESS was awarded the D.S.O. by the C in C on the same day. Battn moved to AVELUY leaving 2 coys in WOLFE HUTS, one in WOLSELEY HUTS and one in AVELUY. Hard frost (27° of frost)	[illegible]
AVELUY	6/2/17		Companies at work under R.E. Hard Frost.	
"	7/2/17		—— do —— — do —	
"	8/2/17		—— do —— — do —	
"	9/2/17		—— do —— — do — CAPT. E.B. METHVEN took over command of A Coy. LIEUT. M C DEMPSEY - - Acting Adjutant.	[illegible]

A5834 Wt. W4973 M687 750,000 8/15 D. D. & L. Ltd. Forms/C.2118/13.

Army Form C. 2118

Instructions regarding War Diaries and Intelligence Summaries are contained in F. S. Regs., Part II. and the Staff Manual respectively. Title pages will be prepared in manuscript.

CONFIDENTIAL

WAR DIARY
or
INTELLIGENCE SUMMARY.

(Erase heading not required.)

SHEET 300

Place	Date	Hour	Summary of Events and Information	Remarks and references to Appendices
AVELUY	10/2/17		Companies at work under R.E. Weather slightly warmer	
"	11/2/17		—— do —— —— do ——	AKK
"	12/2/17		—— do —— Major General PEREIRA cmdg 2nd Division inspected Raiding Party. Slight Thaw during the day.	AKK
"	13/2/17		Companies at work under R.E.	AKK
"	14/2/17		Whole Battn moved to OVILLERS HUTS: move completed by 5 pm. Sapping Platoon returned after spending 18 days in COURCELETTE. Thaw during the day: ground became very wet on surface.	AKK
OVILLERS HUTS	15/2/17		Preparations for forthcoming attack during the morning. The Battn relieved the 17th R.F. in the left subsector, B Company taking over the front line, A, C and D being in support. Relief complete 9.55 pm. Situation quiet.	AKK
COURCELETTE	16/2/17	8pm	B Company moved into battle position with Coy Hdqs at R.29 central and 80 men in the front line to carry ammunition for Stokes Guns. A, C and D moved into their positions in rear. The remaining battalions of the Brigade began to form up for the attack at dawn. There was considerable hostile shelling during the night. Casualties CAPTAIN. N. WEST. Killed. LIEUT J W JEAKES. Wounded. O. Rs 1 Killed and 4 wounded.	AKK

A5834 Wt. W4973/M687 750,000 8/16 D. D. & L. Ltd. Forms/C.2118/13.

Instructions regarding War Diaries and Intelligence Summaries are contained in F. S. Regs., Part II. and the Staff Manual respectively. Title pages will be prepared in manuscript.

CONFIDENTIAL

WAR DIARY
or
~~INTELLIGENCE SUMMARY.~~
(Erase heading not required.)

SHEET 301

Army Form C. 2118.

Place	Date	Hour	Summary of Events and Information	Remarks and references to Appendices
COURCELETTE	17/2/17	5.45 AM	Attack commenced: 99th Brigade having 23rd R.F, 1st KRRC and 2 Companies 22nd R.F assaulting.	
			A Company moved up to O.B.L. carrying up S.A.A. and Water.	
		9.30 AM	A Company commenced carrying SAA & Bombs from OBL to captured position	
		12 noon	C Company carried up SAA and Bombs from Brigade Hdqs to O.B.L, returning on completion of work.	
		3.30 pm	A Company sent 2 Platoons to reinforce K.R.R.C in captured position.	
			The enemy shelled throughout the day, principally on communication trenches, and tracks leading to the rear. Weather - wet and misty.	
			Casualties CAPTAIN E.B. METHVEN wounded	
			ORs 1 Killed and 11 wounded	AKH
— do —	18/2/17		Enemy shelling slackened considerably.	
		6 pm	D Company carried up SAA and water from Brigade Hdqs. to forward dumps, returning on completion of work.	
		10 pm	B, C, and D Companies were relieved by 17th Middlesex and returned to BRUCE HUTS.	
			Casualties O.Rs 1 Killed 7 Wounded 2 Missing	
			Weather wet.	
BRUCE HUTS AVELUY	19/2/17	7 am	A Company arrived having been relieved at 4 AM. Casualties K. 1. W. 7. M. 0. 2/Lieut A J SHIPTON } joined for duty	
			The day was spent in cleaning 200 men on fatigue. — do — F.C. JAMES }	AKH

A5834 Wt. W4973/M687 750,000 8/16 D. D. & L. Ltd. Forms/C.2118/13.

SECRET

SECRET.

2nd.Division.
No.G.S. 1038/op./18

5th Infantry Brigade.
6th Infantry Brigade.
99th Infantry Brigade.
C.R.A.
C.R.E.
10th. D.C.L.I.
"Q"
A.D.M.S.
O.C. 2nd Signal Coy.
2nd.Div. School.

I forward herewith a report on the raid carried out by the 1st Royal Berkshire Regt' on the 5th February.

Lieut-Colonel.
General Staff. 2nd.Division.

7.2.17.

Army Form C. 2118.

Instructions regarding War Diaries and Intelligence Summaries are contained in F. S. Regs., Part II. and the Staff Manual respectively. Title pages will be prepared in manuscript.

CONFIDENTIAL

WAR DIARY
or
INTELLIGENCE SUMMARY.
(Erase heading not required.)

SHEET 302

Place	Date	Hour	Summary of Events and Information	Remarks and references to Appendices
BRUCE HUTS AVELUY.	20/2/17		Weather wet and misty. 200 men on fatigue at night.	
— do —	21/2/17		350 men on fatigue at night.	
— do —	22/2/17		Weather wet. 460 men on fatigue	[illegible]
— do —	23/2/17		Weather misty and colder. 300 men on fatigue at night. Lieut G.O.L. HARRIS proceeded to Fifth Army School for 2 days.	[illegible]
	24/2/17		Battn moved to OVILLERS HUTS - changing billets with 22nd R.F. 300 men on fatigue. 2/Lts: TREMELLEN, GIBBS and BRAZIES joined the Battn	[illegible]
OVILLERS HUTS	25/2/17		Sunday. 250 men on fatigue. Weather much warmer.	
— do —	26/2/17		Battn: were prepared to move at short notice in consequence of the German withdrawal ~~[illegible]~~ behind IRLES and PYS.	[illegible]
— do —	27/2/17		150 men employed in the morning pitching a camp ½ mile S.W. of POZIERES. Battn. moved there in the afternoon. 250 men on fatigue in the evening. 2/Lt BRYAN joined for duty.	[illegible]
POZIERES CAMP	28/2/17		Training of Lewis Gunners and Rifle Grenadiers in the morning. Remainder improving the camp. Inspection of camp by Brigadier in the afternoon. 250 men on fatigue in the evening.	[illegible]

[illegible] Lt Col
Commdg 1st R. Berks Rgt

A5834 Wt. W4973/M687 750,000 8/16 D. D. & L. Ltd. Forms/C.2118/13.

SECRET.

Artillery Programme for Raid. on 4th/5th February.

Ref. Trench Map 1/5,000

1. On the 3rd and 4th February the H.A. to bombard the following localities:-

(E) Posts and trenches from R.12.c.1.9. to R.11.d.7.6.
(F) " " " " M.13.b.4.9. to M.7.d.0.3.
(G) " " " " M.8.c.8.3. to M.8.c.4.0.

NOTE. The enemy to be led to believe that our demonstration at (E) is the most serious.

2. Wire Cutting.
Wire will be cut by Divisional Artillery as under:-

(i) Along line B C on 2nd Feby.
(ii) Along line B C and at point E on 3rd and 4th Feby.

3. At Zero.

Right Group + 17th Battery.

1. 18 pdr.barrage from M.8.c.7.2. to M.8.c.3.0.
2. 18 pdr.barrage from M.3.c.3.0. to M.13.b.5.8. and to include the group of fortified shell holes at M.8.c.0.0.

1 -18 prs and 17th Battery) barrage from M.13.b.5.8. to M.7.d.0.3.
1 - 4.5" How bombards groups of posts etc. at (G) and M.8.c.0.0.
1 - 4.5" How bombards posts etc.along trench at (F)

Left Group (less 17th Bty) - Box barrage on (E)

4. Rates of Fire.

0 - 0.20................ 4 rounds per gun & how per min.
0.20 - 0.30..............3 " " " " " " "
Left Group 2 rounds.
0.30 - 0.60..............1 round per gun a min.
(Left Group ceases firing).

Appendix 11.

STRETCHER BEARERS.

***** ***** *********

1. 2 stretchers and 4 bearers accompanied the party and remained in "No man's land" close to the enemy wire- 1 bearer went forward from each party to look for wounded men.

2. 4 stretchers and 8 bearers in our front line. 100 yards behind.(1)

3. 4 stretchers and 16 bearers at No.19 post about 1,000 yards SW of(2).

4. Stretcher party in (1) carried direct to (3),being replaced at once by a party from (2) at (3) party from (1) was relieved and the stretcher was carried by a party from (3) back to Battn H.Q., where there was a further reserve of 4 stretchers and 16 bearers.

5. As soon as a stretcher party reached a post in rear a similar party was sent up to replace it.

Appendix I

SECRET.

2nd. Division.
GENERAL STAFF.
No.G.S. 1038/Op/8/4.

1st. ROYAL BERKS. Order No. 52.

Reference attached map
and LE SARS 1/10,000.

1. A raid will be carried out by No.16 platoon under 2nd Lt. BURGESS on night 4/5th Feb. 17.

2. Object of raid.

(a) Kill or capture all enemy met with.
(b) Secure identifications and documents.
(c) Bring back or destroy enemy M.Gs and Trench Mortars.
(d) Obtain information about the state of the German trenches.

3. Objective.- Salient in enemy line (M.13.b.7.4.) opposite our posts Nos 5 and 6 and is marked B.C D in attached plan.

4. (a) 50% of the leading wave will carry wire cutters and wear hedging gloves.
(b) All identifications will be removed from those taking part in the raid before they go up into the line.
(c) All members of the raiding party will be warned that if taken prisoner they are only bound to disclose their regimental numbers and names. No other information will be given.

5. Method of carrying out.

(a) Previous to Zero the platoon will be formed up in REGINA Trench between numbers 5 and 6 posts (left resting on No.6 post) ready to advance in two waves-
(b) 1. Leading wave will consist of 2 sections bayonet men (20 O.R.) with bombing party in centre (total 25 other ranks)
2. Second wave will consist of one section bayonet men and one bombing section(less those detailed with the leading wave)
(c) At Zero 4 Stokes Mortars will open rapid fire on B.C.D. for one minute. Directly these Stokes Mortars commence the leading wave will crawl forward on a front of 75 yards towards the enemy's trench B.C to a line not less than 75 yards from it which will be marked by objects put out previously by patrols. The first wave will be followed by second wave at 50 yards distance. The left will direct and move on point O on a true bearing 32°.
(d) Immediately Stokes Mortars fire ceases both waves will move forward as rapidly as possible and rush trench B.C. with the bayonet. (No bombs are to be thrown during the advance.)
(e) The leading wave will pass over B.C. without any pause and rush D.C. The 2nd wave will remain in B.C. and deal with the enemy there.

6. On leading wave entering D.C. they will act as follows :-

(a) Section (10 O.R.) on right will form a picquet at D so as to bring fire to bear from East to N.West.
(b) Bombing party will deal with dug-outs.
(c) Section (10 O.R.) on left will collect prisoners,search dead enemy for documents and search dug-outs in combination with bombing party and will carry back any M.Gs. or small T.Ms. in B.C.D.

7. On 2nd wave entering B.C. they will act as follows:-
(a) Right bombing party will block at B.
(b) Centre bombing party will deal with dug-outs.
(c) Searchers will search all dead enemy in B.C. for documents.
(d) Bayonet men will collect prisoners and bring them to point O.

(e) Left bombing party will move to point C ready to assist leading wave if required. If not required for that purpose they will remain at point C as a reserve.

8. Retirement will be carried out as follows:-

(a) The O.C. platoon will place himself at or near point C and will sound a Klaxon horn to attract attention. It will be very carefully explained to all ranks that the horn is NOT the signal for retirement but merely denotes that orders are being issued near point C.

(b) He will then direct the evacuation of all prisoners, captured M.Gs, wounded ect. Retirement will be made at right angles to B.C. so as to enter our lines between Nos 5 and 6 posts unless for some reason O.C. platoon on the spot prefers to return along line of old trench running from C to our No 7a post.

(c) Bombing post at B and section at D will remain in position until all others (including wounded and prisoners) are back in our lines and in order that they receive orders for retirement will on Klaxon horn sounding, send each one man to point C to report to O.C there. These men will return to their respective parties accompanied by other orderlies with O.C. platoons order.

9. On reaching our lines the O.C. platoon will check the numbers present and inform stretcher bearers of any missing. He will then decide, judging from enemy's barrage whether to immediately return to Advanced Bttn H.Q. (W.MIRAUMONT road) or to remain for a while in REGINA Trench until matters have quitened down. Report to Adv Bttn.H.Q. will in any case be immediately made by FULLERPHONE at No. 8 post.

10. Prisoners and captured documents etc will be sent direct to Adv Bttn H.Q. under reliable sudtody, care will be taken that an officer or senior N.C.O. take charge of documents as soon as collected.

11. Artillery programme attached.

12. (a) 4 stretcher bearers with 2 stretchers will follow 50 yards in rear of 2nd wave. They will halt on reaching enemy's wire and get into communication with platoon in enemy's trenches.

(b) 8 stretcher bearers with 4 stretchers will remain in REGINA Trench between Nos 5 and 6 post ready to assist in bringing in wounded from enemy-s trenches.

(c). All wounded will be carried to No 8 post from whence the M.O. will arrange for their evacuation.

13. Gaps in our wire will be cut between Nos 5 and 6 posts and at No 7a post on evening 4/5th Feb accordance with special instructions to Lieut POCOCK.

14. Advanced Battn H.Q. at W.MIRAUMONT Road.

15. Watches will be synchronized from 99th Inf Bde H.Q. on the afternoon of the 4th February.

16. Zero hour will be communicated later.

(Sd) E.B.Methven. Capt.
a/Adj' 1st Royal Berks.

REPORT ON RAID ON ENEMY SALIENT IN M.13.b by 1/R.BERKS REGt. 99th INFANTRY BRIGADE at 3 a.m. on 5th FEBRUARY 1917

1. The Raiding Party consisted of 2 officers, (2/Lieuts. BURGESS and AVELINE) and 60 O.Rs. exclusive of Stretcher Bearers.

2. The objective embraced the E. and W. arms of salient in M.13.b. for about 150^x along each Arm.

3. The following is a brief description of the raid:-

(a) The objective was decided on after careful reconnaissance, study of Air Maps and Intelligence Summaries.
A copy of the Battalion orders is attached (App. I).

(b) The 1/R.Berks held the Right sub-section, which takes in M.13.b., from night 28th/29th Jan. to night 1st/2nd Feby.

(c) On coming into Support at WOLFE Huts, existing trenches almost identical with the objective were found and improved, and 5 practices were carried out by the Raiding Party, by day and night.

(d) At 6 p.m. 4/2/17 the Party moved to W.MIRAUMONT dug-outs where a meal and accommodation was provided for them.

(e) During the afternoon of 4th Feby. unsatisfactory reports as to t thr state of the wire along the Point and Southern portion of the Eastern face were received: this contingency had been foreseen and the Raiding Party started from a point 100^x to 150^x N. of where they had originally intended and where the wire was known to be insignificant.
Lt. Col. HARRIS, D.S.O., Commdg. 1/R.Berks, went up in advance of the Raiding Party, made a personal reconnaissance of the enemy wire and placed the Raiding Party in position.

(f) 3 small wooden tripods covered with canvas (black on our side white on enemy's side) marking the flanks and centre of the party, had been placed beforehand in No Man's L nd about 30 yards outside our wire and parallel to the enemy trench.
The men, dressed in white smocks with white helmet covers, crawled out in pairs, and were on the alignment (in two waves of about 30 men each, about 15 yards apart) 15 minutes before Zero.

(g) 3 similar tripods had also been placed parallel to the 3 already mentioned and 30^x to 40^x nearer the enemy line. These gave the direction of the advance and proved effective.

(h) At Zero -
(i) 4 Stokes guns 99th T.M.B. opened rapid fire on the objective for one minute.
1 Stokes gun fired rapid on enemy Post at M.13.b.4.9 for one minute.
These guns were brought up near the front line for the occasion and were commanded by Capt. STEED and Lieut. ELLIS, 99th T.M.Bty.
(ii) 2nd Div. Artillery (18 pdrs. and Hows.) formed a Barrage (vide map attached).
(iii) The Raiding Party moved forward to within about 50 yards of the objective (E. Arm) and lay down.

The shooting of the Stokes Guns was very accurate and no casualties from splinters were incurred.

(k).......

(k) At 0.1 - Both waves rushed forward; the leading wave (2/Lt. AVELINE in centre, section Commdrs. on flanks) jumped the E.Arm of the salient on a front of about 40 yards with its left about M.13.b.95.55 formed to the left, and went for the W. Arm of salient, which was its objective.

The rear wave (2/Lt. BURGESS on the left flank- crossed the enemy wire, jumped the trench, turned to the left and ran down outside the parados until they met the enemy, most of whom (including the 2 German officers) they found near the point of the salient.

Any German offering resistance was at once shot, the men then jumped into the trench and in a few minute all resistance came to an end.

2/Lt. BURGESS, commanding the party, was unfortunately severely wounded and the command devolved on 2/Lt. AVELINE.

Prisoners were sent back to our own line under escort, our wounded evacuated, and the party, after remaining 15 - 20 mins. in the objective and after having searched all dug-outs and shelters returned to their own line.

A German machine gun completely smashed was seen at the southern point of the salient.

(l) No German counter-attack was attempted and the blocking parties at N. end of each arm of the salient had consequently nothing to do.

(m) Our artillery barrage was most effective, and the enemy appeared to be quite in the dark as to where the raiding party was.

(n) An enemy barrage started at 2.30 a.m. on a line about 200 - 300 yards in rear of our front line in M.13 and M.14 a. evidently in connection with the raid of the 18th Division on our left.

This barrage slacked off at about 2.50 a.m. and did not re-commence till 3.20 a.m. when it was put down on the same place; it lasted about 20 minutes during which time it was very heavy.

(o) The raid was assisted by 7 machine guns of 99th M.G.Coy. also 6 Lewis guns, 3 on either flank of the Raiding Party. These guns were allotted targets and areas with a view to dealing with a counter attack and to search probable enemy M.G. or T.M. positions and communication trenches.

4. The raid was successful, the enemy garrison amounting to about 65 all ranks being killed or captured except for 1 man who ran away and fell on being fired at.

2 German officers and 49 O.Rs. were brought back to our lines.

5. Our casualties were 2/Lt. BURGESS, Commdg. the party seriously wounded; O.Rs. 1 killed, 11 slightly wounded.

6.....

6. The following information was obtained regarding the enemy's defences:-

(a) WIRE- Three rows of concertina barbed wire 2½ feet high. This proved no obstacle in the moonlight and the men trod it down as they went forward.

(b) TRENCHES - About 8 feet deep, 3 feet wide at bottom, steep sides not revetted. Reported in good order. No continous fire step. Winding but not traversed.

(c) DUG OUTS- Full particupars have not yet been obtained. It was not found necessary to destroy them as the enemy came out and surrendered.

(7) The following points were brought out by the raid:-

(a) The white smocks proved valuable in the snow. Those used had no sleeves. Sleeves 3/4 length of arm would have been better. White rifle covers, but not covering the bolts would have been useful. Faces should be chalked.

Officers wore brown covers to helmets to distinquish them - the men had white covers.

(b) Value of short Stokes barrage - steady platforms and previous registration of each gun necessary.

(c) Position of 2nd in command as well as O.C. the party, should be stated in orders and known to all.

(d) Each Officer's orderly should carry a Klaxon Horn or other instrument used to attract attention.

(e) It was not anticipated that so many prisoners would be taken A N.C.O. and party for escort should remain in No Man's Land otherwise raiding party may be unduly weakened by having to find escorts. Two other ranks to 10 prisoners is sufficient.

(f) All posts in Front line to check number of prisoners passing them on their way back and to take names of raiding party - latter to be at one reported to O.C. party.

(g) Each man carried two bombs but were told to use their rifles. This gives more dash to the attack and prevents hesitation. No bombs were thrown.

8. The arrangements regarding removal of wounded proved satisfactory and are given in Appendix II.

TRENCH MAP

SCALE - 1:5000

CORRECTED FROM AIR PHOTOS TAKEN ON 26-1-17

OFFICE

= H.A on 3rd & 4th Feb.
= 18 Pdr. Barrage.
= 4.5" How.

:REFERENCE:

OLD BATTERY POSITIONS
DUGOUTS
MACHINE GUNS
SUSPECTED MACHINE GUNS
OCCUPIED SHELL HOLES AND POSTS
TRENCH WHICH APPEARS TO BE OCCUPIED OR USED
TRENCH APPARENTLY NOT IN USE OR DAMAGED
TRENCH MORTAR
TRACKS
WIRE

NOTE. DUGOUTS SHOULD BE SUSPECTED WHEREVER BATTERY POSITIONS ARE SHOWN.

— 11 —

99th Brigade / 2nd Division.

1st BATTALION

ROYAL BERKSHIRE REGIMENT

MARCH 1917.

Instructions regarding War Diaries and Intelligence Summaries are contained in F. S. Regs., Part II. and the Staff Manual respectively. Title pages will be prepared in manuscript.

CONFIDENTIAL

WAR DIARY
or
~~INTELLIGENCE SUMMARY.~~
(Erase heading not required.)

Army Form C. 2118.

99/2

Sheet 303.

1/R. BERKS REGT.

Vol 28

Place	Date	Hour	Summary of Events and Information	Remarks and references to Appendices
POZIERES CAMP	1/3/17		Training in the morning. Weather warm and sunny. 50 men on fatigue.	Sen
〃	2/3/17		Training in the morning.	Sen
〃	3/3/17		Battn moved into front line, relieving 24th R Fusiliers. relief complete 10.20 pm. Night quiet. Patrols went out at night to report on enemy's wire. Casualties Nil.	
FRONT LINE B.16 AQUEDUCT RD Nr PYS.	4/3/17		Casualty 1 O.R. Situation quiet; Patrols went out at night and reported several gaps in enemy wire.	Sen
〃	5/3/17		Relieved by 1st K.R.R.C. Relief complete 10 pm. Battn returned to Immediate Support position in the O.B.L. CAPT. NUGENT and 2/LT BAZETT joined the Battn	Sen
O.B.L Nr PYS	6/3/17		Weather cold. 250 men on fatigue at night.	Sen
〃	7/3/17		Snow in the morning. 350 men on fatigue at night in the front line. Casualties 5.	Sen
〃	8/3/17		350 men on fatigue at night.	
〃	9/3/17		Preparations for the forthcoming attack during the morning. At 10 pm the Battn moved up into assembly position.	Sen
FRONT LINE Nr IRLES	10/3/17		At 5.15 am the Battn attacked GREVILLERS TRENCH in conjunction with the 1st K.R.R.C. on the left. The trench was captured at once and a line of posts established in front, to facilitate the digging of a new assembly trench for a future attack. A Company were on the right and established a defensive flank. 100 prisoners (including 1 Officer)	

A5834 Wt. W4973/M687 750,000 8/16 D. D. & L. Ltd. Forms/C.2118/13.

Instructions regarding War Diaries and Intelligence Summaries are contained in F. S. Regs., Part II. and the Staff Manual respectively. Title pages will be prepared in manuscript.

CONFIDENTIAL

WAR DIARY
~~or~~
INTELLIGENCE ~~SUMMARY~~.
(Erase heading not required.)

Army Form C. 2118.

Sheet 304

Place	Date	Hour	Summary of Events and Information	Remarks and references to Appendices
FRONT LINE Nr IRLES	10/3/17 (Cont)		3 Machine Guns* and 2 Light Trench Mortars were captured.	* Numbers of Machine Guns 8248 3395
			Casualties LT BRAZIER killed: 2/Lt LAYERS and 2/LT DENHAM wounded. Other Ranks 10 killed, 83 wounded and 1 missing.	
			The enemy commenced shelling the captured line at about 12 noon and continued throughout the day, but made no effort to recapture the position.	The third was not brought out of the line AEW
"	11/3/17		The enemy continued to shell GREVILLERS TRENCH and the line of posts throughout the day. Patrols were sent out at night to report on the state of the enemy's wire, and found that it had been badly damaged by our artillery fire. The Battn was relieved at night and returned to billets in ALBERT arriving there at about 4 AM. 12/3/17.	
			Casualties Other Ranks 1 killed 12 wounded.	AEW
ALBERT	12/3/17		The Battn rested during the day. 2/LT SIMONS joined the Battn.	AEW
"	13/3/17		Men cleaned up during the morning. 250 men went to CROMWELL HUTS on "permanent fatigue" – having baths before they went.	AEW
	14/3/17		Men had Baths during the morning. Weather wet. Sapping Platoon (50 ORs) went on "permanent fatigue".	AEW
	15/3/17		At 3 pm Battn moved to OVILLERS HUTS via AVELUY, arriving there at 4 pm. Weather fine.	AEW
OVILLERS HUTS	16/3/17		300 men still on "permanent fatigue". Major WESTON returned from leave.	

A5834 Wt. W4973/M687 750,000 8/16 D. D. & L. Ltd. Forms/C.2118/13.

Army Form C. 2118.

Instructions regarding War Diaries and Intelligence Summaries are contained in F. S. Regs., Part II. and the Staff Manual respectively. Title pages will be prepared in manuscript.

CONFIDENTIAL

WAR DIARY
or
~~INTELLIGENCE SUMMARY.~~

(Erase heading not required.)

SHEET 305

Place	Date	Hour	Summary of Events and Information	Remarks and references to Appendices
OVILLERS HUTS	17/3/17		St Patricks Day. Weather fine.	
"	18/3/17		Sunday. 3pm Battn moved to TOFREK CAMP near POZIERES.	SEM.
"	19/3/17		6am Working party under the Commanding Officer left for GREVILLERS. Worked on roads from 10 am till 4pm, arriving back at 7pm.	
			8pm Battn moved into billets at ALBERT.	SEM
ALBERT	20/3/17		200 men still on permanent fatigue. Weather wet and cold.	
"	21/3/17		Men had baths in the morning.	SEM
"	22/3/17		Training of Lewis Gunners and Rifle Grenadiers in the morning. 2/Lts HERBERT, HENLEY, MILES, PALMER joined the Battn.	SEM
"	23/3/17		— do — — do — Weather fine	SEM
	24/3/17		— do — — do — — do —	SEM
"	25/3/17		2nd Division left I Corps. Battn moved by line of march to HARPONVILLE, arriving there at 3pm. Billets good. Weather fine. Lt PUGH to Hospital.	SEM
HARPONVILLE	26/3/17		Battn moved at 10am by line of march to AMPLIER, arriving there at 2.30pm. Billeted in huts. The weather was wet and the roads very bad. 3 ORs fell out on the march.	SEM
AMPLIER	27/3/17		11am, Battn moved by line of march to BONNIERES, arriving there at 4pm. Weather and roads again very bad. Casualties on the march NIL. Billets very crowded.	SEM

A5834 Wt. W4973 M687 750,000 8/16 D. D. & L. Ltd. Forms/C.2118/13.

Instructions regarding War Diaries and Intelligence Summaries are contained in F. S. Regs., Part II. and the Staff Manual respectively. Title pages will be prepared in manuscript.

CONFIDENTIAL

WAR DIARY

~~or~~

~~INTELLIGENCE SUMMARY.~~

(Erase heading not required.)

Army Form C. 2118.

SHEET 306

Place	Date	Hour	Summary of Events and Information	Remarks and references to Appendices
BONNIÈRES	28/3/17		9.40 am. Battn moved by line of march to BLANGERVAL arriving there at 1 pm. Men had dinners outside the village, as billets were not ready when Battn arrived. Weather fine, roads fair. Casualties on the march NIL.	[illegible]
"	29/3/17		Battn rested. Weather wet.	[illegible]
"	30/3/17		9.10 am Battn moved by line of march to TANGRY arriving there at 3.30 pm – dinners on the march. Casualties on the march NIL. Billets fair	
TANGRY	31/3/17		Company training during the morning. several good spaces of ground being available	[illegible]
"	~~1/4/17~~		~~Sunday. Voluntary Service in the morning.~~ [illegible]	
	~~2/4/17~~		~~Company training during the morning. Instruction during the afternoon and night~~ [illegible]	
	~~3/4/17~~ [illegible]			

[signature] Lt Col
Comdg 1st Royal Berks Regt

A5834 Wt. W4973/M687 750,000 8/16 D. D. & L. Ltd. Forms/C.2118/13.

99th Brigade / 2nd Division.

1st BATTALION

ROYAL BERKSHIRE REGIMENT

APRIL 1917.

Instructions regarding War Diaries and Intelligence Summaries are contained in F. S. Regs., Part II. and the Staff Manual respectively. Title pages will be prepared in manuscript.

CONFIDENTIAL

WAR DIARY
or
~~INTELLIGENCE~~ SUMMARY.
(Erase heading not required.)

1/Royal Berks

Sheet No. 307

Army Form C. 2118.

99/2

Vol 30

Place	Date	Hour	Summary of Events and Information	Remarks and references to Appendices
TANGRY	1/4/17		Sunday. Voluntary Service in the morning.	AHM
	2/4/17		Company training during the morning. Snowstorm during the afternoon and night.	AHM
	3/4/17		Heavy snowstorm in the morning. Company training in the afternoon.	AHM
	4/4/17		Company training in the morning and afternoon. Weather fine.	AHM
	5/4/17		Company training in the morning and afternoon. Officers spare kits, one blanket per man and leather jerkins handed in. CAPT F.S. BOSHELL rejoined the Battn. Weather fine and warm. Reinforcements – 47 ORs arrived.	AHM
	6/4/17		Good Friday. Voluntary Service in the morning. CAPT W.J. GREEN and LT. M.P. PUGH awarded the Military Cross.	AHM
	7/4/17		12.40 pm Battn moved by line of march to ORLENCOURT, with C and D Companies at MONCHY BRETON, arriving there at 3.15 pm. Casualties on the march NIL. Weather fine.	AHM
ORLENCOURT	8/4/17		Easter Sunday. Weather fine and warm. Voluntary Service in the morning. LT. M.P. PUGH rejoined from Hospital.	
	9/4/17		Party of 6 Officers 57 ORs under CAPT. V.G. STOKES proceed to XIII Corps Training Depôt. Company training in the morning and afternoon. Weather fine with showers.	AHM
	10/4/17		9.30 am Battn moved by line of march to huts near ETRUN, arriving there at 4.25 pm. Dinners on the march. Casualties on the march NIL. Weather bad, with frequent snow and hail showers.	AHM
ETRUN HUTS	11/4/17		4.30 pm Battn moved to old German front line opposite ROCLINCOURT to relieve 1/6th SEAFORTHS. Relief complete 9.15 pm. Weather very bad with heavy snowstorm in afternoon and evening.	AHM
ROCLINCOURT TRENCHES	12/4/17		Day spent in clearing the trenches, and burying dead. Weather wet in afternoon.	AHM

A5834 Wt W4973/M687 750,000 8/16 D. D. & L. Ltd. Forms/C.2118/13.

Army Form C. 2118.

Instructions regarding War Diaries and Intelligence Summaries are contained in F. S. Regs., Part II. and the Staff Manual respectively. Title pages will be prepared in manuscript.

WAR DIARY
~~or~~
~~INTELLIGENCE SUMMARY.~~

(Erase heading not required.)

Sheet No. 308.

Place	Date	Hour	Summary of Events and Information	Remarks and references to Appendices
ROCKLINCOURT TRENCHES	13/4/17		Weather fine and sunny. A and B companies road-making in the morning. In consequence of German withdrawal opposite Brigade front B Coy moved up to Bn Hq 23rd R.F at 4 pm with SAA and Bombs. D Coy moved up at 8 pm	Sen
"	14/4/17		6.30 AM Bn Hqs. A and C Coys moved up to old German second defence line (KLEEMANN STELLONG) in vicinity of B and D Coys. 8 pm Battn relieved 23 R.F in front line in front of BAILLEUL. Relief complete 9.30 pm. Enemy shelling throughout the night. Casualties NIL	Sen
BAILLEUL TRENCHES	15/4/17		Enemy shelling continued throughout the day. Weather fine. Casualties NIL.	Sen
"	16/4/17		— do — — do — — .. Weather very wet in the afternoon and evening. Casualties 6 ORs. . Left half Battn relieved by 2nd Oxford and Bucks L.I Right half Battn by 1st H.A.C. Relief complete 7 AM 17/4/17. Battn returned to KLEEMAN STELLONG. LT READY joined the Battn.	Sen
ROCKLINCOURT TRENCHES	17/4/17		Battn rested in the morning. Salvage work in the afternoon. Weather very wet in the afternoon.	Sen.
"	18/4/17		11.15 am Battn moved by Companies to MAROEUIL HUTS: last company arriving at 5 pm. Weather wet throughout the day.	Sen

A5834 Wt. W4973/M687 750,000 8/16 D. D. & L. Ltd. Forms/C.2118/13.

Army Form C. 2118.

Instructions regarding War Diaries and Intelligence Summaries are contained in F. S. Regs., Part II. and the Staff Manual respectively. Title pages will be prepared in manuscript.

WAR DIARY

~~or~~

~~INTELLIGENCE SUMMARY.~~

(*Erase heading not required.*)

Sheet No. 309.

Place	Date	Hour	Summary of Events and Information	Remarks and references to Appendices
			Ref Map 51B N.W.	
MAROEUIL HUTS	19/4/17		Battn rested and cleaned up. Men had baths during the day. Weather wet.	AHH
"	20/4/17		Battn on fatigue - road making and laying tracks 7 AM to 5 pm. Weather fine	AHH
"	21/4/17		—— do —— —— do —— Weather fine	
"	22/4/17		C Company and 2 Platoons of D Company on fatigue 7 AM to 5 pm. Weather fine.	AHH
"	23/4/17		A Company and 2 Platoons of B Company on fatigue 7 AM to 2 pm.	
			3 pm Battn. moved to Tent Camp at ROCLINCOURT, changing places with the 23rd R.F. Weather fine.	AHH
ROCLINCOURT	24/4/17		8 pm Battn moved up to front line between BAILLEUL and WILLERVAL to relieve 24th R.F. Bn HQ in SUGAR FACTORY. Relief complete 11 pm. Weather fine	AHH
Front Line BAILLEUL	25/4/17		Enemy shelled front line throughout the day. Casualties LT BACON Killed, LT MASSEY-LYNCH wounded. ORs. 6 killed 6 wounded. CAPT G.H. BISHOP proceeded to XIII Corps Draft training depôt PERNES.	AHH
"	26/4/17		Front line was evacuated by day, as the "Heavies" were wire-cutting. Battn relieved at 9 pm by 2nd HLI. Relief complete 1 AM. Battn returned to Old German front line A.24.c.11. in front of ROCLINCOURT.	AHH
ROCLINCOURT TRENCHES	27/4/17	~~2 AM~~	Battn. rested during the day; weather fine. CAPT V.G. STOKES rejoined from XIII Corps Draft Training Depôt.	
"	28/4/17		2 AM D Coy moved to, and came under orders of, 1/KRRC. 4.25 AM 5th and 6th Brigades attacked OPPY and trench system N and S of the village. 9th Bde were in Reserve.	AHH

A5834 Wt. W4973/M687 750,000 8/16 D. D. & L. Ltd. Forms/C.2118/13.

Army Form C. 2118.

Instructions regarding War Diaries and Intelligence Summaries are contained in F. S. Regs., Part II. and the Staff Manual respectively. Title pages will be prepared in manuscript.

WAR DIARY
or
INTELLIGENCE SUMMARY.

(Erase heading not required.)

Sheet No 310

Ref Map 51B NW

Place	Date	Hour	Summary of Events and Information	Remarks and references to Appendices
ROCLINCOURT TRENCHES	28/4/17	7.30am	20 ORs proceeded to ANZIN to assist 100th F A in evacuating wounded.	[illegible]
	(Cont.)	5AM to 3pm	3 Offs and 85 ORs stood by for use as emergency stretcher-bearers but were not called upon.	[illegible]
		1 PM	Battn moved forward to position in vicinity of A 24 b.6.6.	
		3 PM	Orders were received to prepare for an attack on OPPY WOOD and vicinity that night. The time for attack was eventually put forward to 4 AM.	
		9 PM	The Battn - less D Coy - moved forward by Companies and relieved units of 6th Bde in the front line, which was the same as that held previous to the attack. Relief complete 1 AM 29/4/17.	[illegible]
FRONT LINE E of BAILLEUL	29/4/17	4 AM	Battn - less D Coy - with troops on either flank attacked and captured the OPPY LINE from B.18.d.5.7 to B 18 b 2.8. The troops on our right failed to get on and the right flank was consequently exposed. At about 5 AM the enemy commenced to bomb the right flank and fighting continued until about 10 AM when owing to lack of bombs and SAA we were forced to give way, and withdrew to the jumping off trench via SUNKEN ROAD in B 18 b. C Coy on the left withdrew Northwards along the OPPY LINE and placed themselves under the orders of the 17th R.F., establishing a block at about B.12.d.1.4. taking with them 3 captured Machine Guns. The enemy shelled our front line heavily throughout the remainder of the day and there was a great deal of M G and rifle fire. Patrols were sent out at dark and found the OPPY LINE still held by the enemy.	[illegible]
		11 PM	The Battn was relieved by the 13/E YORKS and returned to the trenches E of ROCLINCOURT through a barrage of gas shells without sustaining any casualties.	[illegible]

A5834 Wt W4973/M687 750,000 8/16 D. D. & L. Ltd. Forms/C.2118/13.

Army Form C. 211

WAR DIARY
or
INTELLIGENCE SUMMARY.
(Erase heading not required.)

Instructions regarding War Diaries and Intelligence Summaries are contained in F. S. Regs., Part II. and the Staff Manual respectively. Title pages will be prepared in manuscript.

Sheet No 311

Place	Date	Hour	Summary of Events and Information Ref Map 51B N.W.	Remarks and references to Appendices
FRONT LINE E of BAILLEUL (cont)	29/4/17		About 70 prisoners and 3 Machine Guns were captured by the Battn during the day, and severe casualties were inflicted on the enemy.	AH
			Casualties Officers Killed 2/Lt M A SIMON. Wounded and Missing 2/Lt H A GIBBS, 2/Lt E C READY. Wounded CAPT V G STOKES, CAPT E L JERWOOD 2/Lt A P AVELINE, 2/Lt G M ARCHDALE.	AH
			Other Ranks Killed 15. Wounded 89. Missing 47 Total 151 casualties out of the 250 who actually attacked.	AH
ROCLINCOURT TRENCHES	30/4/17		Battn rested during the day. Weather fine and warm.	

A H Harris[?] Lt Col
Comdg 1st Royal Berkshire Regt

A5834 Wt. W4973/M687 750,000 8/16 D. D. & L. Ltd Forms/C.2118/13.

99th Brigade / 2nd Division.

1st BATTALION

ROYAL BERKSHIRE REGIMENT

M A Y 1917.

Attached :-

Report on action 3rd May 1917.

Instructions regarding War Diaries and Intelligence Summaries are contained in F. S. Regs., Part II. and the Staff Manual respectively. Title pages will be prepared in manuscript.

CONFIDENTIAL

WAR DIARY ~~or~~ ~~INTELLIGENCE SUMMARY.~~

(Erase heading not required.)

2/99

1st R. Berks

Army Form C. 2118.

Vol 31

Sheet No 312.

Ref Map 51B N.W.

Place	Date	Hour	Summary of Events and Information	Remarks and references to Appendices
ROCLINCOURT TRENCHES	1/5/17		Weather fine, and hot. Battn was formed into 2 Companies of 4 Officers and 100 O.Rs each to be formed into C Battalion with the 23rd R F under the command of Lt Col Vernon DSO. These two companies moved up to the front line at 8 pm: No 1 Coy being commanded by Capt GREEN, No 2 by LIEUT MERRICK. Battalion Hdqrs moved to ~~[illegible]~~ ECURIE CAMP.	
ECURIE	2/5/17		Weather hot. Lt Col. G.P.S HUNT CMG joined the Battalion	Report on Action of 2 Companies in ~~[illegible]~~ 'C' Battn attached.
"	3/5/17		Lt Col G P S HUNT CMG assumed command of the Battalion.	
			Bn HQ with Transport moved at 2 30 pm to 'X' Huts ECOIVRES Weather hot	
ECOIVRES	4/5/17		The 2 Companies from 'C' Battalion rejoined the Battalion at 5 pm.	
	5/5/17		Lt Col A E HARRIS DSO left the Battalion to take over command of 13th ESSEX REGT (6th Bde) with temporary command of 6th Brigade. Battalion bathed during the morning. Weather hot. Ration Strength: 16 Officers (including MO and Padre) 329 O Rs.	
	6/5/17		9 45 am Battn moved to LA COMTE arriving there at 4 30 pm. Dinners were served on the march. Weather hot.	Ref. LENS Map
			1 Warrant Officer and 52 ORs joined the Battn as reinforcements.	
LA COMTE	7/5/17		CAPT BISHOP, 2/Lt ASTLEY, 2/LT DENHAM and 32 ORs rejoined the Battn from XIII Corps Training Depot.	
			122 ORs joined the Battn as reinforcements	

A5834 Wt. W4973/M687 750,000 8/16 D. D. & L. Ltd. Forms/C.2118/13.

Instructions regarding War Diaries and Intelligence Summaries are contained in F. S. Regs., Part II. and the Staff Manual respectively. Title pages will be prepared in manuscript.

CONFIDENTIAL

WAR DIARY
or
~~INTELLIGENCE SUMMARY.~~
(Erase heading not required.)

Army Form C. 2118.

Sheet No 313.

Place	Date	Hour	Summary of Events and Information	Remarks and references to Appendices
LA COMTE	8/5/17		Company Training in the morning and afternoon. 2/Lt FROST rejoined the Battn. from XIII Corps Training Depot. Weather hot. LT PUGH proceeded to LE TOUQUET for Lewis Gun Course.	
"	9/5/17		Company Training in the morning and afternoon. Reinforcements bathed at ROCOURT. Weather hot.	
"	10/5/17		9.30 AM Battn moved to huts at BRAY, arriving there at 4.30 pm. Dinners were served on the march.	Ref. LENS Map
BRAY	11/5/17		11.45 AM. Battn. moved to camp near "LES 4 VENTS" N. of ST NICHOLAS. arriving there at 2.15 pm; coming into Corps Reserve. Weather hot.	Ref. Map 51B NW
ST NICHOLAS	12/5/17		Company Training in the morning and afternoon. Weather hot, with showers in the evening.	
"	13/5/17		Sunday. Church Parade at 9 AM. Inspection of Companies by Commanding Officer 10–12 noon. Sports were held in the evening at 6.30 pm. Weather hot with a thunderstorm at night.	
"	14/5/17		3 Officers and 240 ORs working on roads 8 AM – 3 pm. Training of Lewis Gunners, Snipers and Rifle Grenadiers during the day.	2/Lt W. LEACH joined the Battn.
	15/5/17		3 Officers and 240 ORs working on roads 8.30 AM – 3.30 pm. Training as on 14/5/17	
	16/5/17		— do — do — do — Weather wet.	
	17/5/17		Working parties and Training as on 14/5/17. Weather wet and misty. 2/LT ASTLEY and 2/LT KING went on 3 days leave to PARIS	

A5834 Wt. W4973/M687 750,000 8/16 D. D. & L. Ltd. Forms/C.2118/13.

Instructions regarding War Diaries and Intelligence Summaries are contained in F. S. Regs., Part II. and the Staff Manual respectively. Title pages will be prepared in manuscript.

CONFIDENTIAL

WAR DIARY
or
INTELLIGENCE SUMMARY.
(Erase heading not required.)

Army Form C. 2118.

Sheet No 314

Place	Date	Hour	Summary of Events and Information	Remarks and references to Appendices
ST NICHOLAS	18/5/17		2 Officers and 240 ORs working on roads 8.30 AM – 3.30 PM. Training of Lewis Gunners, Snipers and Rifle Grenadiers. Weather wet.	
	19/5/17		2 Officers and 206 ORs working on roads 8.30 AM – 3.30 PM. Training as on 18/5/17.	
	20/5/17		Sunday. Working and Training as on 19/5/17. Men had baths at ECURIE at 3.30 PM. Sports were held in the evening. Weather hot.	
	21/5/17		Working and Training as on 20/5/17. Weather hot. LT MOUSLEY rejoined the Battn from 15th Prisoners of War Company. LT PUGH rejoined from Lewis Gun Course at LE TOUQUET. LT J.W. JOHNSON and 2/LT T.H. GOWER joined the Battn. Weather hot.	
	22/5/17		1 NCO and 40 working on roads 8.30 AM – 3.30 PM. Training and organisation during the day. Weather wet.	
	23/5/17		Weather fine. CAPT. A.A. MACFARLANE-GRIEVE H.L.I. joined the Battalion.	Ref. Map 51B N.W.
		8 PM.	Battalion relieved 2nd K.O.S.B. in Reserve behind ARLEUX: Btn. Hdqs. at B.15.c 6.3. Relief complete 11.15 PM. Lt Col HUNT C.M.G. in command of the Brigade. The Battalion was organised in two companies A and B forming No 1, C and D forming No 2.	
Reserve TRENCHES Behind ARLEUX	24/5/17		Day quiet, with occasional enemy shelling. Weather fine.	
		9.30 pm	2 Officers and 100 other ranks working under orders of O.C 22nd R.F. carried wire and stakes to the front line. Casualties during the day 2 other ranks wounded.	

A5834 Wt. W4973/M687 750,000 8/16 D. D. & L. Ltd. Forms/C.2118/13.

Army Form C. 2118.

Instructions regarding War Diaries and Intelligence Summaries are contained in F. S. Regs., Part II. and the Staff Manual respectively. Title pages will be prepared in manuscript.

CONFIDENTIAL

WAR DIARY
~~or~~
~~INTELLIGENCE SUMMARY.~~
(Erase heading not required.)

Sheet No 315

Place	Date	Hour	Summary of Events and Information	Remarks and references to Appendices
Reserve TRENCHES Behind ARLEUX	25/5/17		Weather very hot. 9.30 PM 2 Officers and 100 other ranks worked in front line under OC 22nd Royal Fusiliers. Casualties NIL	Ref. Map 51B N W
	26/5/17		Working party as on 25/5/17, but increased to 3 Officers and 150 other ranks. Casualties NIL	
	27/5/17		Weather still very hot. Work as on 26/5/17, but under OC 23rd Royal Fusiliers instead of OC 22nd Royal Fusiliers. Casualties NIL. LT POWELL rejoined the Battalion	
	28/5/17		Work as on 27/5/17. Casualties 14 other ranks wounded, one of whom died of wounds early on 29/5/17. These casualties occurred to the working party on the way up to the front line. Major B G BROMHEAD and Captain H T W QUICK joined the Battalion	
	29/5/17		At 10 pm the Battalion was relieved by the 1st KINGS, and proceeded to Billets at ST AUBIN. Relief complete 11 10 pm. The last platoon arrived at ST AUBIN at about 3 AM 30/5/17	Ref. LENS Map
ST AUBIN	30/5/17		Men had baths at ECURIE during the morning. Weather hot. Swimming Races were held in the SCARPE River in the evening.	
	31/5/17	NOON	Church Parade. Weather very fine and warm. The Battalion relieved 23rd Royal Fusiliers in close support trenches between ARLEUX and OPPY, being still organized in 2 Companies (No1 under command of Capt Pugh M.C and No 2 under command of Capt Green M.C). Relief complete 11.30 pm. Casualties nil. Heavy rain had fallen the previous day and parts of the line were badly flooded. Battn H.Q. at B.10 d 47	Ref Map 51B N.W.

E. P. Hunt Lt Col.
Comdg 1st R Berks Rgt.

A5834 Wt. W4973/M687 750,000 8/16 D. D. & L. Ltd. Forms/C.2118/13.

the trench was fairly strongly held. Some made off across the open and through communication trenches. A good many were shot.

For about an hour the captured trench was consolidated but no block was made the companies having joined hands with units to right & left. Bombs were called for and passed to the left when the bombing died down. To the right a severe bombing fight arose and bombs were called for. These were sent along together with what German bombs had been collected.

5/5 30am After a sharp fight some little distance to the right men were seen to be getting out behind and running along apparently looking for room in the trench but finding it congested they dropped into shell craters. The congestion increased and more men on the right got out and back to shell craters. The companies were at this time without bombs of any sort and only 3 Lewis Guns when a hostile counter attack commenced from the front over the top and along communication trenches. The hostile bombing attack from the right had reached the right of the Companies.

6 10am Considerable casualties were caused to the enemy's frontal attack which however came on and the Companies were driven out, but mainly by the bombing attack from the right.

The men remained in the shell craters all day and were withdrawn at dark.

The majority of the casualties occurred whilst getting back from the German front line and were caused chiefly by machine guns and snipers near OPPY.

8 Officers and 210 N.C.Os + men [illegible] of which 2 officers (both slightly wounded) and 94 O.R. are now with the Battalion.

5/5/17

(Sd) G.R. Hunt Lt Col
Comdg 2nd R Berks Regt

1371

Attached to War Diary Sheet No. 312.

Report on Action 3rd May. 1917.

From information obtained from Capt Green and two composite companies 1st Royal Berkshire Regt.

Ref. Map. OPPY 1/10,000.

1 am — At about 1am 3rd May companies got into line along road from about B.12.b.9. North westward. Capt Bannatynes company of the Kings Regiment was on the right of this but he stated his support and right flank companies were not up as late as 3 am.

2 am — At 2 am Companies went out to the taped line the first wave going about 100 yards in front. This was done to avoid the worst of the hostile barrage which came on. The barrage consisted of heavies on the road mentioned above and lighter guns on the ground nearer the German line. Barrage seemed to be controlled from OPPY village & wood. Our troops must have been seen moving into position as the night was bright - moon behind them.

3 am — Our two companies Royal Berks. were in position lying down in two waves of four platoons each with two special parties for strong points behind. It is stated that troops on the right and left did not seem to be quite ready at 3.45 am when our barrage

3.45 am — commenced but that they all moved forward together. There was a tendency to converge from both sides as the advance was made. Direction was difficult to keep.

The hostile barrage commenced at once and is believed to have caused a considerable number of casualties to the left company and two (at least) Lewis Guns were damaged. There was no rifle or machine gun fire. The wire was well cut and the enemy offered [illegible] resistance though

99th Brigade / 2nd Division.

1st BATTALION

ROYAL BERKSHIRE REGIMENT

JUNE 1917.

1/R Berks 99th Bde. 2nd Div. 2

Army Form C. 2118.

CONFIDENTIAL

WAR DIARY
or
INTELLIGENCE SUMMARY.
(Erase heading not required.)

Instructions regarding War Diaries and Intelligence Summaries are contained in F. S. Regs., Part II. and the Staff Manual respectively. Title pages will be prepared in manuscript.

SHEET No 316

Vol 32

Place	Date	Hour	Summary of Events and Information	Remarks and references to Appendices
Close supp or trenches ARLEUX - OPPY.	1/6/17		Weather fine and warm. Day quiet. Enemy shelled the line occasionally.	
		10.30 pm	100 men of No1 Company (under supervision of East Anglian Field Coy. R.E) commenced digging sumps for drainage of Z trench, the remainder of the Battalion improving KENT ROAD (the O.B.L).	
		11.30 pm	This trench was heavily shelled. Casualties 1 killed & 3.O.R. wounded	
Do	2/6/17		Weather continued dry and warm. Shelling by enemy intermittent. The party of 100 men continued work on Z trench and the remainder of the Battalion improved KENT ROAD, but considerable difficulty was experienced in getting rid of the water by reason of a clay soil and very low lying position. Portions of the trenches were quite impassable. The night was quiet. Casualties NIL.	
Do	3/6/17		Weather cooler, rain threatening in the morning, but by the afternoon it turned fine again. Only slight shelling by the enemy. Work of drainage & improvement of trenches continued at night, but little progress was made in passing the water away. Casualties NIL.	
Do	4/6/17		Weather warm and fine, and very clear visibility. Shelling normal, except that Battalion Headquarters was shelled heavily with 5.9" at 60 secs interval between 1 & 3 pm.	
		11 pm	The Battalion relieved 1st K.R.R. in front line trenches (No1 Coy on Right flank and No 2 coy on the left). A heavy ground mist helped to conceal movement. Relief complete at 1.45 am. Casualties NIL. Bn Hdqrs still at ORCHARD Dug out.	
FRONT LINE between ARLEUX and OPPY	5/6/17		Weather warm and fine. Hostile shelling and sniping continued throughout the day. Trenches improved and deepened during the night. Casualties 1 OR wounded.	
— Do —	6/6/17		Weather warm and fine. Hostile shelling increased slightly during the day. A heavy thunderstorm in the evening flooded the whole trench system. Casualties other ranks 1 killed and 13 wounded. 2/Lt J H SPENCER, 2/Lt J H JOHNSTON } Joined the Battalion.	

A5834 Wt. W4973/M687 750,000 8/16 D. D. & L. Ltd. Forms/C.2118/13.

Instructions regarding War Diaries and Intelligence Summaries are contained in F. S. Regs., Part II. and the Staff Manual respectively. Title pages will be prepared in manuscript.

CONFIDENTIAL

WAR DIARY
or
INTELLIGENCE SUMMARY.
(Erase heading not required.)

Army Form C. 2118.

Sheet No 317

Place	Date	Hour	Summary of Events and Information	Remarks and references to Appendices
FRONT LINE between ARLEUX and OPPY.	7/6/17		Weather cooler. Hostile shelling considerably less throughout the day. Casualties 2 ORs wounded.	Map 51B N.W.
— do —	8/6/17	1.30AM	Gas was projected from our line into OPPY WOOD and vicinity. Weather fine. Hostile shelling slight.	
		10.20pm	Battn was relieved by 22nd R. Fusiliers and returned to BROWN LINE with BN Hdqrs at B. 19. d. 2 6. Relief complete 12.30 am 9/6/17. Casualties during the day, other ranks 1 killed, 3 wounded.	
RESERVE LINE in front of ROCLINCOURT	9/6/17		Men rested during the day. Battn furnished working party of 180 ORs for carrying and digging in the front and support trenches at night. Casualties 1 OR wounded.	
— do —	10/6/17		Weather fine and warm. Working party as on 9/6/17. Casualties NIL.	
	11/6/17		Heavy rain during the morning. The Battn was relieved by 1/K.R.R.C. in the evening and proceeded to billets at ST AUBIN. Relief complete 10 pm. No 1 Company bathed at ECURIE on their way to ST AUBIN.	
ST. AUBIN	12/6/17		Weather fine and very warm. Inspections and training in the morning. No 2 Company bathed in the SCARPE in the afternoon. Battn secured 1st Prize for a Heavy Draught Horse at Divl. Horse Show held at ECURIE.	

A5834 Wt. W4973/M687 750,000 8/16 D. D. & L. Ltd. Forms/C.2118/13.

Army Form C. 2118.

Instructions regarding War Diaries and Intelligence Summaries are contained in F. S. Regs., Part II. and the Staff Manual respectively. Title pages will be prepared in manuscript.

CONFIDENTIAL

WAR DIARY
or
INTELLIGENCE SUMMARY.
(Erase heading not required.)

Sheet No 318

Place	Date	Hour	Summary of Events and Information	Remarks and references to Appendices
ST AUBIN	13/6/17		Weather still fine and very warm. Training in the morning. Battn relieved 14th R WARWICKS at LEEDS CAMP in G 10 b. Relief complete 10.30 pm. 250 ORs worked on TIRED TRENCH under 491 Field Coy R.E. Casualties NIL.	Ref 57 B N.W.
LEEDS CAMP	14/6/17		Weather still very warm. Men rested during the day. Working party at night as on 13/6/17. Casualties NIL	
— do —	15/6/17		Weather still hot. Men rested during the morning, training in the afternoon. No working party at night.	
— do —	16/6/17		Training during the morning. Working party of 125 ORs on TIRED TRENCH at night. Casualties NIL.	
— do —	17/6/17		Working party rested during the morning. Church Parade at 5 pm. Weather still very hot. Working party of 250 ORs under Capt NUGENT worked on TIRED TRENCH at night and stayed in the RED LINE during 18/6/17	
— do —	18/6/17		Working party rejoined Battn during the night. Casualties NIL.	
— do —	19/6/17		10 AM Battn moved from LEEDS CAMP into huts at ACQ arriving at 12.20 pm. 2nd Division transferred from XIII Corps to XI Corps moving by bus to BETHUNE by Brigades. Weather warm with occasional heavy showers.	
ACQ	20/6/17		99th Brigade moved by bus to BETHUNE.	
		8.45 am	Battn marched to ECOIVRES where it embussed.	
		10.30	Busses started, arriving at BETHUNE at 1.15 pm. Route CAMBLAIN L'ABBÉ, HERSIN, NOEUX-LES-MINES. Battn was billeted at the Orphanage, relieving 17th Middlesex.	

A5834 Wt W4973/M687 750,000 8/16 D. D. & L. Ltd. Forms/C.2118/13.

Instructions regarding War Diaries and Intelligence Summaries are contained in F. S. Regs., Part II. and the Staff Manual respectively. Title pages will be prepared in manuscript.

CONFIDENTIAL

WAR DIARY or ~~INTELLIGENCE~~ SUMMARY.

(Erase heading not required.)

Army Form C. 2118.

Sheet No 319

Place	Date	Hour	Summary of Events and Information	Remarks and references to Appendices
BETHUNE	21/6/17		Weather cold. The Battalion moved into Brigade Reserve at NOYELLES, billets in huts, relieving the 2/5th Manchester Regt. The other 3 battalions of the brigade took over the front and support lines.	Ref BETHUNE Combined Sheet Map
NOYELLES	22/6/17		Company Training and Baths in the morning and afternoon. Capt H.T.W. QUICK proceeded to the 2nd Battalion R Berks Regt. Weather cold and wet.	
—	23/6/17		Weather fine. Company Training in the morning. The Officers played the men at cricket in the afternoon, winning by 10 runs.	
—	24/6/17		Sunday. Church Parade at 9.30 am. Sports were held in the evening.	
—	25/6/17		Company Training in the morning. The Battalion played the 24th R Fusiliers at cricket in the afternoon, winning by 75 runs. There was a Concert in the evening.	
—	26/6/17		Weather fine. Company Training in the morning. Company Commanders and Platoon representatives visited the trenches preparatory to relieving the 1st K.R.R.C. The Battalion beat the 483rd Coy R.E. at cricket in the afternoon. Boxing in the evening. Major B.G. BROMHEAD was admitted to hospital.	
—	27/6/17		Weather warm with occasional showers. At 5.30 pm the Battalion relieved the 1st K.R.R.C. in the front line (CAMBRIN RIGHT). Relief complete 7.30 pm. The line was held by a series of posts connected up by tunnels. Casualties NIL.	

A5834 Wt. W4973/M687 750,000 8/16 D. D. & L. Ltd. Forms/C.2118/13.

Instructions regarding War Diaries and Intelligence Summaries are contained in F. S. Regs., Part II. and the Staff Manual respectively. Title pages will be prepared in manuscript.

WAR DIARY

~~or~~

~~INTELLIGENCE~~ SUMMARY.

(Erase heading not required.)

CONFIDENTIAL

Army Form C. 21[illegible]

Sheet No 320

Place	Date	Hour	Summary of Events and Information	Remarks and references to Appendices
FRONT LINE CAMBRIN Right	28/6/17		At 3 am a few gas shells fell on our right front. Weather hot, with some rain in the evening. Day very quiet: a few Trench Mortars fell during the evening. 2/Lt R. G. ROBERTS joined the Battalion. Casualties NIL.	
— " —	29/6/17		L/Cpl J. WELCH was awarded the V.C. for his work during the attack near OPPY on April 29th. Weather fine and warm. 2 deserters (Alsatians) crossed to our lines at about 5.30 PM. Day very quiet. A few rounds of shrapnel burst over Battalion Headquarters between 8 and 10 PM. Casualties 1 OR wounded.	
— " —	30/6/17		Rain the whole morning: and at intervals in the afternoon. Day very quiet. Casualties NIL. During the whole month Battalion was organised as two companies of 4 platoons each. Battalion Headquarters was kept as low as possible. It is not found possible to reduce Battalion Headquarters to any extent. Double-Companies (i.e. A+B and C+D) varied between 110 & 140 each and were therefore at the minimum strength as laid down under G.H.Q. letter O.B. 1919 of February last. The Administrative headquarters including about 20 of the Drums amounted to about 101 which was found to be irreducible. The Drums were used and were fully employed as carrying parties. The battalion did much work whilst out of the trenches in XIth Corps and seldom had any opportunity to train. The Brig. Genl. Comdg. and other officers expressed their appreciation of the work done which generally consisted of carrying [illegible] intermittent shell fire.	

G. Hunt, Lt. Col.
Comdg. 1st Royal Berkshire Regt.

A5834 Wt. W4973/M687 [illegible] 8/16 D. D. & L. Ltd. Forms/C.2118/13.

99th Brigade / 2nd Division.

1st BATTALION

ROYAL BERKSHIRE REGIMENT

JULY 1917.

Instructions regarding War Diaries and Intelligence Summaries are contained in F. S. Regs., Part II. and the Staff Manual respectively. Title pages will be prepared in manuscript.

CONFIDENTIAL

WAR DIARY
or
~~INTELLIGENCE SUMMARY.~~
(Erase heading not required.)

1/R Berks 99/2

Army Form C. 2118.

Sheet No. 321.

Vol 33

Place	Date	Hour	Summary of Events and Information	Remarks and references to Appendices
Front Line Trenches CAMBRIN RIGHT	1/7/17		Weather dull. Day quiet with some Trench Mortar activity in the afternoon and evening. At 7.45 pm our guns and Trench Mortars carried out a retaliatory bombardment. Casualties NIL	
— " —	2/7/17		Weather fine. Enemy slightly more active during the day. Casualties NIL. An S.O.S practice was carried out at 7.45 pm. 2/Lt DOLBY and 2/Lt GRIMES joined the Battalion.	
— " —	3/7/17		Weather hot. Enemy very quiet during the morning. Trench Mortars active in the afternoon. At 5.30 pm the Battalion was relieved by 1st K.R.R.C. and moved into support. Relief complete 7.35 pm. The Battalion was disposed as follows in support. Headquarters at ANNEQUIN. No 1 Company in RESERVE TRENCH. No 2 Company in FACTORY DUG-OUTS with one platoon in ANNEQUIN. Casualties 2/Lt N.G ROBERTS was killed during the relief. 2/Lt ODELL ~~2/Lt~~ joined the Battalion	
ANNEQUIN	4/7/17		Weather dull. 2/Lt ROBERTS was buried at SAILLY-LABOURSE Cemetery in the afternoon. No 1 Company worked in the trenches during the day. No 2 Company bathed at ANNEQUIN	
— —	5/7/17		Weather dull with occasional showers. Working parties of 60 ORs were found during the day. 2/Lt TITLEY joined the Battalion	
— —	6/7/17		Weather hot. No 1 Company and No 2 Company changed places during the afternoon. At 4.30 pm ANNEQUIN was heavily shelled for about 10 minutes.	
— —	7/7/17		Weather hot. No 2 Company bathed at ANNEQUIN in the morning. Working parties of 70 ORs were found during the day.	

A5834 Wt. W4973/M687 750,000 8/16 D. D. & L. Ltd. Forms/C.2118/13.

Instructions regarding War Diaries and Intelligence Summaries are contained in F. S. Regs., Part II. and the Staff Manual respectively. Title pages will be prepared in manuscript.

CONFIDENTIAL

WAR DIARY
or
~~INTELLIGENCE SUMMARY.~~
(Erase heading not required.)

Army Form C. 2118.

Sheet No 322

Place	Date	Hour	Summary of Events and Information	Remarks and references to Appendices
ANNEQUIN	8/7/17		Weather dull, with occasional showers. 70 other ranks on working parties during the day.	
– do –	9/7/17		At 5.30 pm the Battalion relieved the 1/KRRC in CAMBRIN RIGHT sector: relief complete 7 pm. Our Artillery carried out a hurricane bombardment at 11 pm. Casualties NIL.	
Front line trenches CAMBRIN RIGHT	10/7/17		Weather dull. Day very quiet. Casualties 1 OR killed	
– do –	11/7/17		Weather hot. Day very quiet. Casualties NIL.	
– do –	12/7/17		Weather hot. Enemy more active than usual with Trench Mortars. A few gas-shells fell near Battalion Headquarters about mid-night. Casualties NIL.	
– do –	13/7/17		Weather hot. Day quiet. Enemy machine-guns active during the night. Casualties NIL. LT R.G. GREEN, LT J.A. HUGHES, 2/LT W.L. PINNIGER joined the Battalion.	
– do –	14/7/17		Weather hot. thunderstorm in the morning. Day very quiet. Our Artillery carried out a hurricane bombardment on our left at 10 pm. Casualties NIL. LT H.F. COLEMAN joined the Battalion.	
– do –	15/7/17		Weather hot. At 5.30 pm the Battalion was relieved by 1/KRRC. and went into Reserve at ANNEQUIN. Relief complete 7.35 pm. Casualties NIL.	

A5834 Wt W4973/M687 750,000 8/16 D. D. & L. Ltd. Forms/C.2118/13.

Army Form C. 2118.

WAR DIARY
or
~~INTELLIGENCE SUMMARY.~~

(*Erase heading not required.*)

Instructions regarding War Diaries and Intelligence Summaries are contained in F. S. Regs., Part II. and the Staff Manual respectively. Title pages will be prepared in manuscript.

CONFIDENTIAL

Sheet No 323

Place	Date	Hour	Summary of Events and Information	Remarks and references to Appendices
ANNEQUIN	16/7/17		Weather hot. The whole Battalion fired on the range at LE QUESNOY during the morning and afternoon.	
— do —	17/7/17		Lt Colonel Hunt CMG in command of Brigade. The Battalion had baths during the morning, and all gas helmets were tested in the morning and afternoon. ANNEQUIN was heavily shelled with 5.9's between 5.30 pm and 7.10 pm.	
— do —	18/7/17		Weather wet. Training in the vicinity of billets during the morning. Lt CROSBIE, 2/Lt DE VITRE, ~~and~~ 2/LT WELLS and 2/LT MANNING joined the Battalion.	
— do —	19/7/17		Weather dull with occasional showers. The Battalion fired a competition on the range at LE QUESNOY during the morning and afternoon.	
— do —	20/7/17		Weather hot. Company training in vicinity of billets during the morning. A boxing competition was held in the evening.	
— do —	21/7/17		A cinematograph operator from G.H.Q arrived in the morning and took several photographs of the Battalion. At 4.30 pm the Battalion relieved the 1/K.R.R.C. in CAMBRIN RIGHT sub-sector. Relief complete 6.45 pm. Night quiet. Casualties NIL. Capt G.H. BISHOP rejoined the Battalion.	
Front Line Trenches CAMBRIN RIGHT	22/7/17		Weather hot. Day very quiet. Casualties 1 accidentally wounded.	
	23/7/17		Weather hot. Day quiet. At 9.10 pm we released smoke from our front line and put down a rifle grenade barrage on the German front line; in order to draw enemy fire, as a raid was taking place on our right at 9.15 pm. The enemy sent up a large number of S.O.S signals and opened a heavy artillery ~~and~~ trench-mortar and M.G. fire. Casualties 3 other ranks wounded.	

A5834 Wt W4973/M687 750,000 8/16 D. D. & L. Ltd. Forms/C.2118/13.

Instructions regarding War Diaries and Intelligence Summaries are contained in F. S. Regs., Part II. and the Staff Manual respectively. Title pages will be prepared in manuscript.

CONFIDENTIAL

WAR DIARY
or
~~INTELLIGENCE SUMMARY.~~
(Erase heading not required.)

Army Form C. 2118.

Sheet No. 324

Place	Date	Hour	Summary of Events and Information	Remarks and references to Appendices
Front line Trenches CAMBRIN RIGHT	24/5/17		Weather hot. Day very quiet. Casualties NIL.	
	25/5/17		Weather hot. There was a heavy thunderstorm in the afternoon. Day quiet. Casualties NIL.	
"	26/5/17		Weather hot. Day quiet. The enemy shelled our lines about midnight in retaliation for a raid on our left. Casualties 4 other ranks wounded.	
"	27/7/17		Weather very hot. Day quiet. At 4.30 pm the Battalion was relieved by the 1/KRRC. and went into support: Battalion Headquarters at ANNEQUIN. Relief complete 6.50 pm.	
ANNEQUIN	28/7/17		Unusually hot and bright day. Very quiet. Working party 30 or carrying T.M. ammunition at night.	
	29/7/17		Close and dull with heavy thunderstorms. Quiet day. No 2 Coy furnished a working party of 27 or. digging emplacements for 99th T.M.B.	
	30/7/17		Warm and showery. Inter Company relief in support line. A quiet day. Working party for 99th T.M.B as before. Lieut R.C.S. BAKER M.C. joined the Battn.	
	31/7/17		A dull day. ANNEQUIN FOSSE was heavily shelled, the winding gear & power house being frequently hit and the chimney stack brought to the ground. Usual working party found for 99th T.M.B.	

G.P. Hunt Lt. Col
Comdg. 1st Royal Berkshire Rgt.

99th Brigade / 2nd Division.

1st BATTALION

ROYAL BERKSHIRE REGIMENT

AUGUST 1917

CONFIDENTIAL

Instructions regarding War Diaries and Intelligence Summaries are contained in F. S. Regs., Part II. and the Staff Manual respectively. Title pages will be prepared in manuscript.

WAR DIARY
or
INTELLIGENCE SUMMARY.
(Erase heading not required.)

1st Bn ROYAL BERKSHIRE REGT

Army Form C. 2118.

SHEET. No 325

99/2

Vol 34

Place	Date	Hour	Summary of Events and Information	Remarks and references to Appendices
ANNEQUIN	1.8.17		Strength of Battn — EFFECTIVE STRENGTH 39 officers 658 O.R; RATION STRENGTH 25 " 490 O.R	
			A very wet and dull day. Nothing unusual occurred.	
"	2.8.17		Weather unsettled and cooler. ANNEQUIN FOSSE was again heavily shelled. At 4.30 pm the Battn relieved 1/K.R.R.C. in front line CAMBRIN RIGHT. Relief complete 5.45 pm. Night quiet. Casualties nil	
Front line Trenches CAMBRIN RIGHT.	3.8.17		Weather wet and overcast. Trench system found to be very much damaged by rain necessitating constant work. 2 casualties (1 killed + 1 wounded) by enemy "Pineapple". 2/Lieut H A MOSSMAN joined the Battn	
"	4.8.17		Warm + unsettled weather. A quiet day. At 11.30 pm the 8th Bn SHERWOOD FORESTERS (139th I.B) on our RIGHT raided the enemy trenches at about G.5.c.9.3. Our Right Coys (A & B) supported the raid by firing 269 Rifle Grenades on craters in G.5.c. Casualties 2 killed and 1 wounded	
"	5.8.17		Weather fine. Night very dark. 2/Lieut H J ODELL carried out a valuable reconnaissance of enemy line in G.5.c.	
"	6.8.17		Weather fine and warm. An uneventful day. About midnight the enemy fired about 20 .77 mm shells near Battn H.Q. all of which failed to explode or exploded harmlessly in the ground. Subsequent investigation proved these to be shrapnel shell. Casualties 1 OR (A Cpl Rivers) wounded by spent M.G. bullet. 2/Lieut A.J. HARRIS joined the Battn.	

A6834 Wt. W4973/M687 750,000 8/16 D. D. & L. Ltd. Forms/C.2118/13

CONFIDENTIAL.

Army Form C. 2118.

WAR DIARY
or
INTELLIGENCE SUMMARY.
(*Erase heading not required.*)

Instructions regarding War Diaries and Intelligence Summaries are contained in F. S. Regs., Part II. and the Staff Manual respectively. Title pages will be prepared in manuscript.

SHEET N° 326

Place	Date	Hour	Summary of Events and Information	Remarks and references to Appendices
Frontline Trenches CAMBRIN RIGHT	7.8.17.		A Bright warm & uneventful day. At 10 pm a "Gas" warning was received from the 139th Infantry Brigade on our RIGHT, but our front was not affected. Casualties nil. Weather fine until 6 pm. when a heavy thunderstorm burst over the Sector. The	
"	8.8.17		Battn was relieved at 4.30 pm by 1st K.R.R.C. and went into Brigade Reserve at ANNEQUIN. Relief complete at 7.30 pm. Casualties nil.	
RESERVE BILLETS ANNEQUIN.	9.8.17		Weather fine and bright. The morning was spent in cleaning up and fitting the new "Green Tiger" Helmet covers. C.O's inspection in the afternoon. A working party of 20 O.R continued clearing out streams and drains near FOUNTAINS KEEP. ANNEQUIN was shelled during the day & a large number of enemy aircraft was seen.	
"	10.8.17.		A dull day with occasional rain. All C & D Companies employed from 9 am to 2 pm: working in Communication Trenches in CAMBRIN sector. A & B Companies training. After dark a prolonged and successful test of marching, manoeuvring & routine work while wearing Box Respirators was carried out	
	11.8.17.		Fine with slight rain. A & B Companies were absorbed by working parties. C & D Companies executed a Route March. In the afternoon and evening Swimming Sports were held in the LA BASSÉE canal near LE PRÉOL. ANNEQUIN was shelled all day.	
"	12.8.17.		A fine warm day. The Battn (less a platoon of No 2 Coy) spent the day on the Rifle Range LE QUESNOY, carrying out Tests under 2nd Divnl Musketry Competition Scheme. Col G.P.S. Hunt, CMG. went on leave & Major C Nugent assumed command	

A5834 Wt. W4973/M687 750,000 8/16 D. D. & L. Ltd. Forms/C.2118/13.

CONFIDENTIAL.

Instructions regarding War Diaries and Intelligence Summaries are contained in F. S. Regs., Part II. and the Staff Manual respectively. Title pages will be prepared in manuscript.

WAR DIARY
or
INTELLIGENCE SUMMARY.
(*Erase heading not required.*)

SHEET Nº 327.

Army Form C. 2118.

Place	Date	Hour	Summary of Events and Information	Remarks and references to Appendices
RESERVE BILLETS ANNEQUIN.	13.8.17		Fine and warm A & B Companies again furnished large working parties to repair Communication trenches in the CAMBRIN Sector, the remainder of the Battn carrying on the usual training. 2/Lieut D VALENTINE re joined the Battn	
"	14.8.17		Fine and warm. The Battn relieved 1st KRRC. in the front line CAMBRIN RIGHT at 4.30 pm Relief complete 6.30 pm. Casualties Nil Billets in ANNEQUIN taken over by 23rd Bn. Royal Fusiliers.	
Front line trenches CAMBRIN RIGHT	15.8.17.		Weather very fine. Lieut R.C.S. BAKER M.C & No 16153 Pte BARNES. carried out two valuable daylight reconnaissances of the enemy line, crossing HOGS BACK craters from posts L6 and L9. At 11.30 pm D. Special Co R.E successfully projected 10 tons of Lethal Gas on FOSSE 8 and other targets. Enemy's retaliation feeble. Casualties nil.	
"	16.8.17.		Weather very bright and fine. Lt BAKER. with Ptes Barnes and 37618. Pte Harris carried out another daring daylight patrol entering the German lines at MAD POINT & bringing back useful information. At 11.45 pm the 46th Divn on our Right bombarded the enemy lines with Thermite, supported by artillery. Casualties 1 or killed & 2 or wounded by an enemy "pineapple" in L6 post.	
"	17.8.17		Weather fine, visibility exceptionally good. Lieut BAKER. with 2/Lieut A.W. DOLBY Cpl A. HAINGE & Ptes COLLINS & BARNES, completed his daylight reconnaissance of the enemy lines, entering the German trenches at G.5.c.2.4 & walking South for 200x & also investigating the craters and trenches at G.5.c.3.7. A Quiet day. Casualties nil.	

A5834 Wt W4973/M687 750,000 8/16 D. D. & L. Ltd. Forms/C.2118/13.

CONFIDENTIAL

Instructions regarding War Diaries and Intelligence Summaries are contained in F. S. Regs., Part II. and the Staff Manual respectively. Title pages will be prepared in manuscript.

WAR DIARY
or
INTELLIGENCE SUMMARY.
(Erase heading not required.)

Army Form C. 2118.

SHEET. Nº 328.

Place	Date	Hour	Summary of Events and Information	Remarks and references to Appendices
Front line trenches. CAMBRIN RIGHT.	18.8.17.		Weather continued fine and bright. 2/Lieut H.A. MOSSMAN left to rejoin the 2nd Battn Royal Berkshire Regt. A Rifle Grenade fell in Post L.13. killing 1 (Sgt WARD) and wounding 4 of whom 1 (Pte Stevenson) died later in the day.	
"	19.8.17.		Weather fine and warm. About 6 pm Lieut R.C.S. BAKER. M.C. was killed by an enemy sniper whilst observing from L.19 post.	
"	20.8.17.		Weather still fine. A quiet day. At 4.30 pm the Battn was relieved by 1st K.R.R.C. (Relief Complete 7 pm. No casualties) and moved to SUPPORT line. No 1 Co having 3 platoons in RESERVE TRENCH and 1 platoon in CENTRAL KEEP. and No 2 Co having 3 platoons in FACTORY DUG-OUTS. and 1 platoon in ANNEQUIN. Battn H.Q. ANNEQUIN.	
SUPPORT ANNEQUIN	21.8.17.		Weather fine and warm. Lieut R.C.S. BAKER M.C. buried at Cemetery BEUVRY. 2.30 pm the funeral being attended by G.O.C. & staff 99th Infantry Brigade, the C.O. & all available officers of the Battn. No casualties.	
"	22.8.17.		Weather fine. No 2 Coy bathed at ANNEQUIN. An uneventful day.	
"	23.8.17.		Weather boisterous and unsettled with heavy thunderstorms. Companies changed over in Support line. No 1 Company bathed at ANNEQUIN in the afternoon. No casualties.	
"	24.8.17.		Weather bright & very windy. A quiet day. Casualties 1 OR killed by 77 mm shell in RESERVE TRENCH. Orders for relief of 99th Brigade by 139th Brigade received, the Battn to be relieved on 26th August by 5th Bn Sherwood Foresters. C.O. 5th Sherwood Foresters. also B.G.C. 139th Infantry Brigade & staff officers called to discuss details of Relief.	

A5834 Wt. W4973/M687 750,000 8/16 D. D. & L. Ltd. Forms/C.2118/13.

CONFIDENTIAL.

Instructions regarding War Diaries and Intelligence Summaries are contained in F. S. Regs., Part II. and the Staff Manual respectively. Title pages will be prepared in manuscript.

WAR DIARY
or
INTELLIGENCE SUMMARY.
(Erase heading not required.)

Army Form C. 2118

SHEET No 329.

Place	Date	Hour	Summary of Events and Information	Remarks and references to Appendices
SUPPORT. ANNEQUIN.	25.8.17		Weather fine. An uneventful day	
"	26.8.17		Weather continued fine and dry. The Battn was relieved in support line & billets by 5th Bn Sherwood Foresters, and moved into billets at BEUVRY. Relief commenced about 2.30 pm and was complete by 3.45 pm. Casualties nil. Battn Headquarters at ANNEQUIN were handed over to H.Q. of 139th Infantry Brigade. Lieut Col G. P. S. Hunt returned from leave and resumed command	
BILLETS. BEUVRY	27.8.17		A wet day – spent in cleaning up and inspections under Company arrangements. A & B Companies were inoculated in the morning.	
"	28.8.17		A bright windy day with showers of rain occasionally. C & D Companies were inoculated in the morning. At 10.30 am the Divnl Intelligence Officer (Lieut McGOWAN) lectured to the Battn on "The German Army". A & B Companies bathed in the afternoon.	
"	29.8.17		Unsettled weather. Ordinary training was carried on but a number of men were suffering from the effects of inoculation. C & D Companies bathed in the afternoon. In the evening the Commanding Officer gave a lecture on the History of the Regiment	
"	30.8.17		Weather fine but very windy. The Battalion paraded at 9 am. & marched to the Rifle Range "LE QUESNOY. where musketry exercises were carried out. Dinners were eaten on the Range. A successful concert was held in the evening at the Cinema. BEUVRY at which the 2nd Divnl Band played.	
"	31.8.17.		Weather warm and bright with occasional rain. The Battn paraded at 9.30 am and carried out a Route March accompanied by Transport and Drums. Route – BEUVRY	

A5834 Wt. W49, 5/M687 750,000 8/16 D. D. & L. Ltd. Forms/C.2118/13.

CONFIDENTIAL.

Instructions regarding War Diaries and Intelligence Summaries are contained in F. S. Regs., Part II. and the Staff Manual respectively. Title pages will be prepared in manuscript.

WAR DIARY
or
INTELLIGENCE SUMMARY.
(Erase heading not required.)

Army Form C. 2118.

SHEET No 330.

Place	Date	Hour	Summary of Events and Information	Remarks and references to Appendices
BILLETS. BEUVRY.	31.8.17		LE QUESNOY – GORRE – LE HAMEL. LES CHOQUAUX. – BETHUNE Drums were massed at CHAMP DE MARS. BETHUNE. The column left Bethune and returned to Beuvry at 2 pm. In the evening 2/Lt DENHAM gave a lecture to officers & N.C.O.s on Musketry.	
			STRENGTH OF BATTN 31.8.1917 EFFECTIVE 38 officers. 694 O.R RATION. 29 " 527 "	
	21.6.17 to 31.8.17		SUMMARY. The 99th Infantry Brigade took over the CAMBRIN SECTOR on 21.6.1917, and after 6 days in Brigade Reserve at NOYELLES the Battn moved into front trenches of RIGHT sub-sector holding a front of about 1000x extending from RAILWAY ALLEY on N to CLIFFORD ST on S. (both exclusive) and consisting of a number of advanced posts numbered L1 to L19, with NORTHAMPTON TRENCH as support trench, a system of tunnels and dugouts giving covered access to the principal positions. Plans are attached shewing the extent of the front and the positions of the posts and tunnels. The Battn alternately relieved and was relieved by 1st K.R.R.C – each Battn doing 6 days in front line – 6 days in Support – 6 days in front line and 6 days in Reserve until 26.8.1917 when the 99th Brigade was relieved by the 139th Brigade (46th Division). Throughout this period the Battn Trench strength was under 400 and the organization as 2 Companies of 4 platoons each was continued. Owing to this weakness in	

A5834 Wt. W4973/M687 750,000 8/16 D. D. & L. Ltd. Forms/C.2118/13.

CONFIDENTIAL

Instructions regarding War Diaries and Intelligence Summaries are contained in F. S. Regs., Part II. and the Staff Manual respectively. Title pages will be prepared in manuscript.

WAR DIARY
or
INTELLIGENCE SUMMARY.
(Erase heading not required.)

SHEET. No 331.

Army Form C. 2118.

Place	Date	Hour	Summary of Events and Information	Remarks and references to Appendices
			numbers the Battn was not able to effect much in the way of work, but the drainage & revetment of the posts and trenches, and the sanitary condition of the line, were all considerably improved during the period. The Battn carried out some daring and valuable patrols and also gave useful support to operations by units on either flank, but did not take part in any operations. The period was comparatively quiet, our casualties being KILLED. 2 officers and 7 OR, WOUNDED 18. O.R. (2 self inflicted) - all caused by enemy trench mortars and rifle grenades. Very little training was possible, even when in reserve, owing to the nature of the country, observation by the enemy, and the constant demand for working parties.	

G.P. Hunt Lt Col
Comdg 1st Royal Berks Regt
4.9.1917

A5834 Wt. W4973/M687 750,000 8/16 D. D. & L. Ltd. Forms/C.2118/13

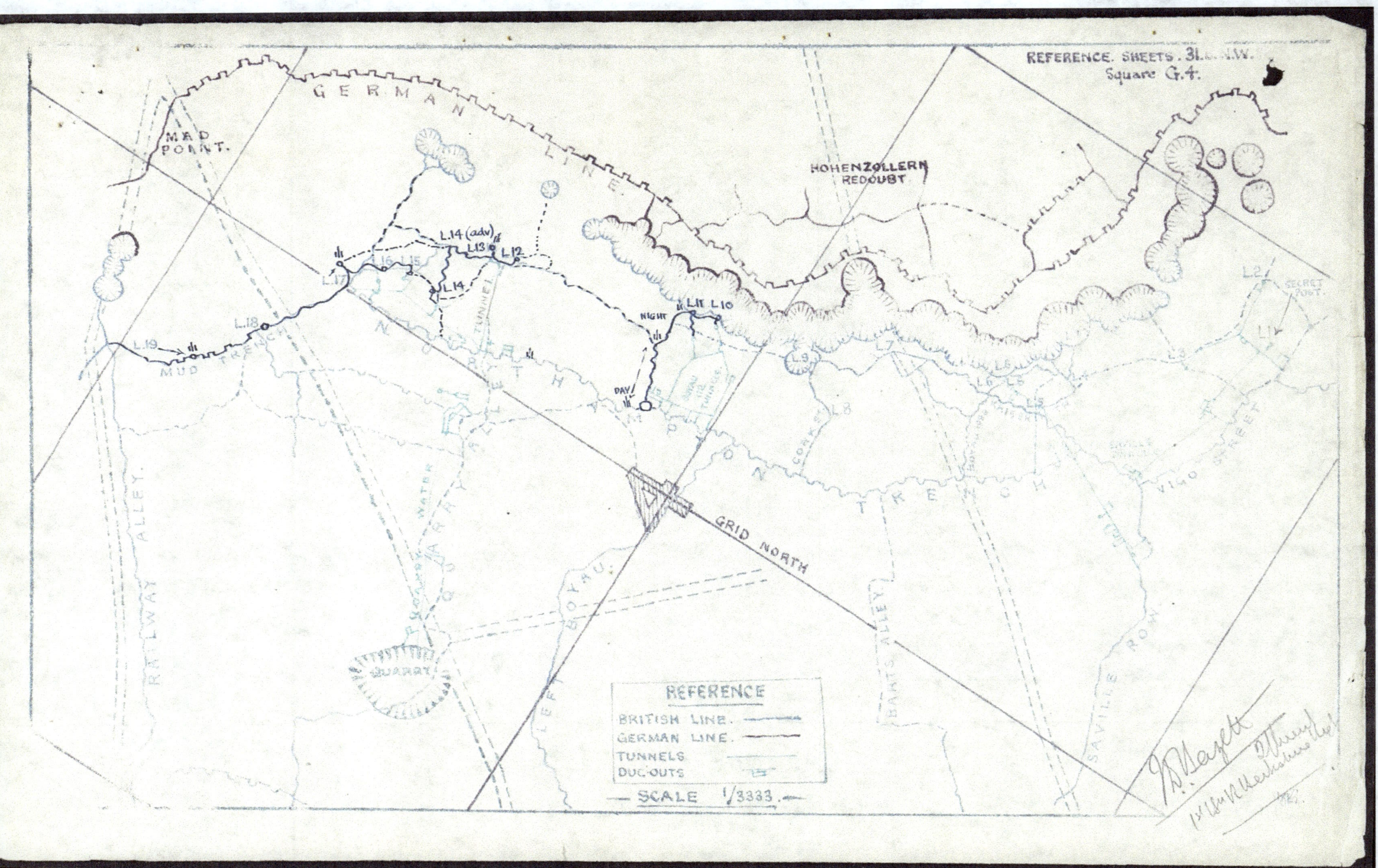

REFERENCE. SHEETS. 31.
Square G.4.
GERMAN LINE.
MAD POINT.
HOHENZOLLERN REDOUBT
L.14 (adv)
L.13
L.12
L.14
L.16
L.15
L.17
L.18
L.19
MUD TRENCH
NORTH
NIGHT
DAY
L.11
L.10
L.9
L.8
L.7
L.6
L.5
L.3
L.2
L.1
SECRET POST.
TUNNEL
CORKS
GRID NORTH
TRENCH
VIGO STREET
SAVILLE ROW
BARTS ALLEY
LEFT BOYAU
RAILWAY ALLEY.
WATER
QUARRY
REFERENCE
BRITISH LINE.
GERMAN LINE.
TUNNELS
DUG-OUTS
SCALE 1/3333.

99th Brigade / 2nd Divison.

1st BATTALION

ROYAL BERKSHIRE REGIMENT

SEPTEMBER 1917.

CONFIDENTIAL

Instructions regarding War Diaries and Intelligence Summaries are contained in F. S. Regs., Part II. and the Staff Manual respectively. Title pages will be prepared in manuscript.

WAR DIARY or INTELLIGENCE SUMMARY.

(Erase heading not required.)

1st Bn ROYAL BERKSHIRE Rt

Army Form C. 2118.

SHEET No 332

Place	Date	Hour	Summary of Events and Information	Remarks and references to Appendices
BILLETS BEUVRY	1.9.17		Weather unsettled. Ordinary training carried on in morning. In the afternoon an inter platoon football competition was started. A number of officers attended the Athletic Sports held by 1/K.R.R.C. at VENDIN LEZ BETHUNE. We entered a team (Capt CASSIDY. RAMC. & 2/Lieuts BRYAN, TITLEY & FROST) for Lloyd Lindsay race, but were unsuccessful.	
"	2.9.17		Church Parade. 10 am in BEUVRY CINEMA. The Divnl Band provided the music. Inter platoon football competition completed & won by a team of "Drums & Stretcher Bearers"	
"	3.9.17		Weather fine & bright. All Companies inoculated a 2nd time. Ordinary training & tests in Divisional Musketry Competition were carried on.	
"	4.9.17		A fine day. Training carried on under Company arrangements, but many men were suffering from effects of inoculation. Lecture in afternoon to all ranks by Capt Anderson (1st Army Physical Training & Bayonet Fighting expert)	
"	5.9.17		Weather fine. The C.O & Adjutant reconnoitred RIGHT sub sector of GIVENCHY sector as held by 2/S/Staffs, whom we were to relieve on 7th inst. Training carried on.	
"	6.9.17		Weather fine at first, rainy & thunder in the afternoon. The Battn bathed. O.C. Companies reconnoitred the line in the morning. Divnl Musketry Competition Tests completed. No 9 Platoon (C.Co) proving best Musketry platoon & No 11 Platoon (C.Co) winning the Battn Lewis Gun competition.	
"	7.9.17		Weather dry but dull & overcast. Battn inspected by C.O. in the morning. In the evening the Battn relieved 2/S/Staffs in GIVENCHY RIGHT sub-sector (the 99th Brigade taking over the whole sector from 6th Brigade). Relief completed 10.30pm. Casualties nil. For the holding of this front the 4 Company organization was retained – each Coy of 2 platoons	

(A7092) Wt. W12839/M1293. 750,000. 1/17. D. D. & L., Ltd. Forms/C.2118/14.

CONFIDENTIAL

Instructions regarding War Diaries and Intelligence Summaries are contained in F. S. Regs., Part II. and the Staff Manual respectively. Title pages will be prepared in manuscript.

WAR DIARY
or
INTELLIGENCE SUMMARY.
(Erase heading not required.)

Army Form C. 2118.

SHEET No 333.

Place	Date	Hour	Summary of Events and Information	Remarks and references to Appendices
FRONT LINE GIVENCHY RIGHT	7.9.17		Companies were disposed as follows:- "A" Co (Capt M.P. PUGH. M.C) in Support in GUNNERS SIDING. "B" Co (Capt STEED) on Right front. "C" Co (Capt E.P. JACKSON) in Centre front and "D" Co (Capt P. MOUSLEY) on Left front ("Islands"). In taking over the line we assumed responsibility for the training of No 1 Coy 13th Bn PORTUGUESE Infantry - 1 platoon being attached "man to man" to each B. C & D Companies.	
"	8.9.17		A fine day. Both G.O.C 2nd Divn & G.O.C 99th Brigade visited the Bn in the line during the morning. At 8 pm No 1 Co. 13th Bn Portuguese Infantry went out and at about 10.30 pm No 3 Co (6 o & 186 o.r.) of same Battn came in and took their place. The relief & change was complicated by the language difficulty & there was considerable confusion in the matter of rations. No casualties however occurred. During the day "BABY" (a heavy T.M) was buried by a 5.9" fired from a Northerly direction & went out of action somewhat to the relief of the Battn as these heavy T.M's always rouse the enemy to retaliation - the infantry suffering!	
"	9.9.17		Early in the morning (2.30 am) about 400 gas shells were fired from 4" Stokes guns by "O" Section No 4 Special Co R.E. on our front. The operation was successfully carried out the enemy retaliation being very slight. Casualties nil. At 10 am Brig. Genl KELLETT (G.O.C. 99th Brigade) conducted Colonel FELISBERTO ALVES PEDROSO (Commanding 6th Portuguese Infantry Brigade) round the trenches. At midday a party of 12 officers and 26 o.R. from Nos 1 & 2 Coys of 2nd Battn (6th Brigade) Portuguese Infantry came in for a 24 hours reconnaissance of the line. 2 officers were attached to each B. C & D Coys & 4 to Battn H.Q.	

(A7092). Wt. W12839/M1293. 750,000. 1/17. D. D. & L., Ltd. Forms/C.2118/14.

CONFIDENTIAL

Army Form C. 2118.

WAR DIARY
or
INTELLIGENCE SUMMARY.
(Erase heading not required.)

SHEET No 334

Instructions regarding War Diaries and Intelligence Summaries are contained in F. S. Regs., Part II. and the Staff Manual respectively. Title pages will be prepared in manuscript.

Place	Date	Hour	Summary of Events and Information	Remarks and references to Appendices
FRONT LINE GIVENCHY RIGHT.	10.9.17		Weather fine and warmer. At 8.30 the Portuguese Reconnaissance party left us. L/C ABROCK & L/C HUMPHRIES, both of D Co. were killed in PRINCES ISLAND during the afternoon by an enemy "pineapple" falling in a grenade dump. At 11 pm the 1st Portuguese Brigade on our left raided the enemy trenches in S.22 c. supported by an artillery barrage. Casualties nil.	
"	11.9.17		Weather fine and warm but misty & cooler at night. Between 10 and 11 am SCOTTISH TRENCH was heavily shelled with 5.9" and practically obliterated for 30x but we suffered no casualties. At 12.30 pm the enemy lines immediately S of our position were bombarded by Medium and Heavy Trench Mortars covered by 18 pounder and 4.5" How fire and by fire of 6th M G Co. About 11 pm 41st Bde R.F.A. fired on the same targets. At 8 pm No 3 Coy 13th Bn. Portuguese Infantry were guided out of the trenches without mishap. At 10 pm Nos 1 & 2 Companies of 2nd Bn Portuguese Infantry (14 O & about 300 OR) came into the line and were attached for instruction, as follows:- B Co. 3 O & 97 OR. C Co. 2 O & 87 OR. D Co. 3 O & 99 OR. Battn H.Q. 6 O & 9 OR.	
"	12.9.17		During the morning BERKELEY ST & PICCADILLY on R Co. front were badly damaged by 5.9" shells. At 11.30 am a Reconnaissance party from 10th Bn. 5th Bde. Portuguese Infantry consisting of 12 O and 36 O.R. came into the line and were attached as follows B Co. 2 O & 11 O.R. C Co. 2 O 10 OR. D Co. 2 O. 11 OR. Bn HQ 6 O. 6 OR.	
"	13.9.17		At 1.30 am gas was successfully projected from same emplacements and on same targets as on the 9th instant. At the same time gas was projected from our right flank on targets in A.16.c. Enemy retaliation to these annoyances was practically nil. At	

(A7092). Wt. W12839/M1293. 750,000. 1/17. D. D. & L., Ltd. Forms/C.2118/14.

CONFIDENTIAL

Instructions regarding War Diaries and Intelligence Summaries are contained in F. S. Regs., Part II. and the Staff Manual respectively. Title pages will be prepared in manuscript.

WAR DIARY
or
INTELLIGENCE SUMMARY.

(Erase heading not required.)

Army Form C. 2118.

SHEET No 335.

Place	Date	Hour	Summary of Events and Information	Remarks and references to Appendices
GIVENCHY RIGHT	13.9.17		9 am the Reconnaissance party from 10th Bn Portuguese Infantry left us. The remainder of the day passed quietly, being fine and warm. At night the Battn was relieved by 1 K.R.R.C and moved to billets at GORRE CHATEAU. Relief complete 11.15 pm. Casualties nil.	
BILLETS GORRE CHATEAU	14.9.17		Battn bathed in the morning. Inspected by Commanding Officer in the afternoon. A working party of 25 employed unloading barges on canal, and a fatigue party of 12 found for sanitary work under Town Major. Weather fine.	
"	15.9.17		Weather warm and fine. We found good training facilities at GORRE – a Bayonet Fighting Course – bombing ground – 30x rifle and revolver ranges – and a good parade ground. Training was carried on all day. Same working parties as previous day.	
"	16.9.17		A fine warm day. Parade Service at 10 am conducted by Padre RAVEN. In the afternoon a spirited football match A & B Cos v C & D Cos ending in a draw. During the night about 11.15 – 12 a number of 5.9" shells, presumably intended for our gun positions, fell near the CHATEAU. The Battn fell in on alarm posts but the bombardment soon ceased causing no casualties. It is related of the GORRE Y.M.C.A. chaplain that, when the shelling commenced, he slipped on his clothes, felt under his bed for his tin hat, clapped it on his head, & got out into the open. Some time afterwards he discovered that his helmet had a handle to it. – Same working parties as the previous day	
"	17.9.17		No 9 platoon of C. Coy practised musketry on LE QUESNOY range. D Coy furnished working party of 50 OR & Town Major's fatigue. 25 per Coy & all officers attended a lecture on "Bullet & Bayonet" by Major Campbell, at LE QUESNOY Theatre. Brig Genl KELLETT entertained to dinner by Officers Mess. The 2nd Divisional Band played	

CONFIDENTIAL

Instructions regarding War Diaries and Intelligence Summaries are contained in F. S. Regs., Part II. and the Staff Manual respectively. Title pages will be prepared in manuscript.

WAR DIARY
or
INTELLIGENCE SUMMARY.
(Erase heading not required.)

Army Form C. 2118.

SHEET NO 336.

Place	Date	Hour	Summary of Events and Information	Remarks and references to Appendices
BILLETS GORRE CHATEAU	18.9.17		Weather continuing warm and fine. Every officer and man with the Battn went through both lachrymatory & Chlorine Gas Tests under supervision of 2nd Divn Gas Officer in the morning. Orders having been received to return to CAMBRIN RIGHT the Battn moved to BEUVRY at noon, handing over GORRE CHATEAU to 2/S/Staffs. In the afternoon the Commdg Officer and Adjutant visited 5/Sherwood Foresters at Battn HQ CAMBRIN RIGHT and discussed preliminary details of relief on 20th.	
BILLETS BEUVRY	19.9.17		A very close warm day. The Battn bathed in the morning, while O C Companies reconnoitred the line. In the afternoon 10 O & 40 OR attended a lecture on the work of the R.F.C. especially the part played by Corps machines	
"	20.9.17		Weather fine but dull. Dinners at noon and at 1 pm the Battn moved off via SAILLY LABOURSE - NOYELLES and relieved 5/Sherwood Foresters in front line CAMBRIN RIGHT. Relief complete 5 pm. Casualties nil, although enemy heavy T M s were very active at the time & later. The Battn took over the exact dispositions of 5/Sherwood F (viz A Coy R front - C Co Centre front - D Co Left Front - B Co in support in RESERVE TRENCH) but on completion of relief reverted to the old dispositions (A & B Coys together as No 1 Coy under command of Capt M.P. PUGH. M.C on RIGHT & C & D Coys together as No 2 Coy under Capt E.P. JACKSON on LEFT). It was found that the 139th Bde had entirely altered the method of holding the line - occupying only 5 advanced posts which they had surrounded by wire, many of the old posts & saps being covered in with barbed wire. A number of the tunnel entrances had also been closed. Our old posts were however practically unaltered & in good condition, but NORTHAMPTON TRENCH had been neglected & was impassable in many places. QUARRY TUNNEL had been blown in near L. Coy H.Q. that morning & was under repair	

(A7092). Wt. W12839/M1293. 750,000. 1/17. D. D. & L., Ltd. Forms/C.2118/14.

CONFIDENTIAL.

Instructions regarding War Diaries and Intelligence Summaries are contained in F. S. Regs., Part II. and the Staff Manual respectively. Title pages will be prepared in manuscript.

WAR DIARY
or
INTELLIGENCE SUMMARY.
(Erase heading not required.)

Army Form C. 2118.

SHEET No 337.

Place	Date	Hour	Summary of Events and Information	Remarks and references to Appendices
FRONT LINE CAMBRIN RIGHT	21.9.17		Weather fine and warm. The enemy sent over a number of heavy Trench Mortar shells in the early evening. otherwise the day passed quietly Casualties nil	
"	22.9.17		Fine weather continued. Enemy heavy T.M again active in the evening, firing about 30 rounds on LEFT BOYAU and QUARRY ALLEY between 5 and 6 pm. Casualties 1 OR. slightly wounded in the hand.	
"	23.9.17		Cooler but fine. Capt Steed took over No 1 Coy & Capt Mousley No 2 Co. G.O.C 99th Brigade visited the line. A quiet day. Casualties nil	
"	24.9.17		Weather continued fine and warm. At 5.30 am: enemy concentrated all his available artillery and T.M's on that part of the Divisional front lying to N of LA BASSEE Canal, and attempted to raid at CANADIAN ORCHARD. The operation was a failure. S.O.S was sent back and our artillery assisted. otherwise all was quiet on our front. the enemy being noticeably inactive. 2/Lt MANNING was slightly wounded by a sniper at 7 am & was sent down. The remainder of the day was uneventful	
"	25.9.17.		A lovely day. Commencing at 3pm, our Medium and Heavy T.M's and Artillery of all calibres carried out an organized shoot on the enemy trenches immediately to our left. All quiet on our front. Casualties nil.	
"	26.9.17		Between 5 and 6 am the enemy fired a large number of large calibre gas shells on our battery positions at ANNEQUIN & VERMELLES and back areas. No trace of the gas was noticeable in the line. The remainder of the day passed without incident. and in the evening the Battn was relieved in the line by 1/K.R.R.C, and moved into Support. The old dispositions were resumed. No 1 Co moving to RESERVE TRENCH, with 1 platoon in CENTRAL KEEP, and No 2 Co in FACTORY DUG OUTS with 1 platoon in	

(A7092). Wt. W12839/M1293. 750,000. 1/17. D. D. & L., Ltd. Forms/C.2118/14.

CONFIDENTIAL

Instructions regarding War Diaries and Intelligence Summaries are contained in F. S. Regs., Part II. and the Staff Manual respectively. Title pages will be prepared in manuscript.

WAR DIARY
or
INTELLIGENCE SUMMARY.

(Erase heading not required.)

Army Form C. 2118.

SHEET. Nº 338.

Place	Date	Hour	Summary of Events and Information	Remarks and references to Appendices
Support. ANNEQUIN.	26.9.17		ANNEQUIN. Battn HQ in ANNEQUIN. Casualties nil. On reaching Annequin we found that on the previous night the enemy had pumped poison gas down the mine shaft of FOSSE 8, and thus filled the numerous ramifications of the BETHUNE mine system with the gas – entrapping a number of British troops, on duty under FOSSE 8, and some French civilian miners in the galleries connecting FOSSE 8 with FOSSE 9. ANNEQUIN. The 170TH Tunnelling Co R.E had organized a rescue party. The Battn was called on to provide a Guard at FOSSE 9. (1.O & 9.OR) relieving 1/K.R.R.C. and our M.O (Capt D.S. CASSIDY) descended the mine to assist the rescue party. Our signallers were in touch with the bottom of the mine. From 12 to 1 that night the enemy shelled FOSSE 9 with 5.9" & 8" gas shells ('Mustard' Gas)	
"	27.9.17		Capt Cassidy & his orderly (Pte Stamp) returned from the mine, badly gassed and were sent down. A number of R.E. personnel also came up badly gassed. Otherwise the day passed without incident. Weather warm and fine. Reinforcements 16 OR joined the Battn. No 2 Coy bathed.	
"	28.9.17.		The fine weather continued. Nothing unusual to record. The mine was still full of gas fumes and efforts to rescue the imprisoned men were unavailing.	
"	29.9.17.		Weather warm and fine – misty at night and in the early morning. Companies changed over in the Support line. No 2 moving up to RESERVE TRENCH under Capt Jackson and No 1 coming back to Factory Dug-outs & Annequin under command of Capt Pugh. Capt G.H. BISHOP rejoined the Battn from ETAPLES.	
"	30.9.17		Considerable artillery activity on part of the enemy. Gun positions in ANNEQUIN being shelled all day with 5.9" x 8". Capt Bishop took over command of B. Coy	

(A7092). Wt. W12839/M1293. 750,000. 1/17. D. D. & L., Ltd. Forms/C.2118/14.

CONFIDENTIAL

Instructions regarding War Diaries and Intelligence Summaries are contained in F. S. Regs., Part II. and the Staff Manual respectively. Title pages will be prepared in manuscript.

WAR DIARY
or
INTELLIGENCE SUMMARY.
(Erase heading not required.)

Army Form C. 2118.

SHEET No 339.

Place	Date	Hour	Summary of Events and Information	Remarks and references to Appendices
Support ANNEQUIN	30.9.17		from Capt Steed. The body of one man of R.E. was recovered from FOSSE 9. Casualties 2 O.R. slightly wounded in LEFT BOYAU and FACTORY DUG OUTS. No 1 Coy bathed during the day. Weather warm and fine.	
	30.9.17		EFFECTIVE STRENGTH 38 O. 708 O.R RATION STRENGTH 23 O. 535 O.R	
			The Battalion benefitted by the change out of the line for 12 days in divisional reserve and 6 days in Brigade reserve. It had not been further back than ANNEQUIN on arriving in this sector in June. Casualties had been comparatively light and the strength of the Battalion had gradually increased during the month from sick and wounded rejoining and from a few men arriving for the first time.	
			The Cambrin Right sub-sector which the Battalion has held alternately with 1st Kings Royal Rifle Corps with a short interval since June, is a somewhat complicated one on account of the numerous craters between the opposing lines and the three tunnel systems leading to our front posts. The view is very limited by the high ground along the craters, the old Hohenzollern Redoubt. Warfare has consisted chiefly of trench mortars, rifle grenades, sniping, overhead machine gun fire + artillery fire. There has been little room for patrol encounters or raids.	
			CASUALTIES during Septr	

	Wounded	Killed
O	2	–
O.R.	3	2

G. P. Hunt Lt. Col
Comdg. 1st Royal Berkshire Regt

(A7092). Wt. W12839/M1293 750,000. 1/17. D. D. & L., Ltd. Forms/C.2118/14.

99th Brigade / 2nd Division.

1st BATTALION

ROYAL BERKSHIRE REGIMENT

OCTOBER 1917.

CONFIDENTIAL.

Instructions regarding War Diaries and Intelligence Summaries are contained in F. S. Regs., Part II. and the Staff Manual respectively. Title pages will be prepared in manuscript.

WAR DIARY
or
INTELLIGENCE SUMMARY.
(Erase heading not required.)

Army Form C. 2118.

1st Bn ROYAL BERKSHIRE REGt.

SHEET No 340.

Vol 36

Place	Date	Hour	Summary of Events and Information	Remarks and references to Appendices
CAMBRIN RIGHT (Support)	1.10.17		Weather continued warm and fine. Nothing unusual occurred.	
	2.10.17		Shortly after 12 M.N. the enemy opened a bombardment with guns of all calibres on our Reserve and Support lines. and battery positions at ANNEQUIN and VERMELLES. and under cover of this, fired a large number of gas shells. chiefly lacrymatory. Box Respirators were adjusted and all ranks stood to. The shelling gradually lessened and ceased about 1 am. The Gas reached our rear H.Q at BEUVRY. Much sneezing was caused. and the use of a new gas "diphenyl chlorarsine" was suspected. At 4 pm the Battn relieved 1/K.R.R.C in front line, taking up same positions as on former occasions. Relief complete 5.40 pm. Casualties nil.	
FRONT LINE CAMBRIN RIGHT.	3.10.17		An uneventful day - weather fine and cool. The attitude of the enemy was unusually quiet.	
	4.10.17.		Some rain. Advance orders for the relief of the 2nd Division by the 25th Division were received. and later in the day. the C.O. of 9th Loyal North Lancashire Regt. with an advance party of officers and N.C.O's. came into the line. and details for our relief by them were discussed. At 11-30 pm gas operations were carried out on a very large scale. On our own front a number of 4" Stokes mortar gas shells were fired from QUARRY. On our immediate left a gas cloud was released from 1200 cylinders in the front line trenches. and to the North and South a large number of gas shells were fired from "projectors". The operation went off without a hitch. & earned the congratulations of the Army Commander, but, in the opinion of experts, the wind was too strong for complete success. Just before M.N. orders received from Brigade giving full details of relief to take place next day.	

(A7092). Wt. W12839/M1293. 750,000. 1/17. D. D. & L., Ltd. Forms/C.2118/14.

CONFIDENTIAL.

Instructions regarding War Diaries and Intelligence Summaries are contained in F. S. Regs., Part II. and the Staff Manual respectively. Title pages will be prepared in manuscript.

WAR DIARY
or
INTELLIGENCE SUMMARY.
(Erase heading not required.)

Army Form C. 2118.

SHEET Nº 341

Place	Date	Hour	Summary of Events and Information	Remarks and references to Appendices
FRONT LINE CAMBRIN RIGHT	5.10.17		Relief by 9/Loyal N. Lancs commenced in the morning and completed by 2 pm. The Battn marched to BETHUNE and occupied billets in MONTMORENCY BARRACKS. Transport. Qr Mrs stores and rear H.Q moving there in advance. The weather was fine. the attitude of the enemy very quiet. and no casualties were suffered. A large reinforcement (253 OR) joined us, consisting of a draft of 100 from Oxford & Bucks L.I. and men combed out from A.S.C and Labour units.	
BETHUNE.	6.10.17		A miserably wet day. The 99th Brigade marched to AUCHEL & RAIMBERT as a Brigade in the following order. 1/K.R.R.C - 99. M.G. Co - 22/R/F - 23/R/F - 1/R.BERKS - 99 T.M. Battery - No 2 Coy Train. Our reinforcements marched as 2 companies. The Battn was allotted billets at AUCHEL, which we reached at 1 pm. The billets were found to be inconvenient and scattered. and sanitary arrangements incomplete. It was impossible to find room for a Battn Mess. + 3 messes were arranged for A & D. Coys. B & C Coys. and H.Q.	
BILLETS AUCHEL.	7.10.17		Weather still wet and cold. Reinforcements were inspected by Commdg Officer and posted to Companies: The 4 company system was again adopted. each company having a strength of about 200. Church parade service in the CINEMA at 11.15 am After dinners reinforcements joined their Companies, and billets were re-allotted so as to centralize the administration of each Company	
"	8.10.17		A Bright. windy day. Training was commenced. reinforcements doing elementary training under Company arrangements. and being absorbed into sections when efficient.	

(A7092). Wt. W12839/M1293. 750,000. 1/17. D. D. & L., Ltd. Forms/C.2118/14.

CONFIDENTIAL

Instructions regarding War Diaries and Intelligence Summaries are contained in F. S. Regs., Part II. and the Staff Manual respectively. Title pages will be prepared in manuscript.

WAR DIARY
or
INTELLIGENCE SUMMARY.
(Erase heading not required.)

SHEET No 342

Army Form C. 2118.

Place	Date	Hour	Summary of Events and Information	Remarks and references to Appendices
BILLETS AUCHEL.	9.10.17		Weather fine and dry. The Battn paraded and marched to RAIMBERT Rifle Range where reinforcements were instructed in musketry and firing. General training was also continued - the training ground being found spacious & convenient.	
"	10.10.17		Weather unsettled. General and specialist training continued. Inoculation commenced.	
"	11.10.17		Weather fine but cold. Training continued under Company arrangements. The Divisional Commander held a conference with Commanding Officers of all units, 2nds in Command, Intelligence Officers &c in AUCHEL CINEMA in the afternoon, during which he explained the experiences gained by the formations fighting near YPRES & said the Divn, after a period of training, would go NORTH & take part in the operations there. In the evening the Commdg Officer lectured to officers & senior N.C.O's on the same subject.	
"	12.10.17		Weather fine in the morning but very wet in the afternoon. Training continued.	
"	13.10.17		Weather unsettled. The Battn paraded and marched to RAIMBERT rifle range where practice with live grenades and general training was carried out. The Range being appropriated for the "Inter Battn" stage of the Divisional Riflemens Competition - result. (1) 1/K.R.R.C (2) 1/R.BERKS (3) 23/R.F. The Commdg Officer and O.C Companies proceeded to XVIII Corps school for 3 days instruction in the latest fighting tactics adopted in the operations in the NORTH. Lecture to officers and senior N.C.O's by Major Wilson D.S.O. (G.S.O. 2nd Divn). on "Training as applied to present operations"	

(A7092). Wt. W12839/M1293. 750,000. 1/17. D. D. & L., Ltd. Forms/C.2118/14.

CONFIDENTIAL

Instructions regarding War Diaries and Intelligence Summaries are contained in F. S. Regs., Part II. and the Staff Manual respectively. Title pages will be prepared in manuscript.

WAR DIARY
or
INTELLIGENCE SUMMARY.
(*Erase heading not required.*)

Army Form C. 2118.

SHEET No 343

Place	Date	Hour	Summary of Events and Information	Remarks and references to Appendices
BILLETS AUCHEL.	14.10.17		Weather fine. Parade service with 1/K.R.R.C. addressed by Rt Rev Bishop L.H. GWYNNE C.M.G. (Bishop of KHARTOUM) Deputy Chaplain General. In the afternoon a football match with 23/R.F. was played, the latter winning 3-2. The "Inter-Battn" stage of Divl Lewis Gun Competition was fired off - result (1) 1/K.R.R.C (2) 1/R.BERKS.	
"	15.10.17		The Brigade, drawn up "in mass" on high ground near RAINBERT Rifle Range, was inspected by the Army Commander (Lt Genl HORNE) who bade us farewell, saying we were leaving his army & were to go NORTH & join in the fighting there. The Brigade then marched past in column of route. Night firing by A & B Coys on the Rifle Range.	
"	16.10.17.		A fine morning. Training carried on under Company arrangements. The afternoon was dull but no rain fell. A Gymkhana was held on the Rifle Range. It was attended by the Divisional Commander, and was very successful. In the evening to officers and senior N.C.O's was given by Col DOONER R.A. on the work of the field guns in connection with modern methods of attack. The Commanding & Company officers returned from XVIII Corps school	
"	17.10.17.		General training carried on. Nothing of unusual interest occurred.	
"	18.10.17		A Route march was carried out via FLORINGHEM. AUMERVAL ANNETTES, BELLERY - FERFAY - CAUCHY-À-LAITOUR. Only one man fell out & condition of the men was generally good.	

(A7092). Wt. W12839/M1293. 750,000. 1/17. D. D. & L., Ltd. Forms/C.2118/14.

CONFIDENTIAL

Instructions regarding War Diaries and Intelligence Summaries are contained in F. S. Regs., Part II. and the Staff Manual respectively. Title pages will be prepared in manuscript.

WAR DIARY
or
INTELLIGENCE SUMMARY.
(Erase heading not required.)

Army Form C. 2118.

SHEET No 344

Place	Date	Hour	Summary of Events and Information	Remarks and references to Appendices
BILLETS AUCHEL.	19.10.17		Weather fine. Training proceeded with under Company arrangements, being based on the tactical conditions prevailing in the YPRES battle.	
"	20.10.17		Training proceeded with. In the evening a successful Regimental concert was held in the CINEMA	
"	21.10.17		Parade Service in the CINEMA at 10 am. In the afternoon a football match v 99th Brigade, which we won 1-0. 2/Lieut C.M. DORMER joined the Battn.	
"	22.10.17		The Battn bathed at RAIMBERT FOSSE during the day, and Companies rehearsed their parts in a Brigade Tactical Scheme which was to take place on the 25th inst. on the high ground N of RAIMBERT Rifle Range. B. Co. were put through gas tests.	
"	23.10.17		A very wet day, interfering considerably with training, which was carried on under Company arrangements.	
"	24.10.17		Musketry practice and general training carried on at RAIMBERT Rifle Range and training ground. Dinners were eaten on the Range. C & D. Companies were put through gas tests.	
"	25.10.17		Weather bright and very windy. Brigade tactical exercise was carried out, practising the tactics which had been evolved during the fighting around YPRES - dealing with Strong points - carrying by "Jump-line" &c.	
"	26.10.17		A very wet day - little training possible. The Commdg Officer inspected kits & equipment in billets.	
"	27.10.17		Weather finer: Training for the attack carried on on the high ground N of RAIMBERT	

(A7092). Wt. W12839/M1293. 750,000. 1/17. D. D. & L., Ltd. Forms/C.2118/14.

CONFIDENTIAL

Instructions regarding War Diaries and Intelligence Summaries are contained in F. S. Regs., Part II. and the Staff Manual respectively. Title pages will be prepared in manuscript.

WAR DIARY
or
INTELLIGENCE SUMMARY.
(Erase heading not required.)

SHEET No 345

Army Form C. 2118.

Place	Date	Hour	Summary of Events and Information	Remarks and references to Appendices
BILLETS AUCHEL.	27.10.17		under Company arrangements. In the afternoon a successful Cross Country race was run off – Result. No 7 platoon. B. Co. 1st. H.Q. No 1 Platoon & No 13 platoon D. Co. tied for 2nd place. In the evening a Regimental Concert was held in the Cinema. Lieut. S.F. HORNE joined the Battn.	
"	28.10.17.		A fine day. Church parade service in the Cinema at 10 am. Capt G. H. Pocock M.C. gave a demonstration of firing the German light and heavy Machine guns.	
"	29.10.17		Firing on RAIMBERT Rifle Range and general Tactical Training under O.C. Companies. A further demonstration of firing the German heavy machine gun was given by 99th M.G. Coy. In the afternoon Capt F.M. Horner (G.S.O. 3) lectured to selected officers and N.C.O.s of the Brigade on "Air photographs"	
"	30.10.17.		Morning fine. but very wet later in the day. Training was carried on and in the evening the Command'g Officer held a conference of Company officers and N.C.O's on the details of the Tactical exercise to be carried out next day.	
"	31.10.17.		A fine warm day. The Battn took part in the 99th Brigade Tactical exercise, being assigned the 2nd & final objective of about 1000x width on the Right – "leap-frogging" the 1/K.R.R.C. at the first objective. The exercise was instructive & fairly successful. A Contact Aeroplane co-operated. The Battn battled at RAIMBERT FOSSE.	
			EFFECTIVE STRENGTH OF BATTN 39 officers 930 other ranks.	
			RATION STRENGTH OF BATTN. 29 " 804 " "	
			Battle Casualties during the month NIL.	

(A7092). Wt. W12839/M1293- 750,000. 1/17. D. D. & L., Ltd. Forms/C.2118/14.

CONFIDENTIAL

Instructions regarding War Diaries and Intelligence Summaries are contained in F. S. Regs., Part II. and the Staff Manual respectively. Title pages will be prepared in manuscript.

WAR DIARY
or
INTELLIGENCE SUMMARY.
(Erase heading not required.)

Army Form C. 2118.

SHEET No 346.

Place	Date	Hour	Summary of Events and Information	Remarks and references to Appendices
OCTOBER 1917.			Except for the first 4 days, the whole of the month was spent at AUCHEL. – The first opportunity the Battn had been given for continuous training since the beginning of the year, except for a few short periods. Billets were poor and scattered and it was found impossible to have a Battalion Officers Mess, and training was somewhat handicapped by these conditions and the bad weather but on the whole progress was good. Nearly 300 reinforcements joined, a large proportion coming from M.T. and Labour units – the elementary training required by these men took up a lot of valuable time. Rumours that we were to "go up North" were very soon confirmed and the XVIII Corps was indicated as our future area. The conditions & tactical considerations experienced in the fighting round YPRES were made the basis of our system of training and necessitated ~~drastic~~ changes in method. Some difficulty had to be overcome in making all ranks realize that the "continuous line of trenches" system had to be abandoned – in teaching the method of tackling strong points and inculcating the "spirit of the bayonet" & "fire and movement". Recreational training was carried out, though the weather was unfavourable, and a number of successful Regimental concerts were held. A number of men went sick with influenza – otherwise the health of the Battn was good.	

[illegible] Lt. Col

(A7092). Wt. W12839/M1293. 750,000. 1/17. D. D. & L., Ltd. Forms/C.2118/14

99th Brigade / 2nd Division.

1st BATTALION

ROYAL BERKSHIRE REGIMENT

NOVEMBER 1917.

99

CONFIDENTIAL.

Instructions regarding War Diaries and Intelligence Summaries are contained in F. S. Regs., Part II. and the Staff Manual respectively. Title pages will be prepared in manuscript.

WAR DIARY
or
INTELLIGENCE SUMMARY.
(Erase heading not required.)

Army Form C. 2118.

1st Bn ROYAL BERKSHIRE REGT.

SHEET No 347.

Place	Date	Hour	Summary of Events and Information	Remarks and references to Appendices
BILLETS AUCHEL	1.11.17		Training carried on - special attention given to intensive digging & working in Box Respirators. C & D Coys carried out night firing on the Rifle Range	
"	2.11.17		"Fire and movement" practise by all Companies on the Rifle Range in the morning. A successful Regimental Concert was held in the Cinema in the evening. Warning Order for move on 5th instant received	
"	3.11.17		Route March carried out AUCHEL - CAMBLAIN CHATELAIN - PERNES - FLORINGHEM - CAUCHY-A-LA-TOUR. Football match against 100th Field Ambulance in afternoon resulting in a win 3-0. 2/Lieut Johnston rejoined the Battn	
"	4.11.17		Church Parade Service at Cinema at 10am. Football match v 23rd R. Fusiliers in the afternoon which we won 1-0	
ROBECQ	5.11.17		The Battn moved, as a unit of 99th Brigade, by march route to ROBECQ. Falling out state. NIL. The weather was fine and the march proved an easy one. The Battn arrived at 1 pm. but found billets had only just been allotted. These proved to be poor and scattered along over 1 mile of road between ROBECQ & BUSNES.	Movement Order No 138.
NEUF BERQUIN	6.11.17		The Battn moved, leading the Brigade, by march route to NEUF-BERQUIN. Falling out state. NIL. Slight drizzling rain. Arrived 1.40 pm. & in billets by 2 pm. Billets found very scattered between NEUF-BERQUIN and ESTAIRES.	Movement Order No 139.
EECKE.	7.11.17		The Battn moved by march route to EECKE area. Falling out state NIL. Marching heavy owing to rain and bad roads. Dinners served en route. The Battn again headed the Brigade. Arrived about 4 pm. Billets poor and very scattered.	Move Order No 140.
HERZEELE.	8.11.17		The Battn marched to HERZEELE area arriving about 1.30 pm. Weather fine but roads in a very bad condition. 2 OR fell out. Billets allotted were very scattered.	Move Order No 141.

(A7092). Wt. W12839/M1293- 750,000. 1/17. D. D. & L., Ltd. Forms/C.2118/14.

1/37

CONFIDENTIAL

Instructions regarding War Diaries and Intelligence Summaries are contained in F. S. Regs., Part II. and the Staff Manual respectively. Title pages will be prepared in manuscript.

WAR DIARY
or
INTELLIGENCE SUMMARY.
(Erase heading not required.)

SHEET Nº 348.

Army Form C. 2118.

Place	Date	Hour	Summary of Events and Information	Remarks and references to Appendices
BILLETS HERZEELE	9.11.17		Weather turned very wet. Billetting was re-adjusted. Training carried on under Company arrangements. + programme for ensuing week settled after conference with Company Commanders.	
"	10.11.17		Training under Company arrangements, but the wet weather made work difficult. Inter Company football in the afternoon.	
"	11.11.17		A very wet day. It was impossible to find cover for a parade service. R.C service in the Orderly Room. Inspection of Lewis Guns and spare parts.	
"	12.11.17		Training under Company arrangements. Capt Porritt R.A.M.C joined the Battn taking over duties of M.O. from Capt Chatfield R.A.M.C.	
"	13.11.17		Battn bathed in baths at WORMHOUDT. Training under Company arrangements. Lieut HORNE went to 2nd Divnl Depot Battn for duty.	
"	14.11.17		Battn Scheme carried out in ST ACAIRE area. Dinners were eaten on the Training ground. Return to billets about 4.30 pm	Scheme + map
"	15.11.17		Weather improving. Training under Company arrangements. In the afternoon a Cross-country race of $3\frac{3}{4}$ miles was run, each platoon entering a team of 6. Won by B Co.	
"	16.11.17		Training under Company arrangements. After dark C + D Companies carried out a Night Assembly practice	Scheme.
"	17.11.17		Training under Company arrangements in morning and inter Company football in the afternoon. After dark A + B Companies carried out a Night Assembly practice similar to that carried out by C + D Companies the night before	Scheme

(A7092). Wt. W12839/M1293. 750,000. 1/17. D. D. & L., Ltd. Forms/C.2118/14.

CONFIDENTIAL

Instructions regarding War Diaries and Intelligence Summaries are contained in F. S. Regs., Part II. and the Staff Manual respectively. Title pages will be prepared in manuscript.

WAR DIARY
or
INTELLIGENCE SUMMARY.
(Erase heading not required.)

SHEET No 349

Army Form C. 2118.

Place	Date	Hour	Summary of Events and Information	Remarks and references to Appendices
BILLETS HERZEELE	18.11.17		A fine Sunday. Church Parade service on "B" Company's parade ground. C Co played D Co at football in the afternoon – a draw. 2/Lieut F T Smeaton joined, posted to A Coy	
	19.11.17		Training under Company arrangements in the morning. Football in afternoon. Experimented successfully with Parachute SOS. signal grenade in daylight	
	20.11.17		Battn bathed at WORMHOODT. Inspection of kit and equipment.	
"	21.11.17		Company training. The Battn was called on to submit names of all desirous of transferring to Tank Corps. A very large number of officers and O.R. sent in their names.	
"	22.11.17		Training under Company arrangements. No laundry arrangements being available. Coys had to wash their own clothes. At 11 pm definite orders received that the Battn would move to CAMBRAI sector with the Division	
	23.11.17		Advance billeting party of an officer and 5 N.C.Os left at 4.45 am. The Divnl General being on leave the Brigadier was in command of Divn and the Commanding Officer had to leave the Battn and command the Brigade. D. Co entrained at ESQUELBECQ station leaving billets at 7 pm. Remainder of Battn marched to same station for entrainment leaving billets at 12 M.N. Falling out state NIL. Lieut A.U.M. HUDSON joined the Battn and posted to "B" Co.	
"	24.11.17		Train left ESQUELBECQ at 4 am – arrived at ACHIET-LE-GRAND at noon. Hot tea issued here. Detrained by 3 pm & marched to BARASTRE arriving about 6.45 pm. Falling out state NIL. Billeted in tents and huts. Commanding Officer re-joined the Battn. Rain	
BARASTRE & BEAUMETZ LES CAMBRAI	25.11.17.		Ordered at 3.30 am to move to BEAUMETZ-LEZ-CAMBRAI. Battn moved off at 9.15 am & arrived at BEAUMETZ at 12.45 p.m. Billeted in tents. Battn officers mess in ruins of village. Weather very windy and cold. Falling-out state NIL. During the night the camp was heavily shelled and was shifted to E side of road VELU-BEAUMETZ. Casualties 3 O.R. wounded.	

(A7092). Wt. W12839/M1293. 750,000. 1/17. D. D. & L., Ltd. Forms/C.2118/14.

CONFIDENTIAL

Instructions regarding War Diaries and Intelligence Summaries are contained in F. S. Regs., Part II. and the Staff Manual respectively. Title pages will be prepared in manuscript.

WAR DIARY
or
INTELLIGENCE SUMMARY.
(Erase heading not required.)

SHEET Nº 350.

Army Form C. 2118.

Place	Date	Hour	Summary of Events and Information	Remarks and references to Appendices
BEAUMETZ LES CAMBRAI.	26.11.17		Orders received at 5 pm & confirmed in detail at 7 pm that the 99th I. Bde would take over that night from 107th Infantry Bde a portion of the new line facing N just W of BOURLON WOOD. The 23/R.F. on R. with this Bn in support and 1/K.R.R.C on L with 22/R.F. in support. The Battn moved off at 9.30 and proceeded by way of main BAPAUME-CAMBRAI road to Sugar Factory E.29 a (Sheet 57 c. N.E. 1/20000). We were supposed to relieve the 2/5 K.O.Y.L.I and 2/5 Y & L by 12 mn. but our march was hindered by other troops on the road and when we reached the FACTORY at about 1 am. we found that the Battns in question were attacking BOURLON village at 6.20 am and had not been notified of the relief. After some delay we found accommodation for the men and eventually took over quarters vacated by 2/5 K.O.Y.L.I & 2/5 Y & L when they went out to the attack. A & B Coys on R. N of road. C & D Coys on L. S of road. Bn H.Q in Chateau E of Sugar Factory. There was no shelling during the move and we suffered no casualties. In this it appears we were very fortunate, favoured perhaps by the weather which was rough and dark owing to heavy snow storms, for the main road was the target for constant shelling and machine gun fire every night during our tour in this sector.	
Support line W of BOURLON WOOD.	27.11.17		The attack on BOURLON village was not a success – Tanks co-operated but were held up by a barricade and the infantry were forced back to their original line on the high ground in the wood. It was feared that 2/5 K.O.Y.L.I had been driven back & that the enemy were advancing to the high ground in E.17 b and E 18 a. and at 10 am we were ordered to move a Company up to the SUNKEN ROAD (E 23.b & E 24.a) on R of 23/RF to prevent this by counter attack if necessary. The 2/8 W YORKS moving up	

(A7092). Wt. W12839/M1293. 750,000. 1/17. D. D. & L., Ltd. Forms/C.2118/14.

CONFIDENTIAL.

Instructions regarding War Diaries and Intelligence Summaries are contained in F. S. Regs., Part II. and the Staff Manual respectively. Title pages will be prepared in manuscript.

WAR DIARY
or
INTELLIGENCE SUMMARY.

(Erase heading not required.)

SHEET No 351.

Army Form C. 2118.

Place	Date	Hour	Summary of Events and Information	Remarks and references to Appendices
SUPPORT LINE W of BOURLON WOOD.	27.11.17		from reserve to reinforce the threatened line. "B" Co under Lieut D. Valentine was moved up suffering 3 OR casualties. Shelling of Factory and road heavy during the night. 2 signallers were wounded. Our M.O. & Stretcher bearers were busy all day and night in R.A.P. at the Chateau dealing with the heavy casualties suffered by the attacking troops, and our H.Q. were made use of by both 2/5 K.O.Y.L.I. and 2/5 Y&L until they were relieved early in the morning of 28th. B Coy also shelled in Sunken Road and suffered 3 O.R casualties.	
			Total casualties.	
"	28.11.17		Bn H.Q. and Regtl A.P. subjected to intensive bursts of shell fire at intervals of about 2 hours until dark, when it became less and intermittent. At 8 pm the Battn relieved 23/R.F. in front line and posts. B Co (Lt Valentine) in R. A Co in centre (Capt Pugh) and C Co (Capt Jackson) on L. in touch with 1/K.R.R.C. We held a line about 1200 yds. D Coy in support in QUARRY GUNPITS (E.23.c.5.3). Bn H.Q. moved to the FACTORY. Relief complete 11.30 pm – casualties NIL. Advance parties from 10/D.C.L.I. and 483 Field Co. R.E., placed at disposal of Brigade to consolidate and wire the trenches and establish two strong points to protect the R flank, came to reconnoitre the line. The Sugar Factory & road were shelled all night and our Regtl A.P. was full of casualties of other troops which were passing to and from relief along main road and considerable difficulty was experienced in evacuating them.	
FRONT LINE W of BOURLON WOOD	29.11.17		At 6.25 am under cover of Artillery and Stokes Gun barrage 1st K.R.R.C. on our LEFT attacked and captured the triangular salient held by the enemy in E.22.b and d. and straightened the line at this point. ½ No Platoon (C Coy) commanded by	

(A7092). Wt. W12839/M1293. 750,000. 1/17. D. D. & L., Ltd. Forms/C.2118/14.

CONFIDENTIAL

Instructions regarding War Diaries and Intelligence Summaries are contained in F. S. Regs., Part II. and the Staff Manual respectively. Title pages will be prepared in manuscript.

WAR DIARY
or
INTELLIGENCE SUMMARY.
(Erase heading not required.)

Army Form C. 2118.

SHEET No 352.

Place	Date	Hour	Summary of Events and Information	Remarks and references to Appendices
FRONT LINE W of BOURLON WOOD.	29.11.17		Lieut. E.C. Dennis de Vitré co-operated in this move, advancing our Battn left flank some 200x and establishing 4 advanced posts. His account is attached. The Factory was persistently shelled all day, and a large number of gas shells were used intermittently throughout the day and night necessitating the wearing of box respirators. 2 Companies 10/D.C.L.I and 2 Sections 483 Field Co. R.E. proceeded with wiring & improvement of trenches and constructing the two strong points N.E of Sunken Road. These strong points were manned by 2 platoons of D Company just before dawn.	Account
	30.11.17		At 8.45 am. the enemy put a terrific "box" barrage of all calibres on the FACTORY and its precincts practically isolating our Bn H.Q., and advanced in force along a line BOURLON village – QUARRY WOOD. As the attack developed we were reinforced by 23/R.F. Along the greater part of the front attacked the enemy attempt to break through was successfully dealt with by Artillery and M.G fire, and never assumed a very serious aspect in our sector except on the R flank held by B Company where very heavy fighting took place. An account and plan of this fighting written by the Commanding Officer is attached. Enemy attacks were renewed in the afternoon but our line was never broken. It was a proud day for the Battn. and congratulatory messages which were received & are attached were undoubtedly well-earned. In the evening B Co 23/R.F. moved up from support & reoccupied the posts on W of Sunken Road without a fight, and the night passed comparatively quietly. Considering the very heavy nature of the fighting our casualties were not heavy.	Account & map Messages

(A7092). Wt. W12839/M1293. 750,000. 1/17. D. D. & L., Ltd. Forms/C.2118/14.

CONFIDENTIAL

Instructions regarding War Diaries and Intelligence Summaries are contained in F. S. Regs., Part II. and the Staff Manual respectively. Title pages will be prepared in manuscript.

WAR DIARY
or
INTELLIGENCE SUMMARY.
(Erase heading not required.)

Army Form C. 2118.

SHEET. N° 353

Place	Date	Hour	Summary of Events and Information	Remarks and references to Appendices
FRONT LINE W of BOURLON WOOD	30.11.17		Capt E.P. JACKSON commanding C Company, was killed instantaneously by a sniper. 2/Lieuts SMEATON and PALMER were wounded. O.R. - 12 killed. 25 wounded. 20 missing. 6 to Hospital. Total 3 officers 63 O.R. 66 EFFECTIVE STRENGTH OF BATTN 41 officers 897 O.R. RATION STRENGTH OF BATTN 32 " 732 O.R. N.B. Casualties on 30th have not been deducted	

E.P. Hunt Lt. Col.
Comdg 1st Royal Berkshire Regt

A5834 Wt. W4973/M687 750,000 8/16 D. D. & L. Ltd. Forms/C.2118/13.

99th Brigade / 2nd Division.

1st BATTALION

ROYAL BERKSHIRE REGIMENT

DECEMBER 1917.

CONFIDENTIAL.

Instructions regarding War Diaries and Intelligence Summaries are contained in F. S. Regs., Part II. and the Staff Manual respectively. Title pages will be prepared in manuscript.

WAR DIARY
or
INTELLIGENCE SUMMARY.
(Erase heading not required.)

1/Royal Berks

Army Form C. 2118.

SHEET No 354

WO 38

Place	Date	Hour	Summary of Events and Information	Remarks and references to Appendices
FRONT LINE NEAR BOURLON	1.12.17.		The shelling of our sector and the SUGAR FACTORY was less intense and we had long periods of comparative peace. Between 8 and 9 pm positions in the line were re-adjusted, as the Battn was mixed up with 23/R.F. by reason of the several reinforcements that had taken place, and our B Company, having taken the weight of the attack on the previous day, was in need of a rest. As a result of the move our C and A Companies remained on L and Centre of the line with D and B Companies in support at the Gunpits and the Quarry respectively. B Coy 23/R.F. re-inforced by 2 Companies of D Co. 23/R.F. held the line between our A Company and the Sunken Road and C Coy 23/R.F. took over the posts and the 2 strong points N.E of Sunken Road. This inter-Battn relief passed off quietly – casualties nil. A quiet night. Good progress was made with wiring & consolidating the front line with the help of 1 Company 10/D.C.L.I and 1 section 483 Field Co. R.E	
"	2.12.17.		A comparatively quiet day on our front – very little shelling, excepting an occasional 77mm or 4.2" on the Sugar Factory and its precincts, until 4 pm when BOURLON WOOD – THE FACTORY and the main road were subjected to a bombardment of gradually increasing intensity, and at 4.30 pm our guns of all calibres opened fire, and continued for nearly an hour. It subsequently transpired that an attack had developed on our left, and had been completely repulsed. There was no hostile movement in our front. At 8-10 pm the 7th & 8th Bns LONDON REGT on our RIGHT attacked and advanced our line to high ground in E.17.d & b and E.	

A7092 Wt. W125.9/M1293 750,000. 1/17. D. D & L. Ltd. Forms/C2118/14.

CONFIDENTIAL

Instructions regarding War Diaries and Intelligence Summaries are contained in F. S. Regs., Part II. and the Staff Manual respectively. Title pages will be prepared in manuscript.

WAR DIARY
or
INTELLIGENCE SUMMARY.
(Erase heading not required.)

1st Bn R. BERKSHIRE REGT

Army Form C. 2118.

SHEET No 355

Place	Date	Hour	Summary of Events and Information	Remarks and references to Appendices
FRONT LINE NEAR BOURLON	2.12.17		18 a. At the same time the 23/R.F. on our immediate RIGHT advanced their right flank. The operation was successful and 8 M.Gs and a number of prisoners were taken. Enemy retaliation was feeble. When this disturbance had settled down D Company relieved C Company on LEFT of our line without casualty. We had no outside help with wiring and consolidating this night, but good progress was made and A Company in the CENTRE established new posts 150x to 200x in front of their original line, with H.Q in a gunpit, and thus secured a far more advantageous position with a first rate field of fire	
"	3.12.17		The morning was quiet until the enemy opened a desultory fire on Factory & road, having probably observed movement. From 1 to 3 pm the enemy bombarded the Factory buildings systematically with aeroplane observation, apparently endeavouring to raze them to the ground and prevent our using them as an O.P. At about 4 pm the enemy were reported to be massing opposite our LEFT Company front. Artillery were informed and fired on S.O.S. lines but nothing further transpired. There was considerable artillery activity between 10 and 11 pm, but the remainder of the night passed quietly.	
"	4.12.17		The morning passed quietly except for occasional artillery duels and the usual shelling of Bn. H.Q and the road with 4.2" & 77 mm. Another reorganization of Brigade front had been ordered to take place this night (Order attached). This was cancelled and orders received for evacuation of the BOURLON SALIENT (Order attached). In accordance with this Order Companies moved out at 15 mins interval betw 1 & 1.45 am.	99. Bde O.O. 198 and O.O. 199

A7092 Wt. W128_9/M1293 750,000. 1/17. D. D & L. Ltd. Forms/C2118/14.

CONFIDENTIAL

Instructions regarding War Diaries and Intelligence Summaries are contained in F. S. Regs., Part II. and the Staff Manual respectively. Title pages will be prepared in manuscript.

WAR DIARY
or
INTELLIGENCE SUMMARY.
(Erase heading not required.)

Army Form C. 2118.

SHEET No 356.

Place	Date	Hour	Summary of Events and Information	Remarks and references to Appendices
FRONT LINE NEAR BOURLON	4.12.17 & 5.12.17		(Notes for Battn Order attached). Bn H.Q. moved off behind the last Company. Rearguards (2 sections and 1 L.G. of A. Co. under 2/Lieut A.J. HARRIS and 2 sections and 1 L.G. of C Co under 2/Lieut A.S. Denham) remained in the line until 3.15 pm and were withdrawn without enemy interference. 1 platoon of C. Co. under Lieut. E.C. Denis de Vitré also remained behind at the SUGAR FACTORY until 5.30 am to protect the left flank of 47th Divn during the withdrawal. They got away without casualties or incident & reached billets at 8.30 am. The only regrettable part of the operation, so far as this Battn was concerned, was that it was found impossible to get our L.G. spare magazines, 2 captured German M.G's and other equipment, all of which had to be thrown away down a well. The Battn moved back to HERMIES. Casualties nil	✓
BILLETS HERMIES	5.12.17		Battn billetted in NISSEN huts, dug-outs and shelters in HERMIES – rested the whole of this day, as many of the men were very worn and fatigued after their trying time in the line, which was spent practically in open trenches, in cold weather, with plenty of hard work and fighting. but, in spite of these hardships, the health of the Battn appeared unimpaired, and the men were in excellent spirits.	
"	6.12.17		Light P.T. and inspections in the morning, but our rest was soon at an end. Working parties to dig new trenches in K.7 and 8 were called for. D.Co. carried 375 picks and shovels to the scene of work, and the whole of A.B. and C Coys were working from 11 pm to 5 am. Casualties nil.	
"	7.12.17		The Battn rested all morning. Baths and cleaning up in the afternoon. Working	

A7092 Wt. W128.9/M1293 750,000. 1/17. D. D & L. Ltd. Forms/C2118/14.

CONFIDENTIAL

Instructions regarding War Diaries and Intelligence Summaries are contained in F. S. Regs., Part II. and the Staff Manual respectively. Title pages will be prepared in manuscript.

WAR DIARY
or
INTELLIGENCE SUMMARY.

(Erase heading not required.)

Army Form C. 2118.

SHEET No 357.

Place	Date	Hour	Summary of Events and Information	Remarks and references to Appendices
BILLETS HERMIES	7.12.17		parties continued at night. all Companies being employed digging communication trenches K.8.a.6.6 to K.14.a.0.3. from 5 pm to 11 pm, carrying tools to the work from HERMIES dump. Casualties 1 OR wounded. Reinforcements of 6 OR arrived and posted to B. Coy.	
"	8.12.17		Bathing of Battn continued under arrangements made by QM. On account of hostile shelling C & D Coys vacated the NISSEN HUTS and moved to safer quarters in the CATACOMBS. Working parties digging C.T. as on previous night. all Coys digging from 11 pm to 5 am. Casualties 10 OR of B. Co. wounded by shellfire while waiting in Sunken Road to proceed to work. Large numbers were reporting sick at this period with diarrhoea and sore feet, the prolonged strain of 9 days fighting in the line and working parties every night beginning to tell on even the strongest men. Reinforcements of 42 OR arrived and posted to B Coy.	
"	9.12.17		Battn rested all morning and at night all Companies were again at work from 5 pm to 11 pm carrying duckboards up to new trenches. Not much was accomplished however by reason of bad organization and congestion of traffic and men at the Dump.	
"	10.12.17		Having been warned that we were to go into front line with 23/R.F. for 48 hours the next day, the Battn rested the whole day, and was spared the usual nightly working party. Details of relief were discussed at H.Q. 142. I. Bde and eventually settled.	

A7092 Wt. W128 9/M1293 750,000. 1/17. D. D & L. Ltd. Forms/C2118/14.

CONFIDENTIAL

Instructions regarding War Diaries and Intelligence Summaries are contained in F. S. Regs., Part II. and the Staff Manual respectively. Title pages will be prepared in manuscript.

WAR DIARY
or
INTELLIGENCE SUMMARY.
(Erase heading not required.)

Army Form C. 2118.

SHEET. No 358.

Place	Date	Hour	Summary of Events and Information	Remarks and references to Appendices
BILLETS. HERMIES.	11.12.17		Order for Relief in the line received (No 201 attached). The Battn rested and drew tools for use in the line. Dinners at 12.30 pm. Moved off by platoons at 1.30. by way of the Canal du Nord. Our disposition in the line is shewn on attached map marked A. Relief was considerably delayed because our guides refused to lead forward until it was quite dark. We found that the Right advanced post had been abandoned during the day. We re-occupied it without incident. Relief finally complete at 9.50 pm.	O.O. 201 " 155 Map. A.
FRONT LINE TRENCHES "CANAL"			Casualties 1.OR wounded. A quiet night. Good work was accomplished consolidating CABLE TRENCH (later named WATSON TRENCH) and clearing out HUGHES SWITCH. which proved to be a very deep and wide trench – almost like a sunken road. The 3 advanced posts were badly sited, shallow and unprotected by wire.	
"	12.12.17		The day passed quietly. Enemy artillery activity noticeably less, though his snipers activity was unabated. The C.O. conferred with 23/R.F (on our Right) and 99th I. Bde at which suggestions were made to alter the method of holding the line, and to withdraw the advanced posts, but these the Divn declined to sanction. At about 8.30 pm S.O.S was sent up from our centre post, numbers of the enemy having been seen approaching. but no attack materialized. A number of our how (4.5") shells fell short and complaint was made to Divl Artillery and Brigades concerned, but noone would accept the blame. Casualties 2/Lt. S.A.E. MILES wounded. 1 OR killed and 3 OR wounded.	
"	13.12.17		A very quiet day. visibility being poor. Orders for Relief received (copy attached). Details arranged between ourselves and 1/K.R.R.C + 22/R.F. in the morning. Our D & B Coys were relieved by 1.K.R.R.C and C & A. Coys by 22/R.F. The B.G.C. Bde made a tour of the line in the morning & was very pleased with the good progress made. The Battn was relieved in	Bde O. 202. Map B.

A7092 Wt. W128 9/M1293 750,000. 1/17. D. D & L. Ltd. Forms/C2118/14.

CONFIDENTIAL.

Instructions regarding War Diaries and Intelligence Summaries are contained in F. S. Regs., Part II. and the Staff Manual respectively. Title pages will be prepared in manuscript.

WAR DIARY
or
INTELLIGENCE SUMMARY.
(*Erase heading not required.*)

Army Form C. 2118.

SHEET Nº 359.

Place	Date	Hour	Summary of Events and Information	Remarks and references to Appendices
FRONT LINE "CANAL"	13.12.17		the evening and the holding of the line re-adjusted (see Map B. attached). Relief complete 7.30 pm. The Battn moved to HERMIES. A & B Coys accomodated in trenches N of Village on each side of HERMIES-GRAINCOURT road. C & D Companies and Bn H.Q in the Village (J.30.a.5.3). Accomodation very poor, though every man had shelter of a kind. Casualties 2 O.R wounded.	
RESERVE. HERMIES	14.12.17		The Battn rested - cleaning up and bathing under arrangements made by Qr Mr.	
"	15.12.17		A quiet day. very cold. D Company found a working party of 3 officers and 100 O.R. carrying gas projectors from K.15.a.1.7 to front line	
"	16.12.17		The Commanding Officer went on leave, and command devolved on Major C. Nugent. Working party 3 officers and 100 O.R. found by Bn HQ. and B. Co. for carrying projectors as on previous night. Orders received for relief of 1/K.R.R.C. astride canal the next day. Advance party sent to reconnoitre (Order annexed). 2/Lieut J.B. Young joined the Battn and posted to A. Company.	No 156.
"	17.12.17		The Battn relieved 1/K.R.R.C in the line. Relief complete 7 pm. Casualties nil. Gas projection under Bde Order No 205 (annexed) postponed on account of relief. When we took over we found that the combined post at K.9.b.5.9. had been evacuated. We re-occupied same without a fight and held same day and night during our tour. Dispositions as per statement and plan attached.	O.O. 205. Plan.
FRONT LINE. CANAL	18.12.17		Day and night quiet. Good work accomplished, and a lot of wire staked out. A new post (afterwards called NUGENT) commenced at K.9.b.2.8. Gas projection again postponed. the wind being unsuitable.	

A7092 Wt. W128 9/M1293 750,000. 1/17. D. D & I. Ltd. Forms/C2118/14.

CONFIDENTIAL.

Instructions regarding War Diaries and Intelligence Summaries are contained in F. S. Regs., Part II. and the Staff Manual respectively. Title pages will be prepared in manuscript.

WAR DIARY
or
INTELLIGENCE SUMMARY.

(Erase heading not required.)

Army Form C. 2118.

SHEET No 360

Place	Date	Hour	Summary of Events and Information	Remarks and references to Appendices
FRONT LINE CANAL	19.12.17		Quiet both day and night. Sergeant post completed and manned, also a post at DUG OUT (K.9.a 55.80) manned and approved by Bde. Gas projection again postponed.	
"	20.12.17		An uneventful day. Plan and Report annexed showing work done during tour. Relieved by 17 Middlesex Regt (Bde. O.O annexed) & moved into Divnl Reserve in O'SHEA CAMP, near LEBUCQUIERE. Casualties during tour and relief NIL. The whole Battn was in camp by 12 M.N. Accommodation was found to be very poor - the men were crowded in NISSEN huts, and the Camp was dirty & neglected. Lieut A.V. RAPER joined Bn and posted to C. Coy	O.O. 206
O'SHEA CAMP. LEBUCQUIERE	21.12.17		Weather very cold. No work was done during the day. The Battn rested and commenced cleaning up the camp as far as possible, but the hard frost and snow made this difficult	
"	22.12.17		Very cold, but fortunately ample fuel was available from ruins of adjacent villages. Company Commanders inspected their Companies, and the day was spent in cleaning up and re-organization. The ground was too hard for recreation.	
"	23.12.17		Parade Service at 11am in the Cinema, attended by B. Genl Kellett, at that time in temporary command of Divn. After the service the General addressed the Battn in laudatory terms, especially congratulating B Company on the fine work done in the fighting near BOURLON on 30th ultimo.	
"	24.12.17		The whole Battn marched to SPOIL HEAP (J.35.d) and worked from 9am to 4pm on	

A7092 Wt. W128.9/M1293 750,000. 1/17. D. D & L. Ltd. Forms/C2118/14.

1 R Berks

answered
RMK

99' Infantry Brigade.

I have established a new post at K. 9 b 2.8. this will be completed by dawn tomorrow the 20.12.17. and fit for day occupation. i.e. sanitary arrangements etc.

The Garrison will be 2 Sections with a Lewis Gun.

Jervis Post is being connected with the new post thence E to the Canal.

The New Post is covered by the thick belt of Boche Wire shown on Air Photo: No 15. L B. 231 d/15-12.17.

The post will be handed over to the 17' Middlesex Regt. as one in the Divisional line.

On the night of the 17/18.12.17 before the situation of Steve post was cleared a post was established at K. 9. b 45-80. I would suggest that ~~the~~ Kellet trench be continued eastward through Jervis - New Post temporary post K. 9 b 45. 80. - Allen.

This line would be covered by the present Boche wire.

Stene post to be connected with Allen on the right. A second post established on the West Bridge head thence to Jarvis Post. thus ensuring our line not being overlooked from the West of the Bridge.

Clmgean Major

19.12.17. O.C. 1st Royal Berkshire Rgt.

CONFIDENTIAL.

Instructions regarding War Diaries and Intelligence Summaries are contained in F. S. Regs., Part II. and the Staff Manual respectively. Title pages will be prepared in manuscript.

WAR DIARY
or
INTELLIGENCE SUMMARY.
(Erase heading not required.)

Army Form C. 2118.

SHEET Nº 361

Place	Date	Hour	Summary of Events and Information	Remarks and references to Appendices
O'SHEA CAMP. LEBUCQUIERE	24/12/17		construction of shelters for use as Battn H.Q. Good work was accomplished. Dinners and teas were served on the scene of work. D Company sent a party of 20 O.R. to 2nd Divnl R.E YARD at YTRES. and 2 complete L.G. teams to Divnl Dump. RUYAULCOURT (P.10.a) relieving 1/K.R.R.C.	
"	25/12/17		Christmas Day. Voluntary service at Cinema Hall. The men had their dinners at 1pm in 10 messes. A great deal of trouble had been taken to give the bare NISSEN huts a comfortable and festive appearance, and, considering the conditions, the arrangements proved very successful. The Quartermaster (Capt F.S. BOSHELL) had provided ample fare – pork beef & plum puddings and a liberal supply of beer and cigarettes. The Commdg Officer (Major C. Nugent) visited each mess. and addressed the men. At 6pm the Sergeants had their dinner in their mess. and at 8pm the officers wound up the day with an exceeding cheery dinner. Altogether the day passed merrily – a certain amount of conviviality and goodfellowship but no trouble. The spirit and discipline of all ranks proved to be excellent.	
"	26/12/17		Morning and afternoon spent quietly preparing to move up into the front line again. (Bde O.O's 207 & 207a). In the evening the Bn relieved 52/L.I. in SUPPORT LINE. C & D Companies moved off early at 2.30 pm. relieving the 2 forward Companies of 52/L.I., having been detailed for working party (100 O.R) at FORT GEORGE, but their trouble was all for nothing, as the R.E supervising officer failed to rendezvous and no work was possible. The remainder of the Battn moved off at 5 pm. Relief complete at 8 pm. Casualties Nil. Accommodation for A.B & D fair – for C. poor	Bde O.O's 207 & 207a. Bn O.O. 157

A7092 Wt. W128 9/M1293. 750,000. 1/17. D. D & L. Ltd. Forms/C2118/14.

CONFIDENTIAL

Instructions regarding War Diaries and Intelligence Summaries are contained in F. S. Regs., Part II. and the Staff Manual respectively. Title pages will be prepared in manuscript.

WAR DIARY
or
INTELLIGENCE SUMMARY.
(*Erase heading not required.*)

Army Form C. 2118.

SHEET No 362

Place	Date	Hour	Summary of Events and Information	Remarks and references to Appendices
SUPPORT LINE 'CANAL'	27/12/17		Location Statement annexed. Very early in the morning the enemy commenced a very heavy bombardment of our front and support lines & communication trenches – this continued throughout the day and night – the enemy appearing to fire at haphazard – searching our lines, but probably registering under cover of what seemed to be loose & inaccurate shooting. A & B Coys each found working parties of 50 O.R. to work in FORT GEORGE from 6–10 pm. Casualties 1 OR killed & 1 OR wded	✓
"	28/12/17		Weather very cold – sharp frost and blizzard at night. A & B Companies again found working parties as in the previous night. Enemy artillery fire less severe but still persistent. A quiet day – casualties nil.	
"	29/12/17		A quiet day. Advance party visited the front line to prepare for relief in accordance with Bde. O.O. 208 (attached). A & B Companies again furnished large working party as in preceding 2 nights. C Company furnished a party of 40 O.R. to carry material & work on construction of dug-outs in KELLETT and BULLEN TRENCHES from M.N.	Bde O.O 208
" & FRONT LINE	30/12/17		D. Co furnished a working party of 24 O.R. at 8am to work under 2nd Australian Tunnelling Co on dug-outs in the front line. In the evening the Battn relieved 1/K.R.R. in front line as per Battn O.O. No 158 attached. Relief was complete by 7pm. and no casualties were suffered. Companies and Bn H.Q. located as per statement and map attached. At night small working parties were found by B and C Coys digging Medium Trench Mortar emplacements under supervision of a N.C.O. of T.M. Battery and dug-outs under R.E. supervision.	O.O 158 ✓
"	31/12/17		A quiet day and night. The enemy shelled D Companies lines persistently the	

A7092 Wt. W128 9/M1293 750,000. 1/17. D. D & I. Ltd. Forms/C2118/14.

Instructions regarding War Diaries and Intelligence Summaries are contained in F. S. Regs., Part II. and the Staff Manual respectively. Title pages will be prepared in manuscript.

WAR DIARY
or
INTELLIGENCE SUMMARY.
(Erase heading not required.)

Army Form C. 2118.

Place	Date	Hour	Summary of Events and Information	Remarks and references to Appendices
FRONT LINE. CANAL.	31.12.17		whole day. Casualties 1 O.R. wounded. B and C Companies found the same working parties as on the previous day. Companies did good work strengthening the wire and improving the front line at night. A new post (VALGRIM) was established on Bridgehead opposite STEVE post.	
			Total Casualties for December: Officers — KILLED: –; WOUNDED: 2. O.Rs — KILLED: 6; WOUNDED: 58.	
			EFFECTIVE STRENGTH OF BATTN 31-12-17: 37 officers. 729 O.R.	
			RATION " " ": 28 officers. 630 O.R.	
			[signature] Major, Commdg 1st Bn R. Berkshire Regt.	

2nd Division
99th Infantry Bde.
War Diaries

1st Royal Berks

January - To December
1918

~~[illegible]~~

CONFIDENTIAL.

Instructions regarding War Diaries and Intelligence Summaries are contained in F. S. Regs., Part II. and the Staff Manual respectively. Title pages will be prepared in manuscript.

WAR DIARY
or
INTELLIGENCE SUMMARY.
(Erase heading not required.)

1st Bn ROYAL BERKSHIRE REGT.

Army Form C. 2118.

SHEET No 364

Vol 39

Place	Date	Hour	Summary of Events and Information	Remarks and references to Appendices
FRONT LINE. CANAL DU NORD	1/1/18		A quiet day and night. Good progress was made with wiring and other work, and the usual working parties were found. Casualties 1 OR wounded. Lieut Col HUNT rejoined from leave	
	2/1/18		Nothing unusual occurred. Under Brigade Order No 209 (copy attached) preliminary details of relief on night 3/4.1.18 were discussed with C.O.s of 8/S/Staffs and 10/Sherwood Foresters (51st Infantry Bde). A quiet night.	
	3/1/18		A Bright day. Visibility very good and both sides were very active in the air and registration of heavies. The Battn was to be relieved in the line under Bde O.O. No 209a and Battn Order No 159 (copies attached). but at 4.30 pm the enemy suddenly opened a very heavy bombardment of our front line and communication trenches with his Trench mortars and artillery, and shortly after attacked in numerous parties, each about 30 strong, on our front and to our Right. The garrisons of our two unprotected sentry posts (VALGRIM and STEVE) were taken unawares and were in danger of being cut off, so were withdrawn behind our belt of wire without casualties, and the enemy occupied these positions in force and commenced to consolidate them. Meanwhile our relief proceeded. B and D Companies sent out patrols to clear up the situation and found the posts occupied. By 10 pm all Companies had left the trenches except 2 platoons of B Coy and Battn H.Q. The situation was reported to Brigade and at 10.30 instructions were received to evacuate NUGENT. CROSSE and STEVE SUPPORT posts – that the	

A7092 Wt. W128 9/M1293 750,000. 1/17. D. D & L. Ltd. Forms/C2118/14.

CONFIDENTIAL

Instructions regarding War Diaries and Intelligence Summaries are contained in F. S. Regs., Part II. and the Staff Manual respectively. Title pages will be prepared in manuscript.

WAR DIARY
or
INTELLIGENCE SUMMARY.
(Erase heading not required.)

Army Form C. 2118.

SHEET No 365.

Place	Date	Hour	Summary of Events and Information	Remarks and references to Appendices
			artillery would fire for 30 minutes, and we were then to send out strong officer patrols and reoccupy the lost positions if possible. Posts were cleared by 12.5 am - the artillery fired from 12.25 - 12.55, but the bombardment was feeble and inaccurate, and when our patrols went out under 2/Lieut GRIMES on W side of Canal and Lieut HUDSON on E side, they were immediately fired on by enemy machine guns. The night was moonlit and it was impossible to approach unseen, because on both sides a thick belt of old German wire had to be passed in single file. Patrols therefore returned in accordance with Brigade orders. Relief was finally completed at 2.30 am. Casualties 2 OR killed and 5 O.R wounded. The Battn moved to huts at BARASTRE, by march route to the Spoil Heap HERMIES and thence by Motor lorries to billets. 2/Lieut BUSH joined the Battn and was posted to "C" Coy.	
BILLETS. BARASTRE.	4/1/18		The Battalion rested and commenced cleaning up billets and 2 companies bathed in the afternoon. Weather very cold. The huts were found to be almost without any provision for heating. Generally the camp was very dirty and neglected and the accommodation poor.	
	5/1/18		Companies were given light training under Company arrangements. Lieut Col Hunt took over command of 99th I. Bde. in absence of B.G.C. on leave and command devolved on Major C. Nugent. The weather was still very cold making training difficult and games practically impossible. The work of	

A7092 Wt. W128 9/M1293. 750,000. 1/17. D. D & L. Ltd. Forms/C2118/14.

CONFIDENTIAL

Instructions regarding War Diaries and Intelligence Summaries are contained in F. S. Regs., Part II. and the Staff Manual respectively. Title pages will be prepared in manuscript.

WAR DIARY
or
INTELLIGENCE SUMMARY.
(Erase heading not required.)

SHEET No 366

Army Form C. 2118.

Place	Date	Hour	Summary of Events and Information	Remarks and references to Appendices
BILLETS			cleaning up the Camp was proceeded with, but progress was very slow.	
BARASTRE	6/1/18		Sunday. Parade Service was held in the morning, and cleaning camp was continued. In the afternoon 2 O.R. killed on night 3/4 were buried at LEBUCQUIERE.	
"	7/1/18		Frost and snow unabated. Training almost impossible, and had to be restricted to conferences and lectures under cover. 2nd. Division Conference at ROCQUIGNY in the afternoon.	
"	8/1/18		Frost continued. Commenced digging drains and building protective walls round hutments, but the ground was too hard for real progress. 2/Lieut. H.B Reynolds joined the Battn and posted to D Company.	
"	9/1/18		Arrangements for sending O.R. on short leave to Paris were made, and a first party of 12 went on this day. During the night the frost broke & some rain fell, making the Camp a sea of mud	
"	10/1/18		Companies were at work all day, attempting to drain the camp which was nearly flooded by the melting snow and rain.	
"	11/1/18		A party of 18 O.R. sent on ~~[illegible]~~ pass to AMIENS, starting 5 a.m. returning from Amiens 5.30 p.m. This was continued throughout our stay at BARASTRE – about 10 O.R. under an officer being sent every morning. Owing to thaw precautions the lorries were not available, but we used our own transport vehicles to railhead at ACHIET-LE-GRAND and back.	
"	12/1/18		Special instruction in "rapid wiring" by R.E. commenced. A party of observers and orderlies under 2/Lieut ODELL reconnoitred routes to the front line. Remainder of	

A7092 Wt. W.128 9/M1293. 750,000. 1/17. D. D & L. Ltd. Forms/C2118/14.

CONFIDENTIAL

Instructions regarding War Diaries and Intelligence Summaries are contained in F. S. Regs., Part II. and the Staff Manual respectively. Title pages will be prepared in manuscript.

WAR DIARY
or
INTELLIGENCE SUMMARY.
(Erase heading not required.)

Army Form C. 2118.

SHEET N° 367.

Place	Date	Hour	Summary of Events and Information	Remarks and references to Appendices
BILLETS BARASTRE	13/1/18		Battn went for a Route March via HAPLINCOURT – BANCOURT – RIENCOURT and VILLERS-AU-FLOS, practising simple manoeuvres en route.	
"	13/1/18		Sunday. Parade Service in Camp. Remainder of morning spent in cleaning up Camp and draining. Football match v 22/R.F. in afternoon, which we won 8–0. The Aldershot R.A. Band was playing in the area and gave an enjoyable concert at the Cinema. BARASTRE. in the afternoon, which was attended by a number of the Battn	
"	14/1/18		Training carried on. 10 officers and 25 OR. received instruction in care & handling of carrier pigeons. A Co instructed in rapid wiring.	
"	15/1/18		A very wet and miserable day, making training & games practically impossible.	
"	16/1/18		A & B Coys & Transport bathed at BARASTRE. C Company received instruction in rapid wiring. Lewis Gun teams for A.A. work at Divisional H.Q. provided by A & C Companies.	
"	17/1/18		D Company instructed in rapid wiring. The whole Battn witnessed a demonstration in the use of the Flammenwerfer. All Companies in night operations.	
"	18/1/18		Route March into BAPAUME via ROCQUIGNY – LETRANSLOY – BEAULENCOURT. Dinners outside BAPAUME. The whole Battn witnessed a special performance of the pantomime "Cinderella" by the TONICS. (A Balloon section R.F.C). Return via BANCOURT and HAPLINCOURT. Special performance had been arranged for one franc a head.	
"	19/1/18		C & D Companies and H.Q. bathed at BARASTRE. 6 officers and 19 OR instructed in care and handling of carrier pigeons. Football match v 5th Brigade H.Q. in first	

A7092 Wt. W128 9/M1293 750,000. 1/17. D. D & L. Ltd. Forms/C2118/14.

CONFIDENTIAL

Instructions regarding War Diaries and Intelligence Summaries are contained in F. S. Regs., Part II. and the Staff Manual respectively. Title pages will be prepared in manuscript.

WAR DIARY
or
INTELLIGENCE SUMMARY.
(Erase heading not required.)

SHEET. Nº 368.

Army Form C. 2118.

Place	Date	Hour	Summary of Events and Information	Remarks and references to Appendices
BILLETS BARASTRE	19/1/18		round 2nd Divisional Football competition. Won 1-0 after playing extra time.	
"	20/1/18		Sunday. Parade service in camp. A quiet day.	
"	21/1/18		Training proceeded with under Company arrangements. Divisional Point to Point Meeting. 2/Lts Bryan & Tilley rode ~~but had no success~~ [and came in 3rd in flat race & 2nd in steeplechase respectively]. 2/Lt R. Frost was thrown during practice and seriously injured.	
"	22/1/18		Company and Battalion Drill, and inspection of all Companies by Commanding Officer. Rest of day spent cleaning up and completing re organization. A successful concert held in 'A' Company's hut in the evening. The band of 1/60th Rifles gave their services, and was much appreciated. 2/Lt Bush & 25 OR attached 2nd AUST Tunnelling Co	
"	23/1/18		Morning spent clearing camp & preparing for move. Dinners 12 noon. Battn marched to ROCQUIGNY & entrained (Bde & Battn Orders attached). Owing to congestion of the line trains were late and the Battn reached its new billets at METZ-EN-COUTURE just before dark, relieving ANSON Battn. 63rd Divn. Accommodation ample but very dirty & neglected. Location statement attached.	
BILLETS METZ-EN-COUTURE	24/1/18		Except for a little P.T. and Specialist training the day was spent in making a commencement of cleaning and draining camps and collecting salvage. The village was littered with discarded equipment, especially clothing. Lt Col Hunt rejoined the Battn and took over command. Brig. Genl G. B. Barker (formerly commanding 22/R F) took over command of Brigade.	

A7092 Wt. W128.9/M1293. 750,000. 1/17. D. D & I. Ltd. Forms/C2118/14.

CONFIDENTIAL.

Instructions regarding War Diaries and Intelligence Summaries are contained in F. S. Regs., Part II. and the Staff Manual respectively. Title pages will be prepared in manuscript.

WAR DIARY
or
INTELLIGENCE SUMMARY.
(Erase heading not required.)

Army Form C. 2118.

SHEET. No. 369.

Place	Date	Hour	Summary of Events and Information	Remarks and references to Appendices
BILLETS. METZ-EN-COUTURE.	25/1/18		G.O.C. Divn inspected the billets. O.C. Companies went up the line after dusk and reconnoitred LEFT sector of RIGHT section of LA VACQUERIE line. which the Battn was to take over next day. Considerable bombing by enemy air-craft in the early evening, but METZ escaped damage. A very warm spring like day. A Lewis Gun team of B Coy. attached to R.F.A. for A.A. work. became casualties owing to their having used shell-hole water, tainted with mustard gas, for washing.	
FRONT LINE. LAVACQUERIE RIGHT.	26/1/18		Morning spent collecting salvage. In afternoon the Battn relieved 1. K.R.R.C in front line. Relief complete 9.15 pm - casualties nil. (Bde & Battn orders attached). Relief was aided by a heavy mist, but delayed by the breakdown of a L.G. limber. Location Map attached. Night quiet and warm.	
	27/1/18		Very misty morning, allowing free movement above ground the whole morning. The trenches were full of mud & practically impassable - but the posts were dry and provided with fairly good shelter. In the afternoon the mist cleared. and all movement had to cease. Casualties 1 OR wounded. After dusk A & D Coys relieved B & C Coys. 2/Lieut Johnston & 25 OR left for 1 months attachment to 483 Field Co R.E. for training as Sappers Mates. We were ordered by Brigade to reconnoitre German post in sap opposite No 29 post, with a view to a silent raid, and the capture or extermination of the garrison. but a patrol under 2/Lieut Gitley (D.Co) found the wire too thick to allow the approach of any numbers in the bright moonlight, and the project was postponed.	

A7092 Wt. W123.9/M1293 750,000. 1/17. D. D & L. Ltd. Forms/C2118/14.

CONFIDENTIAL.

Instructions regarding War Diaries and Intelligence Summaries are contained in F. S. Regs., Part II. and the Staff Manual respectively. Title pages will be prepared in manuscript.

WAR DIARY
or
INTELLIGENCE SUMMARY.
(Erase heading not required.)

SHEET. Nº. 370.

Army Form C. 2118.

Place	Date	Hour	Summary of Events and Information	Remarks and references to Appendices
FRONT LINE LA VACQUERIE RIGHT	28/1/18		Very bright and clear all day, and enemy balloons were up observing all our front, movement being impossible. Night quiet except for a little gas shelling. Casualties one OR wounded.	
	29/1/18		A quiet day. Weather still bright. In the evening the Battn was relieved by 1/K.R.R.C (Battn O. 161 attached). Relief complete 9.30 pm. Casualties NIL. Accomodation in Brigade Reserve good and comfortable.	
	30/1/18		Working parties found as detailed in Schedule to Battn O. 161. Weather bright but Companies succeeded in amassing a large amount of valuable salvage in the valley & village of VILLERS PLOUICH. The amount of material awaiting reclamation was found to be very considerable – amongst other valuable equipment, over 1500 9.2" shells were found, but, owing to their weight, could not be removed.	
	31/1/18		Working parties continued. Advantage was taken of the misty weather to collect salvage further afield, from positions normally in full view of the enemy.	
			CASUALTIES during JANUARY Officers. Wounded. NIL. Killed. NIL. O.R. Wounded. 12 Killed 2.	
			EFFECTIVE STRENGTH. 31-1-18 36 officers 722 O.R.	
			RATION STRENGTH 31-1-18 25 officers 554 O.R	

A7092 Wt. W128 9/M1293 750,000. 1/17. D. D & I. Ltd. Forms/C2118/14.

CONFIDENTIAL

Instructions regarding War Diaries and Intelligence Summaries are contained in F. S. Regs., Part II. and the Staff Manual respectively. Title pages will be prepared in manuscript.

WAR DIARY
or
INTELLIGENCE SUMMARY.
(Erase heading not required.)

SHEET Nº 371.

Army Form C. 2118.

Place	Date	Hour	Summary of Events and Information	Remarks and references to Appendices
			From a fighting point of view the month of January was uneventful. The Battn came out of the line into Corps Reserve on night 3-4th, having the misfortune to lose 2 outpost positions while the relief was in progress. From 4th to 23rd was spent in camp at BARASTRE. When taken over this camp was in a delapidated and unfurnished condition, and our energies during our stay there were divided between training & attempting to repair, drain, and render the camp habitable, but both were seriously interfered with by weather conditions – hard frost and snow alternating with sudden thaws and rain. In spite of these difficulties good work was done – vide congratulatory messages attached. Some benefit was derived from the period of training, especially from R.E. instruction in rapid wiring. Recreation was restricted, not only by the weather, but also by the desolate & ruined nature of our surroundings. Three days (24. 25 & 26) were passed at METZ-EN-COUTURE under similar conditions, though the weather was more gracious, & good work was accomplished in cleaning up the billets and in salvaging the astounding amount of waste clothing & equipment there. The remainder of the month was spent in the front line and in Brigade Reserve, in LEFT sub-section of LA VACQUERIE RIGHT sector. The trenches were found to be very wet and impassable, and advantage was taken of the peaceful attitude of the enemy & several misty days, to improve the defences & accomodation and to salve a large quantity of derelict material, with which VILLERS PLOUICH and its surroundings was littered.	

G A Hunt Lt Col
Comd 8th Royal Berkshire Regt

A7092 Wt. W125 9/M1293 750,000. 1/17. D. D & L Ltd. Forms/C2118/14.

CONFIDENTIAL

Instructions regarding War Diaries and Intelligence Summaries are contained in F. S. Regs., Part II. and the Staff Manual respectively. Title pages will be prepared in manuscript.

WAR DIARY
or
INTELLIGENCE SUMMARY.
(Erase heading not required.)

1st Bn R. BERKSHIRE REGT

Army Form C. 2118.

SHEET No 372

Vol 40

Place	Date	Hour	Summary of Events and Information	Remarks and references to Appendices
			Further congratulatory messages and publications with reference to the BOURLON WOOD fighting are attached.	Misc.
FEBRUARY				
SUPPORT VILLERS PLOUICH	1.		Under cover of a thick mist free movement was possible and all available men were employed in salvage, and improving the roads. – cross roads in village drained and repaired. In the evening the Battn relieved 1/K.R.R.C in front line (O. No 162 attached) Relief complete 7pm. Casualties 2 O.R accidentally wounded in dark	O 162.
FRONT LINE - LA VACQUERIE	2.		A Bright day – movement impossible. Artillery & aerial activity very pronounced. Night quiet. Patrols reconnoitred the enemy sap running E and W opposite No 29 post but found no signs of the enemy. The line was reconnoitred by an advance party of 2/H.L.I. Reorganization of Brigades into 3 Battn formations took place about this date. the 22nd R.F being disbanded and disappearing from the 99th Infantry Brigade. This incident evoked the real sympathy of all ranks in the Battn – the two units having lived and fought side by side in complete harmony for well over 2 years. An appreciation by the Brigadier General. formerly in command of 22/R.F. is attached	Letter.
	3.		Colder. Counter-battery work by artillery on both sides. The Battn was relieved by 2/H.L.I (Bde O. 212 and Bn O. 163 attached). Relief complete 9pm Casualties 1 O.R accidentally injured – run over by a limber. The Battn was fortunate in	Bde 212 O 163

A7092 Wt. W128 9/M1293 750,000. 1/17. D. D & L. Ltd. Forms/C2118/14.

CONFIDENTIAL.

Instructions regarding War Diaries and Intelligence Summaries are contained in F. S. Regs., Part II. and the Staff Manual respectively. Title pages will be prepared in manuscript.

WAR DIARY
or
INTELLIGENCE SUMMARY.
(Erase heading not required.)

Army Form C. 2118.

SHEET Nº 373

Place	Date	Hour	Summary of Events and Information	Remarks and references to Appendices
			getting away from the line without more casualties. The incoming unit made free use of electric torches when approaching the line, and the enemy, scenting a relief, bombarded all roads and approaches with 5.9. Entraining and detraining arrangements were good and caused no delay, and the last	
BILLETS MANANCOURT	4.		Company was in billets at MANANCOURT by 2 am. Work report for the tour — also a letter from the Brigadier, written on his return to the Brigade, attached. The Battn rested the whole day & cleaned up their arms and equipment. A commencement was made with the protection of huts against A.A fire by building walls round same.	
"	5.		Working parties 50 and 30 strong respectively were found for A.A protection of 2nd Div HQ and the construction of 2nd Div Signal School. The whole Battn bathed at ETRICOURT baths. Revetment of huts continued	
"	6		Same working parties as on previous day. Remainder of Battn detailed to pitch tents under orders of Area Commandant. C.S.M. Brooks & Woodley reported relieving C.S.M. Inman (D) and Haynes (C) to England war-worn	
"	7		Working parties as before, also 2 sections per Company clearing salvage and rubbish from MANANCOURT – LE MESNIL road to 300x from each side. Reinforcements 5 officers and 138 o.r. (part of 10 officers and 160 o.r.) arrived from 6th	

CONFIDENTIAL

Instructions regarding War Diaries and Intelligence Summaries are contained in F. S. Regs., Part II. and the Staff Manual respectively. Title pages will be prepared in manuscript.

WAR DIARY
or
INTELLIGENCE SUMMARY.
(Erase heading not required.)

Army Form C. 2118.

SHEET No 374.

Place	Date	Hour	Summary of Events and Information	Remarks and references to Appendices
BILLETS	7		Battn which had been disbanded	
MANANCOURT	8.		Reinforcements posted to Companies – the officers as follows. 2/Lieuts W.T. LORD and H.M. AVERY to A Co. 2/Lieuts C.H. BEER and J.A. WRIGHT to B Co and 2/Lieut J.T. MOLD to D. Co. Usual working parties found. Lewis Gun teams from A and D Coys went ahead of the Battn for A.A protection of Artillery positions near BEAUCAMP.	
	9.		Working parties cancelled by arrangement. Battn relieved in Brigade Reserve. (Bde Warning Order in reference to reorganization of Divnl front and Bde Order No 213 & Bn O. No 164). 1 officer and 50 OR from D Company proceeded by march route at midday for work wiring LINCOLN RESERVE. Relief complete 8.30 pm. Casualties nil. Col Hunt left for M.G. demonstration at CAMIERS and Major Nugent being in leave, command devolved on Capt M.P. PUGH M.C.	
BRIGADE RESERVE HAVRINCOURT WOOD and VILLERS PLOUICH.	10.		Four working parties each of 1 officer and 40 OR found for work on communication and support trenches under supervision of 483 Field Co. R.E found by B and C Coys. A. Co found a party of 1 officer and 100 OR wiring LINCOLN RESERVE.	
	11		A quiet day. Working parties of previous day repeated.	
	12.		Nothing remarkable occurred. Working parties found as on previous day, and on completion of the night parties inter relief of Companies took place (Order attached) Relief complete by M.N. Commanding Officer and 2nd in Command both returned.	

A7092 Wt. W128.9/M1293 750,000. 1/17. D. D & L. Ltd. Forms/C2118/14.

CONFIDENTIAL

Instructions regarding War Diaries and Intelligence Summaries are contained in F. S. Regs., Part II. and the Staff Manual respectively. Title pages will be prepared in manuscript.

WAR DIARY
or
INTELLIGENCE SUMMARY.

(Erase heading not required.)

SHEET No 375.

Army Form C. 2118.

Place	Date	Hour	Summary of Events and Information	Remarks and references to Appendices
BRIGADE RESERVE	13		A quiet day - Working parties under R.E. provided as before. Commdg Officer went to demonstration of cooperation of TANKS with Infantry. Major NUGENT assuming command. The following officers joined from England and were posted to Companies:- Lt W.L. HUMBLEY to D Co. 2/Lt T.M. GOWER to D Co. 2/Lieuts S.C. BERESFORD and H. STREET to C Co. 2/Lieuts G.H. HERRING and L SAVILLE to A Coy and 2/Lieut E.E. KERBY to B Coy.	
"	14		Nothing unusual occurred. Same working parties found.	
"	15		Day uneventful. In the evening the Battn was relieved in ~~reserve~~ support by 1. K.R.R.C and relieved 23/R.F in the line. (Bde O. 214 and Bn O. 165 attached) Relief was complete by 8 pm. Casualties Nil. A quiet night. Report on work done while in RESERVE is attached	
FRONT LINE	16		A quiet day. A patrol from D Co left SYME SAP and investigated the derelict TANK at JAM SAP which was found occupied. A patrol of A Co under 2/Lieut LORD worked up the LA VACQUERIE reentrant as far as the deserted gunpits, but encountering the enemy in strength were compelled to withdraw	
"	17		Nothing occurred during the day. A patrol of A Company moved N of JAM SAP to ascertain whether enemy were working on their new trench at this point, but could trace no movement. A fighting patrol of A Co under 2/Lieut LORD again searched the neighbourhood of the gunpits on VILLAGE ROAD in the hopes of securing an	

A7092 Wt. W128 9/M1293 750,000. 1/17. D. D & I. Ltd. Forms/C2118/14.

CONFIDENTIAL

Instructions regarding War Diaries and Intelligence Summaries are contained in F. S. Regs., Part II. and the Staff Manual respectively. Title pages will be prepared in manuscript.

Army Form C. 2118.

WAR DIARY
or
INTELLIGENCE SUMMARY.
(Erase heading not required.)

SHEET No 376

Place	Date	Hour	Summary of Events and Information	Remarks and references to Appendices
FRONT LINE	18		identification, but were unsuccessful. The patrol was fired on by enemy M.G's. Other patrols were also sent out by D Co on the right.	
"	18.		A Daylight patrol under 2/Lieut REYNOLDS and Sgt Jenkins reached the enemy dug out on PARTRIDGE ROAD (R.20.d.73.13) and shot a sentry. The enemy, alarmed by the shot, drove our patrol off, and in the subsequent fighting we accounted for at least two other Germans, but no identification was secured. Casualties 1 OR (L/C DAVY killed). In the evening C & B Companies relieved D & A Coys in the line. Casualties NIL. D.C. and A Companies all had patrols out on our front watching enemy work and movement and endeavouring to secure prisoners, dead or alive, but met with no success	
	19		A quiet day. A patrol of B Company found the enemy at work near the gunpits on VILLAGE RD — a pre-arranged artillery bombardment was put on at 11pm, and, under cover of this, a strong patrol of A Coy under 2/Lieut LORD entered & ransacked the gunpits and adjacent shelters, but, although a lighted brazier and other signs of occupation were found, no prisoner was forthcoming. Casualties NIL. Other patrols were out on our RIGHT front, but their efforts were equally unavailing. During the day 2/Lieut WRIGHT was wounded by an enemy "pineapple" which fell right in the entrance to H.Q. of LEFT Co (B).	

A7092 Wt. W128 9/M1293. 750,000. 1/17. D. D & L. Ltd. Forms/C2118/14.

CONFIDENTIAL

Instructions regarding War Diaries and Intelligence Summaries are contained in F. S. Regs., Part II. and the Staff Manual respectively. Title pages will be prepared in manuscript.

WAR DIARY
or
INTELLIGENCE SUMMARY.
(Erase heading not required.)

SHEET No 377.

Army Form C. 2118.

Place	Date	Hour	Summary of Events and Information	Remarks and references to Appendices
FRONT LINE			In the early morning patrols reconnoitred the enemy lines in the neighbourhood of SYME SAP and PARTRIDGE Rd. and at night the same ground was kept constantly observed, and every movement of the enemy watched. Casualties 1 O.R. wounded	
"	21		An uneventful day. Under para 1 of Bde O. 215. annexed A Company moved up from close support and relieved a Company of 52. L.I. on LEFT, thus extending our frontage to 2000x held by 3 Companies in the line, supported by the remaining Company and 3 Companies of Batt. in Brigade Reserve. Relief complete 7 pm – Casualties NIL. Patrols were again out at night along the whole front trying to get into touch with the enemy, but without success	
	22		Our relief was due this day, and as a last effort to secure a prisoner, a small organized raid was made at 3 am. on the enemy dug out which had been the scene of the patrol encounter on morning of 18th. Instructions for this raid and other documents relating to same, are annexed. The raid was not a success. The enemy having erected a barricade on the road during the night which practically neutralized the tactics of the parties approaching from the N, at the same time adding to the strength of the enemy position. The L.T.M bombardment was also disappointing – all 4 guns "jamming" owing to the long range and the enforced use of additional charge "rings". and only 38 rounds were fired. The enemy	

A7092 Wt. W128 9/M1293 750,000. 1/17. D. D & L. Ltd. Forms/C2118/14.

CONFIDENTIAL

Instructions regarding War Diaries and Intelligence Summaries are contained in F. S. Regs., Part II. and the Staff Manual respectively. Title pages will be prepared in manuscript.

WAR DIARY
or
INTELLIGENCE SUMMARY.
(Erase heading not required.)

Army Form C. 2118.

SHEET No 378

Place	Date	Hour	Summary of Events and Information	Remarks and references to Appendices
FRONT LINE	22		held the position by means of a machine gun & bombs. and a lucky shot with one of the latter wounded 7 of the party. In addition, on calling the roll, 2 OR were found missing though no one could explain their disappearance.	
DIVN L RESERVE METZ			At night we were relieved in the line by 1/K.R.R. and moved into Divnl Reserve at METZ-EN-COUTURE. Relief complete 8.15 pm. Casualties NIL. Last Company arrived in billets 10.30 pm (Bde and Bn Relief orders are attached). No sooner were Companies in billets than the enemy fired some 20 or 30 H.V shells into the Village. but caused us no casualties. Work Report attached. This ended a memorable tour – 6 days in close support and 7 days in the line – in all 13 days without respite. The Battn can look back with pride on these 13 days, for an immense amount of very useful wiring and digging was accomplished. as the work reports attached will testify. and at the same time, when in the front line, not a night passed without fighting & reconnoitring patrols going out on the whole front, and, by skill and boldness, obtaining valuable information and securing for us the absolute mastery of "No Man's land". This activity was inspired by a hint that an "identification" from the Divisional front was needed – and it was a genuine disappointment to all ranks that, in spite of our efforts. we were unable to secure a prisoner.	

CONFIDENTIAL

Instructions regarding War Diaries and Intelligence Summaries are contained in F. S. Regs., Part II. and the Staff Manual respectively. Title pages will be prepared in manuscript.

WAR DIARY
or
INTELLIGENCE SUMMARY.

(*Erase heading not required.*)

Army Form C. 2118.

SHEET No 379.

Place	Date	Hour	Summary of Events and Information	Remarks and references to Appendices
METZ	23.		The village was again shelled in the early morning. The day was spent by Companies in cleaning up and tidying billets, and revetting the huts against shell and bomb splinters.	
"	24.		The village was shelled about 3am, and C & D Companies billets were very nearly hit, but no casualties caused. All Companies bathed. A working party of 1 platoon found for cleaning up the Brigade area. Some salvage collected.	
"	25.		METZ escaped its usual night bombardment and the enemy utilized his long range guns to pour an enormous number of gas shells into HAVRINCOURT WOOD at 2am. the bombardment lasting nearly an hour. Companies were inspected by the Commanding Officer. Specialist training commenced. Both our own and enemy artillery displayed unwonted activity both by day and night. Working party found as on previous day.	
"	26		The Battalion (full strength) was employed the whole day in digging a cable trench, returning to billets about 4.30pm. The work was carried out without any molestation from the enemy.	
			2Lieuts W. S. WINSTANLEY and A.E. FOSTER from 6th Batton joined the battalion and were posted to D & B Coys respectively.	

A7092 Wt. W128 9/M1293 750,000. 1/17. D. D & L. Ltd. Forms/C2118/14.

CONFIDENTIAL

Instructions regarding War Diaries and Intelligence Summaries are contained in F. S. Regs., Part II. and the Staff Manual respectively. Title pages will be prepared in manuscript.

WAR DIARY
or
INTELLIGENCE SUMMARY.
(Erase heading not required.)

Army Form C. 2118.

SHEET No 380

Place	Date	Hour	Summary of Events and Information	Remarks and references to Appendices
METZ	27		The day was spent in training under Coy. arrangements and a conference for all officers in the afternoon.	
"	28		The morning was employed in cleaning up billets and preparing for the batt^n to go up into Brigade Support to relieve the 23rd R. Fusiliers (See attached Order)	
			2/Lieut. W. S. HUSSEY joined the batt^n from 6th Batt^n and posted to "C" Coy.	
			The body of Pte Burman, one of the men missing in the raid of 22nd Inst. was found by 1st R.R.R. a few nights later near our wire undisturbed by the enemy. Pte Fox is still unaccountably absent.	
			Total Casualties for February. Officers wounded 1. O.R's { Killed – 2, Wounded – 13, Missing 1 }	
			Effective Strength 46 officers 860 O.R's	
			Ration Strength 31 " 604 "	
			G.P. Hunt Lt. Col. Comd'g. 1st Royal Berkshire Regt.	

A5834 Wt. W4973/M687 750,000 8/16 D. D. & L. Ltd. Forms/C.2118/13.

99th Brigade.

2nd Division.

1st BATTALION

ROYAL BERKSHIRE REGIMENT

MARCH 1 9 1 8

Appendix attached:-

Report on Operations 21st-31st March.

CONFIDENTIAL.

Instructions regarding War Diaries and Intelligence Summaries are contained in F. S. Regs., Part II. and the Staff Manual respectively. Title pages will be prepared in manuscript.

WAR DIARY
or
INTELLIGENCE SUMMARY.
(Erase heading not required.)

1st Bn ROYAL BERKSHIRE REGt

SHEET No 381.

Army Form C. 2118.

99/2

Vol 41

Place	Date	Hour	Summary of Events and Information	Remarks and references to Appendices
BRIGADE SUPPORT. VILLERS PLOUICH.	1/3/18		The Battn had moved into Support, relieving 23/R.F. on previous night without Casualties. Weather dull with occasional snow and sleet. All Companies were occupied day and night with large working and carrying-parties. Rumours that an attack by the enemy was imminent were spreading. 2/Lieut. L. SAVILLE to Hospital, sick	
"	2/3/18 3/3/18 4/3/18 5/3/18		These days passed quietly and without incident. The usual working parties were found, and a considerable quantity of salvage was collected. 200 men were working daily under R.E. supervision. Rumours of the coming attack were persistent, but no definite information was given, and nothing but the usual artillery activity took place	
FRONT LINE - LA VACQUERIE RIGHT	6/3/18		As soon as it was dusk the Battn relieved 23/R.F. in the front line. Companies being disposed in platoon posts as follows. C on RIGHT, B in CENTRE, D on LEFT, and A in SUPPORT. Relief complete 9 pm. Casualties nil. Capt Valentine went on short leave and 2/Lieut J.A. GRIMES took over command of "B" Company	
"	7/3/18		At 12.35 am the enemy "projected" gas on our front. The projection was by means of "Rum-jar" T.M's. H.E was used, and the detonations were terrific, damaging the trenches badly and veiling the fact that gas was present. The gas was of the Phosgene type. 2/Lieut. J.A GRIMES. M.C. died from the effects of the gas, after	

A5834 Wt. W4973/M687 750,000 8/16 D. D. & L. Ltd. Forms/C.2118/13.

CONFIDENTIAL

Instructions regarding War Diaries and Intelligence Summaries are contained in F. S. Regs., Part II. and the Staff Manual respectively. Title pages will be prepared in manuscript.

WAR DIARY or INTELLIGENCE SUMMARY.

(*Erase heading not required.*)

Army Form C. 2118.

1st Bn ROYAL BERKSHIRE REGT
SHEET No 382

Place	Date	Hour	Summary of Events and Information	Remarks and references to Appendices
FRONT LINE. LA VACQUERIE RIGHT	7/3/18		gallantly endeavouring to rescue his orderly who had been buried in the trench. 2/Lieuts C.H. BEER and FOSTER and 29 O.R were also casualties (wounded 'gas') The effects of the projection were chiefly felt by RIGHT, CENTRE and SUPPORT Companies	
"	8/3/18.		A quiet fine day. At night our patrols were very active, every endeavour being made to procure enemy identifications, but without success. 2/Lieut A.J. HARRIS Sgt CRAWLEY and Sgt McCANN played a prominent part in these patrols. Work in the line was concentrated on erection of shelters in the platoon posts.	
"	9/3/18		Another fine uneventful day. Our patrols were again very active at night but were unable to accomplish their object. At about 10pm our guns on the RIGHT opened a heavy bombardment.	
"	10/3/18		At 3am troops of the VII CORPS on our right carried out a raid towards GONNELIEU under cover of an artillery barrage. A patrol of ours under 2/Lieut A.J. HARRIS went out and cut gaps in the enemy wire in preparation for a raid by 23/R.F. Listening patrols were also out until dawn, but no identification was obtained. The day was fine and uneventful. At night the holding of the line was re-adjusted. A and C Coys taking over the whole line, in posts, with B and D Coys in reserve. At this time the policy of defence appeared to be that, in event of attack, our main line of resistance would be the HIGHLAND RIDGE and BILHEM SWITCH system, and that the advanced line or posts were to be abandoned. For this reason the line was very lightly held.	

A5834 Wt. W4973/M687 750,000 8/16 D. D. & L. Ltd. Forms/C.2118/13.

CONFIDENTIAL

Instructions regarding War Diaries and Intelligence Summaries are contained in F. S. Regs., Part II. and the Staff Manual respectively. Title pages will be prepared in manuscript.

WAR DIARY
or
INTELLIGENCE SUMMARY.
(Erase heading not required.)

Army Form C. 2118.

SHEET No 382.

Place	Date	Hour	Summary of Events and Information	Remarks and references to Appendices
FRONT LINE LA VACQUERIE RIGHT.	11/3/18		Frosty morning and a very fine day. Very little activity during daylight, except with aircraft of both sides. The Divl Commander visited the line in the morning. At about 7.15 pm the enemy commenced an intense bombardment with "MUSTARD GAS" over a large front – this continued unabated for about $3\frac{1}{2}$ hours, intermixed with H.E. The Rations convoy reached the line in spite of the gas and got away again with comparatively slight casualties. The gas hung about in dangerous strength the whole night	
"	12/3/18		The effects of the gas bombardment began to be manifest during this and subsequent days. Casualties were heaviest in B and D Companies (in SUPPORT) – the troops in the front line posts suffering comparatively slightly. Our total casualties from the gas were eventually found to be 11 Officers wounded (Capts M.C. DEMPSEY and R.N. PORRITT our M.O. Major C. NUGENT. Lieut J.W. JOHNSON (attd 99 T.M.B) and 2/Lieuts W. LEACH E.E. KIRBY. A.J. HARRIS J TITLEY A.S. DENHAM T.M. GOWER & W.S. WINSTANLEY) and 257 O.R. wounded. The bulk of these casualties were not serious and few would have been evacuated to England had it not been necessary to clear the hospitals for the reception of wounded in subsequent fighting. In the evening we were relieved in the line by 1/K.R.R.C (see Bde O.O. No 218 and Bn O.O attached), and moved into Divisional Reserve at METZ. Relief complete at 10.5 pm. Casualties NIL. Arrived in billets at about 12 midnight. A few gas shell fell during the move, but stringent precautions were observed. WORK REPORT during tour is attached.	

A7092I. Wt. W12839/M1293 750,000. 1/17. D. D & L., Ltd. Forms/C2118/14.

CONFIDENTIAL

Instructions regarding War Diaries and Intelligence Summaries are contained in F. S. Regs., Part II. and the Staff Manual respectively. Title pages will be prepared in manuscript.

WAR DIARY
or
INTELLIGENCE SUMMARY.
(Erase heading not required.)

Army Form C. 2118.

SHEET Nº 383.

Place	Date	Hour	Summary of Events and Information	Remarks and references to Appendices
DIVISIONAL RESERVE METZ	13/3/18		The day was spent in resting the men, reorganizing Companies so far as possible, and cleaning up. Signs of gas were noticed during the day and evening blowing over METZ, and the hutments were shelled at 11pm and again at 5.20 am next day. The Battn bathed and re-clothed during the day.	
"	14/3/18		Reinforcements (125 O.R. from the BUCKINGHAMSHIRE Territorials) joined and were posted to B and D Coys. which had been practically wiped out by the gas attack. The day was spent in digging in a new Tented Camp owing to the frequent & heavy shelling of the existing hutted camps. We learnt here that the enemy had continued his bombardment of the line with mustard gas practically without ceasing ever since we left the line, and that other units had also suffered severely.	
"	15/3/18.		The attached "intelligence" from Divn is interesting in view of subsequent events. The enemy at this time was expected to launch his attack at any moment, and, attached Bde Order No 219 having been received at about 7pm, the Battn was kept practically 'standing to' and at midnight A & B Coys were ordered to move up to the support positions. During the day the Battn was again employed digging in the Tented camp.	
"	16/3/18		A & B Companies reached their new positions at 3am. No attack developed and they returned at about 8.30 am, having spent the early hours digging and improving the trench system. A & B Coys rested. C & D, after a little P.T. continued work on the	

A7092. Wt. W12839/M1293 750,000. 1/17. D. D & L., Ltd. Forms/C2118/14.

CONFIDENTIAL

Instructions regarding War Diaries and Intelligence Summaries are contained in F. S. Regs., Part II. and the Staff Manual respectively. Title pages will be prepared in manuscript.

WAR DIARY
or
INTELLIGENCE SUMMARY.
(Erase heading not required.)

Army Form C. 2118.

SHEET No. 384

Place	Date	Hour	Summary of Events and Information	Remarks and references to Appendices
DIVISIONAL RESERVE METZ	16/3/18		Tented camp. In the evening C and D Companies moved up into Support positions as on previous night, but, though warning was received to "stand by" on ½ hours notice, nothing developed, and C and D Companies returned to billets	
"	17/3/18		arriving at about 8.45 am. and spent the morning resting. A and B Coys did a little P.T. and general training. Church service in the afternoon. A and B Coys again moved up into the Support Line in the evening, returning early next morning	
"	18/3/18		A fine day. In the evening the Battn relieved 23/R.F in support in accordance with Bde and Bn orders 220 and 168 attached. Casualties nil.	
IN SUPPORT. HIGHLAND LINE	19/3/18		A wet day. Nothing of note occurred. In the evening the Division was relieved by 47th (LONDON) Divn. The Battn was relieved by 15/London, and moved back into Corps Reserve at MANANCOURT. Arrived in billets at 2 am. Casualties NIL. Bde Order attached.	
CORPS RESERVE MANANCOURT.	20/3/18		A dull day. The Battn rested and cleaned up.	
"	21/3/18		At 5 am. we received warning to "Stand by". The enemy attack developed at dawn, and very heavy gunfire was heard on all sides of the salient. The whole day passed in suspense – orders to move up being expected at any moment. In the evening the Commdg Officer inspected Companies. We were told we were certain to move during the night, and every man stood to arms, but no definite orders were received.	

A7092). Wt. W2839/M1293 750,000. 1/17. D. D & L., Ltd. Forms/C2118/14.

CONFIDENTIAL

Instructions regarding War Diaries and Intelligence Summaries are contained in F. S. Regs., Part II. and the Staff Manual respectively. Title pages will be prepared in manuscript.

WAR DIARY
or
INTELLIGENCE SUMMARY.
(Erase heading not required.)

Army Form C. 2118.

SHEET. Nº 385.

Place	Date	Hour	Summary of Events and Information	Remarks and references to Appendices
CORPS RESERVE. MANANCOURT	22/3/18		The Battn was still under short notice, but no definite news of the progress of the enemy attack could be obtained, though many uncomfortable rumours were rife. Emphasis was given to these by the order to move the 1st line transport back to LE MESNIL-EN-ARROUAISE. MANANCOURT was intermittently shelled by the enemy H.V. guns throughout the day but little damage and no casualties were caused. At about 10.45 pm warning was received to stand by and be prepared to defend the village. Strong patrols were sent out towards EQUANCOURT and ETRICOURT on both sides of the CANAL DU NORD, and every man was kept on the alert. but, although there was considerable movement back along the roads of artillery, transport and miscellaneous troops, and rumours of disaster and general "wind-up" were prevalent, no further developments took place during the night and no official news reached us.	
"	23/3/18		The morning dawned a fine day. The intensity of enemy shelling increased every hour, and the general uneasiness grew, though everyone was in the dark as to the actual position. Soon it was rumoured that FINS had been occupied by the enemy. This was difficult to believe, though it proved to be true. We received absolutely no official enlightenment as to the situation. The disintegration of the Division had commenced, the 5th & 6th Brigades having moved NORTHWARDS	

CONFIDENTIAL

Instructions regarding War Diaries and Intelligence Summaries are contained in F. S. Regs., Part II. and the Staff Manual respectively. Title pages will be prepared in manuscript.

WAR DIARY
or
INTELLIGENCE SUMMARY.
(Erase heading not required.)

SHEET No 386

Army Form C. 2118.

Place	Date	Hour	Summary of Events and Information	Remarks and references to Appendices
CORPS RESERVE MANANCOURT	23/3/18		to support the 17th Divn near HERMIES. while our Brigade was left at disposal of 5th Army. This day saw the commencement of further confusion and disorganization. For subsequent movements of the Battn - Refce Maps 57c & 57D 1/40000. At 9.30 am A & B Companies were moved to EQUANCOURT to strengthen the line held by 23/R.F. and were soon in touch with the enemy, fighting a stubborn rearguard action all day and withdrawing by stages through VALLULART WOOD - YTRES - BUS - ROCQUIGNY, whence the survivors rejoined 1st line Transport near LE TRANSLOY at night.	Movements of A & B Coys under Capts M.P. PUGH & Capt VALENTINE
			At midday Battn H Q. and C and D Companies were moved to hold a line from BEETROOT FACTORY (V.2. central) EASTWARD to the Railway - they had scarcely got into position when the enemy came in sight and a rearguard action commenced, and we withdrew by stages via the Cemetery at ETRICOURT (where Capt P.L MOUSLEY was wounded) LECHELLE WOOD (where the Commanding Officer Lt Col. G.P. HUNT. CMG. DSO. was killed while gallantly rallying all troops within reach) - LE MESNIL-EN-ARROUAISE - ROCQUIGNY, where the residue attached themselves to troops of the 47th Divn commanded by Lt Col DAWES, and spent the night.	Movements of Bn H.Q & C & D. Coys. under Lt Col G.P. HUNT & Capt MOUSLEY.
			Soon after noon details moved to join 1st line Transport at LE MESNIL - being sped on their way by a sudden increase in the intensity of the hostile bombardment of MANANCOURT which the enemy occupied only a few minutes later. In less than an	Movements of 1st line Transport & details.

CONFIDENTIAL.

Instructions regarding War Diaries and Intelligence Summaries are contained in F. S. Regs., Part II. and the Staff Manual respectively. Title pages will be prepared in manuscript.

WAR DIARY
or
INTELLIGENCE SUMMARY.
(Erase heading not required.)

Army Form C. 2118.

SHEET No 387.

Place	Date	Hour	Summary of Events and Information	Remarks and references to Appendices
IN CONSTANT MOVEMENT	23/3/18		Lorr Transport & Details were forced to leave LE MESNIL by the enemy shelling and moved back, by order of Brigade, through SAILLY SAILLISEL to a point just SOUTH of LETRANSLOY, where the night was spent. Capt M.P. PUGH M.C. here assumed command.	
"	24/3/18		In the early morning Battn H.Q. and C & D Coys at ROCQUIGNY were involved in fierce fighting, and with troops on their flanks, were forced back during the day WESTWARD through GUEUDECOURT to LE SARS, where they rejoined A & B Coys in the evening. At 3 am A & B Coys. 1st line Transport and Details moved back, by order of Brigade, through LE TRANSLOY - LES BOEUFS - GINCHY - LONGUEVAL - FLERS. Here the Transport was halted, and during this & subsequent days, moved back through LE SARS - MIRAUMONT - AUCHONVILLERS - MAILLY-MAILLET - BERTRANCOURT - to LEALVILLERS. From FLERS, after replenishing with S.A.A. water and rations. A & B Coys & details moved up to GUEUDECOURT, and, with the 23/R.F. held a line E of the Village until about 4 p.m. They were then relieved and moved back to a line on the sunken road between EAUCOURT L'ABBAYE & LIGNY THILLOY. Here C & D Companies rejoined and the Battn was practically intact again, holding 600 yards of the line with 23/R.F. on the RIGHT and 10/D.C.L.I on LEFT facing EAST. The night was spent in this line, and the men rested as far as possible, though the cold was intense. At GUEUDECOURT Brigr Genl. R. BARNETT-BARKER and Staff Captn (Capt E.S. BELL) were killed by one shell.	

A7092. Wt. W12839/M1293 750,000. 1/17. D. D & L., Ltd. Forms/C2118/14.

CONFIDENTIAL.

Instructions regarding War Diaries and Intelligence Summaries are contained in F. S. Regs., Part II. and the Staff Manual respectively. Title pages will be prepared in manuscript.

WAR DIARY
or
INTELLIGENCE SUMMARY.
(*Erase heading not required.*)

Army Form C. 2118.

SHEET No 388.

Place	Date	Hour	Summary of Events and Information	Remarks and references to Appendices
IN CONSTANT MOVEMENT	25/3/18		At dawn our line was fiercely attacked by the enemy. The troops on our LEFT were forced back, and in spite of efforts to reorganize and control the fire, the whole line, after resisting some 2 hours, was compelled to withdraw. This was accomplished without much confusion, notwithstanding the lack of cohesion and command, and a spirited resistance was offered wherever the situation allowed – particularly at LE SARS and the high ground WEST of that Village. Here units became more and more scattered, and our own Companies lost touch with Battn H.Q. and were not re-united until evening. The withdrawal continued slowly as far as the high ground between PYS and COURCELETTE, which we found to be held by units of the 5th Infantry Bde. Companies passed through this line right back to the ANCRE valley at BEAUCOURT. Battn H.Q and some 20 O.R. attached themselves to 1/K.R.R. and moved back to MIRAUMONT. Here orders were received to return to the PYS line and reinforce the troops there, but before reaching it were ordered to move back through GRANCOURT to the high ridges W of the ANCRE near BEAUCOURT. This point was reached at dusk. The Brigade was here re-organized, issued with S.A.A and food and held the line for the night, which was again intensely cold. During the day reinforcements (200 O.R.) from 6/SOMERSETS were posted to the Battn. These men were absorbed into a composite Battn under command of Major Smith 1/K.R.R. and were put into the line near AUCHONVILLERS, where they were in action this day	

A7092. Wt. W12839/M1293 750,000. 1/17. D. D & L., Ltd. Forms/C2118/14.

CONFIDENTIAL.

Instructions regarding War Diaries and Intelligence Summaries are contained in F. S. Regs., Part II. and the Staff Manual respectively. Title pages will be prepared in manuscript.

WAR DIARY
or
INTELLIGENCE SUMMARY.

(Erase heading not required.)

Army Form C. 2118.

SHEET No 389.

Place	Date	Hour	Summary of Events and Information	Remarks and references to Appendices
IN CONSTANT MOVEMENT.	26/3/18		At dawn, with other units of the Brigade, the Battn moved back to the O.B.L. near BEAUMONT HAMEL (HAWTHORN RIDGE), taking over 200 yards of the trenches from Q.10. central to Q.10.d. 2.6. This line the Battn held all day without coming into close contact with the enemy, though the inter-change of rifle and machine-gun fire at long range was ceaseless and the hostile artillery fire gradually increased in intensity. In this position the feeling was at last prevalent that the final line of resistance had been reached, and that our own artillery was again in position behind us, and re-organized to support the infantry. Rumours were also current that fresh divisions were close at hand to take over the line. In the afternoon these rumours were confirmed by the appearance of parties of the N.Z.R. (ANZAC CORPS) in our midst. These troops came to us "over the top", under the impression that no troops were holding the line, and they suffered more casualties than they need have for this reason. At 10.30 pm we received orders to move back to MAILLY-MAILLET. We reached this village at midnight, but the troops were condemned to spend yet another night in the open. - but it was a quiet night, and the men had fair rest and hot food.	
MAILLY-MAILLET. & FORCEVILLE	27/3/18		The morning was spent in cleaning up and resting, and some reorganization was attempted. In the afternoon the Battn moved back to billets at FORCEVILLE. Here	

A7092). Wt. W12839/M1293 750,000. 1/17. D. D & L., Ltd. Forms/C2118/14.

CONFIDENTIAL

Instructions regarding War Diaries and Intelligence Summaries are contained in F. S. Regs., Part II. and the Staff Manual respectively. Title pages will be prepared in manuscript.

WAR DIARY
or
INTELLIGENCE SUMMARY.
(Erase heading not required.)

Army Form C. 2118.

SHEET No 390.

Place	Date	Hour	Summary of Events and Information	Remarks and references to Appendices
FORCEVILLE	27/3/18		The men had a good night's rest, under cover for the first time since leaving MANANCOURT on the 23rd instant. The 200 reinforcements with 2/Lieuts SPENCER, BUSH, REYNOLDS and DORMER, had joined us at MAILLY-MAILLET, and, in spite of casualties, our numbers were still fairly useful, though a thorough reorganization was necessary before we could be a useful fighting unit again.	
"	28/3/18		During the morning, thorough inspections were carried out, and an attempt was made to organize into 2 Companies (A with B and C with D), and to ascertain our actual casualties, but before this was completed, we were ordered to provide 2 companies, each 130 strong, as part of a composite Battn of the 99th Infantry Brigade. These were hurriedly made up, one (C) under command of Lieut ASTLEY, and the other (D) under Lieut CROSBIE, and the 2 Companies moved off after dinners through ENGELBELMER to a position under AVELUY WOOD, N of MARTINSART, which was held all this night and next day. Lt Col WINTER, D.S.O. (23/R.F.) was in command. At 4 pm the remainder of the Battn moved back to LEALVILLERS where 1st Line Transport was established. To day the long spell of fine weather, which had been so favourable to the enemy plans, broke up, and heavy rain fell during the afternoon and night.	
LEALVILLERS	29/3/18		The morning was wet and stormy, but later the weather improved. The enemy activity was very slight. During the night the Composite Battn of 99th Bde was relieved in AVELUY WOOD and moved back to billets in ENGELBELMER.	

A7092. Wt. W12839/M1293 750,000, 1/17. D. D & L., Ltd. Forms/C2118/14.

CONFIDENTIAL

Instructions regarding War Diaries and Intelligence Summaries are contained in F. S. Regs., Part II. and the Staff Manual respectively. Title pages will be prepared in manuscript.

WAR DIARY
or
INTELLIGENCE SUMMARY.
(Erase heading not required.)

Army Form C. 2118.

SHEET No 391.

Place	Date	Hour	Summary of Events and Information	Remarks and references to Appendices
LEALVILLERS.	30/3/18		More rain fell during the night and day, but the weather was warmer. The day was uneventful. Another Composite Battn was formed out of the Division, consisting mainly of reinforcements, under command of Lt Col MURRAY-LYON D.S.O. Two of our officers (2/Lieuts H.J. ODELL and G.H. HERRING) were attached to this Battn, which moved up to the line during the afternoon. The Brigade Composite Battn remained in support at ENGELBELMER.	
"	31/3/18		Heavy rain during night - but the day was fairly fine tho stormy & unsettled. The Bde Composite Battn remained in bivouac on outskirts of ENGELBELMER. The village was shelled intermittently all day. Major R.J. BRETT (2/Oxford & Bucks L.I.) was appointed to temporary command of the Battn, and during the afternoon established Battn H.Q. at ENGELBELMER. The Composite Battn pending relief of the Divn, was divided into 2 units - CERT Battn (1/R.BERKS) under command of Major Brett, and CIN Battn (23/R.F. and 1/K.R.R.C) under command of Lt Col Winter D.S.O. M.C. During the night LEAVILLERS was shelled with H.V. and bombed by enemy aircraft.	
			Casualties during the month of MARCH	
			OFFICERS. ——— KILLED 2. WOUNDED 16 . MISSING — .	
			O.R. ——— " 23. " 439 " 62.	

A7092). Wt. W12839/M1293 750,000. 1/17. D. D & L., Ltd. Forms/C2118/14.

CONFIDENTIAL

Instructions regarding War Diaries and Intelligence Summaries are contained in F. S. Regs., Part II. and the Staff Manual respectively. Title pages will be prepared in manuscript.

WAR DIARY
or
INTELLIGENCE SUMMARY.
(*Erase heading not required.*)

Army Form C. 2118.

SHEET No 392

Place	Date	Hour	Summary of Events and Information	Remarks and references to Appendices
	31/3/18		EFFECTIVE STRENGTH 28 OFFICERS 720 O.R	
			RATION STRENGTH 21 OFFICERS 548 O.R.	
			R.D. Birtt, Major Cmdg 1/R. Berkshire Regt	

A7092. Wt. W12839/M1293 730,000. 1/17. D. D & L., Ltd. Forms/C2118/14.

1st Battn Royal Berkshire Regt.

R E P O R T on Operations from 21 - 31/3.1918.

19/3/18. The Battn was relieved in support by 15/London Regt, 47th Divn, and moved into Corps Reserve at MANANCOURT. Arrived in billets at 2 am.

20/3/18 A dull day. The Battn rested and cleaned up.

21/3/18 At 5 am warning was received to stand by. The enemy attack developed at dawn and very heavy artillery fire was heard on all sides of the salient. The whole day was passed in suspense, orders to move up being expected at any moment. In the evening the Commanding Officer inspected Companies. Owing to heavy casualties from enemy gas the Battn was very weak and was organized in two Companies, No 1 comprising A and B Coys commanded by Capt M.P.PUGH M.C., and No 2 comprising C and D Coys commanded by Capt P.L. MOUSLEY. Fighting Strength about 20 officers and 404 O.R. We were told that we were certain to move during the night and every man stood to arms, but no definite orders were received.

22/3/18. The Battn was still held at short notice, but no definite news of the progress of the enemy attack could be obtained, though many disquieting rumours were rife. Orders were received to move 1st Line Transport back to LE MESNIL EN ARROUAISE, and this was done during the evening in 3 journeys. Manancourt was intermittently shelled by the enemy H.V. guns during the day but little damage and no casualties were caused. At about 10.45 pm warning was received to stand by and be prepared to defend the village of Manancourt. Strong pattols were at once sent out towards EQUANCOURT and ETRICOURT on both banks of the CANAL DU NORD and every man was kept on the alert, but, although there was considerable movement back along the roads of Artillery, transport, and miscellaneous troops, and rumours of disaster were generally prevalent, no further developements took place duging the night and no official news reached us.

23/3/18 The day dawned fine. Enemy shelling increased every hour and the general uneasiness grew, though everyone was in the dark as to the actual position. It was rumoured that FINS had been occupied by the enemy. This was difficult to believe but it proved to be substantially true. We received absolutely no official enlightenment as to the true situation, except that the Division had been split up, the 5th and 6th Brigades having moved NORTH to support the 12th Divn near HERMIES, and that our Brigade had been left at disposal of 5th Army. This day saw the commencement of still further disintegration. Reference Maps for subsequent movements of the Battn 57c and 57d, scale 1/40000. At 9.30 am No 1 Coy was moved to EQUANCOURT to strengthen the line held by 23 /R.F. and 1/K.R.R.C. and was almost immediately at grips with the enemy, fighting a stubborn rearguard action all day and withdrawing by stages through VALLULART WOOD. YTRES. BUS. to ROCQUIGNY, whence the survivors rejoined 1st Line Transport near LE TRANSLOY during the night.

At noon Battn H.Q. and No 2 Coy were moved to hold a line from the BEETROOT FACTORY (V.2 central) EASTWARD to the Railway - they had scarcely got into position than the enemy came into sight and a rearguad action commenced, withdrawal being carried out by stages via THE CEMETERY at ETRICOURT (here Capt P.L.MOUSLEY was wounded) LECHELLE WOOD (here the Commanding Officer Lt Col G.P.HUNT C.M.G. D S.O. was killed, shot through the head, while gallantly endeavouring to rally and reorganize the troops in his vicinity, with absolute disregard for his personal safety) LE MESNIL EN ARROUAISE, to ROCQUIGNY, where the survivors attached themselves to troops of the 47th Divn commanded by LT Col DAWES. Here they spent the night.

Soon after noon Details of the Battn left MANANCOURT to join 1st Line Transport at LE MESNIL, sped on the their way by a sudden increase in the intensity of the enemy shelling. The enemy occupiesd the Village of MANANCOURT only a few minutes later. In less than an hour Transport and Details were compelled to leave LE MESNIL by the enemy shelling and moved back, by order of Brigade, through SAILLY SAILLISEL to a point on the main road SOUTH of LE TRANSLOy, where the night was spent. Capt M.B.PUGH M.C. here assumed command .

24/3/18 In the early morning Battn H.Q. and No 2 Coy at ROCQUIGNY were involved in fierce fighting, and, with the troops on their flanks, were forced back during the day WESTWARD through GUEUDECOURT to LE SARS where they rejoined No 1 Coy in the evening. At 3 am No 1 Coy, Transport and Details moved back by order of Brigade through LE TRANSLOY. LESBOEUFS. GINCHY. LONGUEVAL. FLERS. Here the Transport was halted and, during this and subsequent days, moved back through LE SARS. MIRAUMONT. AUCHONVILLERS. MAILLY-MAILLET. BERTRANCOURT to LEALVILLERS. From FLERS, after replenishing with S.A.A. water and rations No 1 Coy and Details (Total strength about 150 o.r.) moved up to GUEUDECOURT, and, with XXXXXXX 23/R.F. held a line EAST of the Village until about 4.0 pm, but did not come into close contact with the enemy who could be seen coming over the ridges at about 3000 yards. We then moved back to a line on the Sunken Road between EAUCOURT L'ABBAYE and LIGNY THILLOY. Here C and D Coys rejoined and the Battn was again intact, holding 600 yards of the line with the 23/R.F. on the RIGHT and 10/D.C.L.I. on the LEFT facing EAST. The night was spent in this line and the men rested as far as possible though the cold was intense.

25/3/18 At dawn our line was fiercely attacked by the enemy. Troops on our left were forced back, and, in spite of efforts to re-organize the line and control reckless and ineffective fire, the whole line, after some 2 hours resistance, withdrew in fair order considering the lack of cohesion & command. A spirited resistance was offered whenever the situation allowed - particularly at LE SARS and the high ground WEST of that Village. Here units became more and more scattered and Companies lost touch with Battn H.Q., until re-united in the evening. The withdrawal continued slowly as far as the high ground between PYS and COURCELette, which we found to be held by Units of the 5th Infantry Brigade. Our 2 Companies had passed right through this line back to the ANCRE valley at BEAUCOURT. Battn H.Q. and about 20 o.r. attache d themselves to 1/K.R.R.C. and moved back with them to MIRAUMONT. Here orders were received to return to the PYS line and to reinforce the line there, but before reaching it orders were given to move back through GRANCOURT to the high ridges WEST of the ANCRE near BEAUCOURT. This point was ~~xxxxxx~~ reached at dusk. The Brigade was here re-organized issued with S.AA and food and held the line for the night which was again intensely cold. During the day reinforcements, about 200 o.r., from 6/SOMERSETS had arrived for the Battn. These men were absorbed into a Composite Battn under command of Major SMITH of 1/K.R.R.C. and were put into the line near AUCHONVILLERS where they were in action during this and the next day.

26/3/18 At dawn, with other units of the Brigade, the Battn moved back to the O.B.L. on HAWTHORN RIDGE near BEAUMONT HAMEL, taking over 200 yards of the trenches from Q.10 central to Q.10.d. ~~XX~~ 2. 6. This line the Battn held all day, exchanging fire with the enemy at about 1000 to 1500 yards range. The enemy artillery fire gradually increased in intensity during the day. In this position it was at last felt that the real line of resistance had been reached, and that our own artillery was again in position behind us and reorganized. Rumours also reached us of fresh divisions close at hand ready to take over the line. During the afternoon these rumours were confirmed by the appearance in our midst of parties of N.Z.R. (ANZAC CORPS). These troops came to us "over the top" and under the impression that no troops were holding the line. Their casualties on this account were far heavier than they need have been. At 10.30 p.m. we received orders to move back to MAILLY-MAILLET. We reached this village at midnight, but the troops were condemned to spend yet another night in the open But it was a quiet night and they had a real rest, fires, and hot food.

27)3/18 The morning was spent in cleaning up and resting and some re-organiztion was attempted. The party of reinforcements joined us here. In the afternoon the Battn moved back to billets at FORCEVILLE. Here the men had a good night's res under cover for the first time since leaving MANANCOURT on 23rd instant.

F.D. Hazett
Capt & A/Adjt
2/4/18

//

99/2

Instructions regarding War Diaries and Intelligence Summaries are contained in F. S. Regs., Part II. and the Staff Manual respectively. Title pages will be prepared in manuscript.

WAR DIARY
or
INTELLIGENCE SUMMARY.
(Erase heading not required.)

CONFIDENTIAL

Army Form C. 2118.

1st Battalion Royal Berkshire Rgt
Sheet No 400

Vol 43

Place	Date	Hour	Summary of Events and Information	Remarks and references to Appendices
Front Line (Left) BOIRY ST MARTIN	1/5/18		Fine day. Enemy Machine Guns very active. 1 Other Rank wounded	
"	2/5/18		Fine day. Inter Company Relief. "D" Coy relieved "A" on the Right "B" Coy relieved "C" on the left. "A" Coy to Support "C" Coy to Reserve. 2/Lieuts A. P. BURNET. O. F. WOODCOCK and H. B. LEVER joined Battalion for duty. Sgt Rumble D.C.M. M.M (i/c Stretcher Bearers) wounded	
"	3/5/18		Fine day. Considerable Trench Mortar & Artillery Activity. Boundary adjusted. Nos 1 & 2 Posts handed to Right Battn. 2/Lt F. H. BROWN to Hospital	
"	4/5/18		Fine day. Artillery & T. M. activity. Organised retaliation by 18 pounders & 6" guns. Not very satisfactory. Readjustment of left Boundary. See O.O. 176 attached. Two American officers attached for instruction. During night 4 horses killed & 3 wounded at Forward Transport	

A7092). Wt. W12839/M1293 750,000. 1/17. D. D & L., Ltd. Forms/C2118/14.

CONFIDENTIAL

Army Form C. 2118.

WAR DIARY
or
INTELLIGENCE SUMMARY.
(*Erase heading not required.*)

Instructions regarding War Diaries and Intelligence Summaries are contained in F. S. Regs., Part II. and the Staff Manual respectively. Title pages will be prepared in manuscript.

Sheet No 401

Place	Date	Hour	Summary of Events and Information	Remarks and references to Appendices
Front Line (Left) BOIRY ST MARTIN	5/5/18		Dull day. Some rain. A few Trench Mortars otherwise quiet. Relief by 1st Bn K.R.R.C. Operation Order No 177 attached. Relief complete 1-45 a.m. Casualties 1 killed & 1 wounded	
BRIGADE RESERVE PURPLE LINE	6/5/18		Back Areas shelled by enemy. Direct hit on Gunpit occupied by "B" Coy. 3 Killed 1 wounded. Captain BAZETT goes on Sniping & Scouting course & relinquishes appointment of Acting Adjutant. Captain PUGH takes over Acting Adjutant. Captain F. D. BAZETT LIEUT SHIPTON 2/Lt SPENCER & LORD & the REV. C. H. BELL C.F. awarded the Military Cross	
"	7/5/18		Back areas shelled by enemy. 2/Lieuts SPENCER & LORD appointed Acting Captains. Battalion Headquarters moved from BLAIREVILLE to trench at X 14 b 1.6 LIEUT H. E. BALDWIN 2/Lieuts J. S. PEARCE A. L. ROW F. H. McGEE joined Battn 2/Lt F. B. REYNOLDS to Hospital	
"	8/5/18		Quiet day. Relieved 23rd R.F. in Front Line Right Sector. Companies disposed of as follows. "A" Coy Right Front "B" Coy Support "C" Coy Left Front "D" Coy Reserve	

A7092) Wt. W12839/M1293 750,000. 1/17. D. D & L., Ltd. Forms/C2118/14.

Instructions regarding War Diaries and Intelligence Summaries are contained in F. S. Regs., Part II. and the Staff Manual respectively. Title pages will be prepared in manuscript.

WAR DIARY
or
INTELLIGENCE SUMMARY.
(Erase heading not required.)

CONFIDENTIAL Army Form C. 2118.

Sheet No 402

Place	Date	Hour	Summary of Events and Information	Remarks and references to Appendices
Front Line (Right) BOIRY-ST-MARTIN	9/5/18		Weather continues fine. Quiet day. Raid by 1st K.R.R.C. on left. No result. Casualties 6 wounded by our own barrage. Tremendous "Wind" from behind	
"	10/5/18		Weather dull. Situation normal. "Wind" from rear increases. 2/Lt FEATHERSTONE & 11 other ranks go on fighting patrol to secure an identification. No identification secured. Left Coy. heavily shelled but no enemy action followed. Casualties 4 other ranks	
"	11/5/18		Very quiet day. HENDECOURT gassed (mustard). Reconnoitring Patrol 2/Lt BERESFORD & 3 other ranks. Enemy work discovered & rifle (new) brought in. 2/Lt REYNOLDS rejoined from Hospital	

A7092I. Wt. W12839/M1293 750,000. 1/17. D. D & L., Ltd. Forms/C2118/14.

Instructions regarding War Diaries and Intelligence Summaries are contained in F. S. Regs., Part II. and the Staff Manual respectively. Title pages will be prepared in manuscript.

WAR DIARY
or
INTELLIGENCE SUMMARY.
(Erase heading not required.)

CONFIDENTIAL

Army Form C. 2118.

Sheet No 403

Place	Date	Hour	Summary of Events and Information	Remarks and references to Appendices
Frontline (Right) BOIRY ST MARTIN	12/5/18		Very quiet day. Relieved by 10th Bn Argyle & Sutherland Highlanders. Relief complete 2 a.m. See O.O. No 178. Battalion embussed at RANSART & debussed at Billets in LAHERLIERE	
LAHERLIERE CORPS RESERVE	13/5/18		Arrived in billets 6 a.m. Cleaning up. Capt B. BARNFATHER M.C. joined Battalion	
"	14/5/18		C Coy bathed in afternoon. Training 9 - 12 - 30 Fine weather.	
"	15/5/18		Training 9 - 12 - 30. Inspection by B. General IRONSIDE commanding 99th Bde. 2/Lt KOTCHIE joined Battn & posted to "A" Company	

CONFIDENTIAL

Army Form C. 2118.

Instructions regarding War Diaries and Intelligence Summaries are contained in F. S. Regs., Part II. and the Staff Manual respectively. Title pages will be prepared in manuscript.

WAR DIARY
or
INTELLIGENCE SUMMARY.
(*Erase heading not required.*)

Sheet No 404

Place	Date	Hour	Summary of Events and Information	Remarks and references to Appendices
LAHERLIERE CORPS RESERVE	16/5/18		Very hot day. Inspection by Maj. Gen. PEREIRA commanding 2nd Division. Test have successfully carried out. Troops stopped on way to rendezvous & inspected by Brig Gen IRONSIDE	
			Training 9 - 12 - 30.	
			Riding school commenced under 2/Lt BRYAN Transport Officer.	
			Gas Test all Companies & Headquarters in afternoon.	
			Concert given by "D" Coy in evening.	
	17/5/18		Training 9 - 12 - 30. Inspection by Major General PEREIRA commanding 2nd Div. Bombed in evening by enemy. Casualties 2 Killed (Sgt Hearn & Pte Clark) 7 Wounded. Very hot day. American platoon with 1 officer attached for training.	
	18/5/18		Training 9 - 12 - 30. A & D Companies changed billets going under Canvas in order to avoid enemy aeroplane bombs. Brig Gen IRONSIDE	

A7092). Wt. W12839/M1293 750,000. 1/17. D. D & L., Ltd. Forms/C2118/14.

Instructions regarding War Diaries and Intelligence Summaries are contained in F. S. Regs., Part II. and the Staff Manual respectively. Title pages will be prepared in manuscript.

WAR DIARY
or
INTELLIGENCE SUMMARY.
(Erase heading not required.)

CONFIDENTIAL Army Form C. 2118.

Sheet No 405

Place	Date	Hour	Summary of Events and Information	Remarks and references to Appendices
LAHERLIERE			dined with Battalion. Very hot day. Concert in evening by	
CORPS	18/5/18		2nd Div. Troupe & Band. Band played at Mess in	
RESERVE			evening. American platoon returned. Lorries very late in arriving	
	19/5/18		Very hot day. Divine Service 10-45 a.m. limited to	
			50 per company. Concert in evening by 2nd Div Troupe and	
			Band. Band played at Mess in evening	
	20/5/18		Training 9-12-30. Very hot day. Another American	
			Platoon arrived (attached to "D" Company for training). 2 officers (1 Capt & 1 Lieutenant of American	
			Army attached for instruction)	
			Boxing competition in evening. Guest night ~~[illegible]~~.	
			Very hot day. Lt E. J. Cox joined Battalion & posted	
			to "C" Coy	

A7092. Wt. W12839/M1293 750,000. 1/17. D. D & L., Ltd. Forms/C2118/14.

Instructions regarding War Diaries and Intelligence Summaries are contained in F. S. Regs., Part II. and the Staff Manual respectively. Title pages will be prepared in manuscript.

WAR DIARY
or
INTELLIGENCE SUMMARY.
(Erase heading not required.)

CONFIDENTIAL

Army Form C. 2118.

Sheet No 406

Place	Date	Hour	Summary of Events and Information	Remarks and references to Appendices
LAHERLIERE CORPS RESERVE	21/5/18		Training 9-12-30. American platoon attached to "C" Coy. Very hot day. American platoon returned to Billets at MONDICOURT	
	22/5/18		Another American platoon attached for training to "C" Coy. Training 9-12-30. Inspection by G.O.C VIth Corps (Lt-Gen HALDANE). Capt BARNFATHER M.C. attached to 2nd South Staffords	
	23/5/18		Training commenced at 7-30 a.m. Tactical scheme carried out. Brig-Gen present. Inspection of Brigade (99th) by Corps Commander in afternoon. American platoon returned to Billets at MONDICOURT. A little cooler but still very hot weather	

A7092). Wt. W12839/M1293 750,000. 1/17. D. D & L., Ltd. Forms/C2118/14.

CONFIDENTIAL

WAR DIARY
or
INTELLIGENCE SUMMARY.
(*Erase heading not required.*)

Sheet No 407

Army Form C. 2118.

Instructions regarding War Diaries and Intelligence Summaries are contained in F. S. Regs., Part II. and the Staff Manual respectively. Title pages will be prepared in manuscript.

Place	Date	Hour	Summary of Events and Information	Remarks and references to Appendices
LANERUERE CORPS RESERVE	24/5/18		Wet day. Training in the morning. American platoon attached for training with "C" Company. Guest night. Maj-General PEREIRA dined with Battalion.	
	25.5.18		Fine day, rather cool. Training in the morning. Lieut F. LAWSON transferred to 2nd Batt. R. Berks. R. American Platoon returned to Billets at MONDICOURT	
	26.5.18		Fine day. Church Parade in the morning.	
	27.5.18		Training in the morning. 23rd Royal Fusiliers & 2nd Division H.Q held sports in the afternoon. Tug of War at 23rd R. F. sports won by Battalion Team. Fine day American Company (Capt STURGIS in command) attached to Batt. for training	
	28.5.18		Fine day. Training in the morning. Commanding Officer (Lt Col. R. J. BRETT) Capt F. D. BAZETT MC & No 8985 C.S.M. J. CLARKE mentioned in despatches. American Company returned to Billets at MONDICOURT	

A7092) Wt. W12839/M1293 750,000. 1/17. D. D & L., Ltd. Forms/C2118/14.

Instructions regarding War Diaries and Intelligence Summaries are contained in F. S. Regs., Part II. and the Staff Manual respectively. Title pages will be prepared in manuscript.

WAR DIARY
or
INTELLIGENCE SUMMARY.
(Erase heading not required.)

CONFIDENTIAL

Army Form C. 2118.

Sheet No 408

Place	Date	Hour	Summary of Events and Information	Remarks and references to Appendices
LAHERLIERE CORPS RESERVE	29.5.18		Fine day. C & D Coys occupied an outpost Line & were attacked by A & B Coys. Corps Commander (Lt Gen HALDANE) was present. Outpost Line in LABAZEQUE WOOD. Dinners were had in the wood after the scheme. Lieut R. E. POWELL rejoined Battalion & posted to "D" Coy	
	30.5.18		Fine day. Training in the morning. 1st K. R. R. held sports in the afternoon. LLOYD - LINDSAY Race for N. C. O's won by team from this Battalion.	
	31.5.18		Fine day. Training in the morning	
Synopsis 13.5.18 to 31.5.18			During this period of Corps Reserve progressive training was carried out (Training programmes attached). The weather was very fine & the ~~marked~~ difference in the military Knowledge & physical fitness of the men was most marked. On coming into ~~the line~~ Corps Reserve the Battalion consisted mainly of Raw material but at the	

A7092. Wt. W12839/M1293 750,000. 1/17. D. D & L., Ltd. Forms/C2118/14.

Army Form C. 2118.

WAR DIARY

or

~~INTELLIGENCE SUMMARY.~~

(Erase heading not required.)

Sheet No 409

Instructions regarding War Diaries and Intelligence Summaries are contained in F. S. Regs., Part II. and the Staff Manual respectively. Title pages will be prepared in manuscript.

Place	Date	Hour	Summary of Events and Information	Remarks and references to Appendices
LAHERLIERE CORPS RESERVE			time of writing the majority of the men are well trained and efficient soldiers.	
			A Platoon Football Competion was held & was won by No 13 Platoon.	
			The Company Football competition was won by "D" Coy.	
			A Lorry was allotted to the Battalion every third day to take 25 men to DOULLENS	
			Casualties during the month of May	
			Officers Killed NIL Wounded NIL Missing NIL.	
			O. R's " 6 " 20 " NIL.	

A7092/. Wt. W12839/M1293 750,000. 1/17. D. D & L., Ltd. Forms/C2118/14.

11

Instructions regarding War Diaries and Intelligence Summaries are contained in F. S. Regs., Part II. and the Staff Manual respectively. Title pages will be prepared in manuscript.

Army Form C. 2118.

WAR DIARY
or
~~INTELLIGENCE SUMMARY~~.
(Erase heading not required.)

Sheet No 410

Place	Date	Hour	Summary of Events and Information	Remarks and references to Appendices
LAHERLIERE CORPS RESERVE	31/5/18		EFFECTIVE STRENGTH 1/5/18 Officers 33 O. R's	1197
			EFFECTIVE STRENGTH 31/5/18. — " — 39 — " —	1165
			RATION STRENGTH 1/5/18 Officers 25 O R	771
			RATION STRENGTH 31/5/18 — " — 28 — " —	1076
			Lieut (a/Captain M.P. PUGH) M.C was awarded the D.S.O for conspicuous gallantry and good work when he took over command of the battalion on March 23rd when Lieut. Colonel Hunt was killed.	

VM Anderson Major
1/R. Berks. Regt.

A7092). Wt. W12839/M1293 750,000. 1/17. D. D & L., Ltd. Forms/C2118/14.

99/2

Instructions regarding War Diaries and Intelligence Summaries are contained in F. S. Regs., Part II. and the Staff Manual respectively. Title pages will be prepared in manuscript.

WAR DIARY
or
~~INTELLIGENCE SUMMARY.~~
(Erase heading not required.)

CONFIDENTIAL
1st Batt. Royal Berkshire Regt
Sheet No 411.

Army Form C. 2118.

Vol 44

Place	Date	Hour	Summary of Events and Information	Remarks and references to Appendices
LAHERLIÈRE	1/6		Village shelled in the morning with high velocity 5.9s. Capt Astley and 2 O.Ranks killed, 8 O.Ranks wounded. Usual training carried out in the morning. Battalion moved billets in the afternoon to wood near LA BAZEQUE with majority of the men in shelters constructed in trenches, remainder under canvas. C.O. Adjutant and Signal Officer on Brigade Staff ride in the afternoon. Battalion H.Q. V.20 c 8.2.	BUCQUOY Combined Sheet 1/40,000.
LA BAZEQUE	2/6		No training – C of E Church parade in woods in the morning. Funeral in the afternoon WARLINCOURT HALTE Cemetery (Capt ASTLEY and 2 O.Ranks) – a fine day.	
	3/6		Training continued – A and C Companies to Baths at LAHERLIÈRE. B and D Company rifle meeting.	
	4/6		Fine day. Training as usual. B and D Companies to Baths.	
	5/6		C.O. and one officer per company reconnoitred forward area prior to relieving Guards Division – 2/Lieuts. H.M. AVERY, S.C. BERESFORD, A.L. ROW. M.M. killed, 2/Lieut (Act/Capt) J.H. SPENCER. M.C. wounded & died of wounds later at C.C.S. Lt Col R.J. BRETT wounded.	

A5834. Wt. W4973/M687 750,000 8/16 D. D. & L. Ltd. Forms/C.2118/13.

Army Form C. 2118.

Instructions regarding War Diaries and Intelligence Summaries are contained in F. S. Regs., Part II. and the Staff Manual respectively. Title pages will be prepared in manuscript.

WAR DIARY
or
INTELLIGENCE SUMMARY.
(Erase heading not required.)

Sheet. N° 412

Place	Date	Hour	Summary of Events and Information	Remarks and references to Appendices
			In the evening Concert given to battalion by Divisional troupe and band - Stage erected by pioneers in the wood.	
LA BAZEQUE	6/6		Fine day - Training, as usual, carried out, with particular attention paid to Open Warfare - Major G.B. ANDERSON M.C. and one Officer per Company reconnoitred forward areas.	
	7/6		Fine - The day devoted to cleaning up and resting - In the morning funeral of three deceased Officers (2/Lieuts Avery, Beresford and Row.) In the evening battalion left LA BAZEQUE at 7 pm. and proceeded to MONCHY-AU-BOIS by light Railway - Relieved	BUCQUOY. Combined Sheet 1/40,000
	8/6		2nd battalion Scots Guards in the Right Sector - Casualties Nil.	
In The Line			Relief Complete 12.30 am - Operation Order N° 179 attached - B and D Companies front line - C in Support, A in Reserve Battalion HQ. F.15.c.2.1 - Slight shelling of batt. HQ from 9 to 10 am	
	9/6		Transport & details moved to St AMAND - Good billets - Casualties Nil	
	9/6		Fine day - Hostile artillery active on back areas - Quiet day on battalion front. Casualties - Nil -	

Instructions regarding War Diaries and Intelligence Summaries are contained in F. S. Regs., Part II. and the Staff Manual respectively. Title pages will be prepared in manuscript.

WAR DIARY
or
~~INTELLIGENCE SUMMARY.~~

(Erase heading not required.)

Army Form C. 2118.

Sheet No 413

Place	Date	Hour	Summary of Events and Information	Remarks and references to Appendices
	10/6		Hostile artillery still very active on back areas especially round QUESNOY FARM – D Company worried by T.M's in the morning – Inter Company relief in the Evening A and C front line B Support, D Reserve Casualties 2 OR killed. Capt LORD MC. MM. rejoined from leave, Capt TALBOT M.C. from 2nd Army School 2nd Lieut V.G. STOKES M.C. from England took over Command of D Company.	
	11/6		Fine day – Quiet on battalion front, usual shelling of back areas Lieut Col D.W. POWELL Northamptonshire Regt joined battalion to Command Casualties Nil –	
	12/6		Quiet day – 100 O.Ranks proceeded to join 5th Bn Royal Berkshire Regt. Casualties Nil.	
	13/6		Quiet day – The battalion relieved by 23rd R. Fusiliers and went into Brigade Reserve – B and D Companies forward in the PURPLE System with Company HQ near QUESNOY FARM, C and D Companies in Old German line in E 11 b battalion HQ E.5.d 2.1.	

A5834 Wt. W4973/M687 750,000 8/16 D. D. & L. Ltd. Forms/C.2118/13.

Army Form C. 2118.

Instructions regarding War Diaries and Intelligence Summaries are contained in F. S. Regs., Part II. and the Staff Manual respectively. Title pages will be prepared in manuscript.

WAR DIARY
~~or~~
~~INTELLIGENCE SUMMARY.~~ WM Sheet No. 414
(*Erase heading not required.*)

Place	Date	Hour	Summary of Events and Information	Remarks and references to Appendices
	14/6		Relief Complete and Companies Settled in new areas 3 am. Fine day - resting and cleaning up. Casualties - Nil.	WMM
	15/6		Fine - Companies bathed at MONCHY - B and D Companies reserve platoons shelled in the morning - 3 OR Killed - 6 OR wounded. Lieut E. J. Cox, Mtd. Duty, to England for transfer to M.G. Corps.	WMM
	16/6		Fine. Burial of 3 OR at St AMAND (Killed previous day). Battalion relieved 1/K.R.R.C in the LEFT Subsector - 2/Lieuts LEVER WOODCOCK, KOTCHIE [illegible] to 2nd Northamptonshire Regt - Lieut THORBY and BOORA joined battalion	WMM
	17/6		Relief Complete 12 20 am - Quiet day on battalion front. Capt E M ALLFREY DSO joined for duty. Casualties. Nil	WMM
	18/6		Quiet day on battalion front. Artillery of both sides active on back areas. 2/Lieut BOORA to hospital	WMM
	19/6		Weather showery, Enemy artillery active round QUESNOY FARM during the morning - Capt E M ALLFREY DSO took over Command of A Company in the line. Casualties. Nil -	WMM
	20/6	1.30am	Enemy Commenced Shelling Right battalion HQ and JEWEL Valley with HE and	

A5834 Wt. W4973/M687 750,000 8/16 D. D. & L. Ltd. Forms/C.2118/13.

Army Form C. 2118.

Instructions regarding War Diaries and Intelligence Summaries are contained in F. S. Regs., Part II. and the Staff Manual respectively. Title pages will be prepared in manuscript.

WAR DIARY
or
~~INTELLIGENCE SUMMARY.~~ [initials]

(*Erase heading not required.*)

Sheet No 415.

Place	Date	Hour	Summary of Events and Information	Remarks and references to Appendices
			Gas Shell – Gas blew down Valley – Grade Concentration near Support HQ. All clear as far as battalion was concerned 2.15 am	
	20/6		Dull day. Boche aeroplane low over our lines from 9.30 am to 10 am. MG, Lewis Guns opened fire, also a battery of 18 pdrs – 2/Lieuts Featherstone & Ayres left line in the evening for Course of instruction. "L" Cpl Wells to transport prior to proceeding to Signalling Course at DUNSTAPLE. Casualties Nil	[initials]
	21/6		Weather Showery – Quiet day on battalion front	[initials]
	22/6		Dull day – Trenches very sticky – usual low flying boche plane in morning – fired on by Lewis and Machine Guns. Relieved by 23rd R. Fusiliers and moved into Reserve.	[initials]
	23/6		Relief complete in the line 12.15 am. Day rather cold. Nothing of note happened – 1/Kings band played a programme during afternoon and evening at [illegible] HQ	[initials]
	24/6		Weather Cold and dull. Reorganisation of battalion under GHQ letter – double Lewis Gun sections in platoons.	[initials]

Instructions regarding War Diaries and Intelligence Summaries are contained in F. S. Regs., Part II. and the Staff Manual respectively. Title pages will be prepared in manuscript.

WAR DIARY
or
INTELLIGENCE SUMMARY
(*Erase heading not required.*)

Army Form C. 2118.

Sheet No 416

Place	Date	Hour	Summary of Events and Information	Remarks and references to Appendices
	25/6		Weather fine but cold. Battalion relieved 1/KRRC in Right Sub Sector in the Evening – Quiet relief – MM	
	26/6		Relief Complete 12.40 am – ~~weather cold windy~~ MM Quiet Day on battalion front – 1 OR wounded, but remained at duty. MM	
	27/6		Weather fine – nothing of note happened. MM	
	28/6		Fine Day, Enemy shelled vicinity of HQ with about 60, 105 mm shell mostly instantaneous fuze. no damage – A patrol of B Company under 2/Lieut MURRAY, having completed their reconnaissance, encountered a large enemy patrol about 20–25 strong near our line – Enemy patrol at once threw a shower of bombs – wounding 2/Lieut Murray and 2 O.Ranks – Our patrol at once opened rapid fire and threw several bombs. Enemy fled – Ground was searched but no identification was obtained – A later patrol discovered a body killed about 7 to 10 days previously – Shoulder straps marked 7, cap, and oddments were brought in. MM	

A5834 Wt. W4973/M687 750,000 8/16 D. D. & L. Ltd. Forms/C.2118/13.

Instructions regarding War Diaries and Intelligence Summaries are contained in F. S. Regs., Part II. and the Staff Manual respectively. Title pages will be prepared in manuscript.

WAR DIARY
or
INTELLIGENCE SUMMARY
(Erase heading not required.)

Sheet No 417.

Army Form C. 2118.

Place	Date	Hour	Summary of Events and Information	Remarks and references to Appendices
	29/6		Fine day. Five men commenced to complain of severe headaches & pains. 3 men to hospital. Quiet day in the line	
	30/6		Fine day. Nothing of special note happened. Battalion relieved by 23rd R Fusiliers. 6 men to hospital with Epidemic.	
			Effective strength 1st week in June — Officers 33, O Ranks 1145	
			Ration " — 21, 949	
			Effective 11th " — 35, 999	
			Ration " — 24, 790	
			Killed in action 1st " — 5, 3	
			Wounded " — 1, 7	
			Killed in action 2nd " — 2	
			Wounded — 1	
			Killed in action 3rd — 3	
			Wounded " — 7	
			Wounded 4th " — 2	
			Casualties for Month of June — K W M.	
			Officers — 5 1 0	
			O Ranks — 8 17 0	

K. W. Powell Lt Col
Cmdg 1/Royal Berkshire Regt

A5834 Wt. W4973/M687 750,000 8/16 D. D. & L. Ltd. Forms/C.2118/13.

Instructions regarding War Diaries and Intelligence Summaries are contained in F. S. Regs., Part II. and the Staff Manual respectively. Title pages will be prepared in manuscript.

WAR DIARY
or
INTELLIGENCE SUMMARY.
(*Erase heading not required.*)

Army Form C. 2118.

Confidential
1 R Berks R
Sheet No 418
Vol 45

Place	Date	Hour	Summary of Events and Information	Remarks and references to Appendices
BRIGADE RESERVE near MONCHY	July 1		Day fine & bright but very cold. The influenza epidemic still prevailing 29 reporting sick of whom 10 were admitted to Hospital	
	2		Nothing of importance happened throughout the day. Very cold & windy. 37 O.R. reported sick with the epidemic 17 being admitted to hospital	
	3		Large numbers again on sick parade. Companies getting rather weak in numbers. 10 men admitted to hospital & the Commanding Officer & Adjutant confined to bed	
	4		Nothing of importance happened. 15 O.R admitted to hospital with epidemic	

A5834 Wt. W4973/M687 750,000 8/16 D. D. & L. Ltd. Forms/C.2118/13.

Instructions regarding War Diaries and Intelligence Summaries are contained in F. S. Regs., Part II. and the Staff Manual respectively. Title pages will be prepared in manuscript.

WAR DIARY
or
INTELLIGENCE SUMMARY.
(*Erase heading not required.*)

Army Form C. 2118.

Sheet No 419.

Place	Date	Hour	Summary of Events and Information	Remarks and references to Appendices
	July ~~4~~ 5		Epidemic still very prevalent. following Officers having to go to Transport Capts Allfrey, Pugh & Talbot. 2/Lieut Herring admitted to Hospital. 2/Lieut Catchpole joined Battalion from Base, taken on strength & posted to 'A' Coy. 13 O.R admitted to hospital with epidemic. Battalion relieved 1/K.R.R.C in Left Sub-sector. Relief complete 12-40 a.m 6th July	
IN THE LINE LEFT SECTOR	6		Weather fine and bright, nothing of importance happened throughout the day. 7 O.R. to hospital	
NEAR DOUCHY	7		Fine day. Very quiet in the line. Aerial activity on both sides during the morning. Slight decrease in number of	

A5834 Wt. W4973/M687 750,000 8/16 D. D. & L. Ltd. Forms/C.2118/13.

Instructions regarding War Diaries and Intelligence Summaries are contained in F. S. Regs., Part II. and the Staff Manual respectively. Title pages will be prepared in manuscript.

WAR DIARY
or
INTELLIGENCE SUMMARY.
(Erase heading not required.)

Army Form C. 2118.

Sheet No 4 20

Place	Date	Hour	Summary of Events and Information	Remarks and references to Appendices
	7		influenza cases. Capt Allfrey & 2/Lt Bryan admitted to hospital. 2/Lieut Catling joined Battalion & posted to D Coy	
	8		Weather still fine & bright. Everything very quiet. Capt Allfrey rejoined from Hospital	
	9		Weather dull and threatening with rain, slight drizzle in afternoon for about an hour. Hostile aeroplane crossed our lines at a low altitude but was driven away by 18 pounders and Machine Guns. 8 extra Lewis Guns drawn thus bringing the number up to 36 for the Battalion	

A5834 Wt. W4973/M687 750,000 8/16 D. D. & L. Ltd. Forms/C.2118/13.

Instructions regarding War Diaries and Intelligence Summaries are contained in F. S. Regs., Part II. and the Staff Manual respectively. Title pages will be prepared in manuscript.

WAR DIARY
or
INTELLIGENCE SUMMARY.
(Erase heading not required.)

Army Form C. 2118.

Sheet No 421

Place	Date	Hour	Summary of Events and Information	Remarks and references to Appendices
	July 10		Weather fine and bright but very windy. Enemy shelled vicinity of QUESNOY FARM with gas shells at 8 a.m. Our aeroplanes very active over enemys' line during the morning. Throughout the remainder of the day nothing else of importance happened	
	11		Enemy aerial activity. One flew over our lines at a very low altitude & was driven off by Rifle and Machine Gun fire. Nothing of importance happened for the remainder of the day. At 10-15 p.m a test S.O.S was sent up by "B" Coy. The grenade was a Dud: Another was sent up by Batt. H.Q at 10-22 p.m. and taken up from QUESNOY FARM and RESERVE Batt H.Q. Batteries opened very rapidly & the test was quite successful	

Instructions regarding War Diaries and Intelligence Summaries are contained in F. S. Regs., Part II. and the Staff Manual respectively. Title pages will be prepared in manuscript.

WAR DIARY
or
INTELLIGENCE SUMMARY.
(*Erase heading not required.*)

Army Form C. 2118.

Sheet No 422

Place	Date	Hour	Summary of Events and Information	Remarks and references to Appendices
	JULY 12		Nothing of importance happened throughout the day with exception of aerial activity on both sides. 2 Lieut G. Byst joined Battalion & posted to "B" Company	
	13		All quiet throughout the day with exception of aerial activity which was very marked.	
	14		Weather dull with occasional showers throughout the day. Hostile artillery active on our batteries at intervals during the day. Battalion on our LEFT (1st KINGS. 6th Brigade) carried out a raid on the enemy outpost line. Result. 9 prisoners taken enemy work destroyed.	

Instructions regarding War Diaries and Intelligence Summaries are contained in F. S. Regs., Part II. and the Staff Manual respectively. Title pages will be prepared in manuscript.

WAR DIARY
or
INTELLIGENCE SUMMARY.
(*Erase heading not required.*)

Army Form C. 2118.

Sheet No. 423.

Place	Date	Hour	Summary of Events and Information	Remarks and references to Appendices
	JULY 15		Fine day. Visibility poor owing to low clouds. Artillery quiet on both sides throughout the day. Battalion relieved by 23rd Royal Fusiliers. Relief complete 10-25 p.m.	
BRIGADE RESERVE NEAR MONCHY	16		Fine day. Battalion having been ordered to carry out a raid in the near future, B & D Coys selected to do same with Capt V. G STOKES M.C. in command. Tapes were laid out & practice for the raid commenced. BRIG. GEN. IRONSIDE (Cmdg 99th Bde) was present at practice	
	17		Fine day. Practice for raid continued	
	18		do do	

Army Form C. 2118.

Sheet No 424

WAR DIARY
or
INTELLIGENCE SUMMARY.
(Erase heading not required.)

Instructions regarding War Diaries and Intelligence Summaries are contained in F. S. Regs., Part II. and the Staff Manual respectively. Title pages will be prepared in manuscript.

Place	Date	Hour	Summary of Events and Information	Remarks and references to Appendices
	July 19		Fine day. GENERAL BYNG (Cmdg 3rd Army) LIEUT GEN HALDANE (Cmdg VIth Corps)	
			MAJ. GEN PEREIRA (Cmdg 2nd Div) & the Brigadier were present at the practice for the raid. Everything was considered satisfactory & valuable suggestions made which were incorporated in the scheme	
FRONT LINE RIGHT SUB SECTOR	20		Batt. Relieved 1/K. R. R. C in Right sub-sector. Relief complete at 9-15 p.m	
	21		Very quiet day. 2 O. R wounded coming up with rations. Artillery active on back areas	
	22		Fine day one O. R. wounded. Nothing of importance happened. Lieut DEMPSEY. 2/Lts KIRBY. TITLEY. GREAVES. JACOBS & WINSTANLEY joined Battalion	

A5834 Wt. W4973/M687 750,000 8/16 D. D. & L. Ltd. Forms/C.2118/13.

Instructions regarding War Diaries and Intelligence Summaries are contained in F. S. Regs., Part II. and the Staff Manual respectively. Title pages will be prepared in manuscript.

WAR DIARY
or
INTELLIGENCE SUMMARY.
(Erase heading not required.)

Army Form C. 2118.

Sheet No 425

Place	Date	Hour	Summary of Events and Information	Remarks and references to Appendices
	July 23		At 12-30 a.m. a raid was carried out by the Battalion against enemy lines in vicinity of ABLAINZEVILLE. The party consisted of 6 officers and 203 other ranks with Capt V. G. STOKES M.C. in command. The raid was very successful. 5 prisoners being obtained & about 50 killed exclusive of those killed by our barrage. Our casualties were 1 Officer killed 2/Lt F. S. BOSHELL. 1 Officer wounded 2/Lt BYSH & 31 O.R. wounded. Most of the wounds were very slight indeed. The enemy put down a heavy barrage ~~but all w~~ & some gas shells but all was quiet about 2 a.m.	
	24		Very dull day. Nothing of importance happened	
	25		Dull day, occasional showers. Nothing of importance happened	

A5834 Wt. W4973/M687 750,000 8/16 D. D. & L. Ltd. Forms/C.2118/13.

Instructions regarding War Diaries and Intelligence Summaries are contained in F. S. Regs., Part II. and the Staff Manual respectively. Title pages will be prepared in manuscript.

WAR DIARY
or
INTELLIGENCE SUMMARY.
(Erase heading not required.)

Army Form C. 2118.

Sheet No 426

Place	Date	Hour	Summary of Events and Information	Remarks and references to Appendices
	July 26		Very dull & showery. Artillery active on back areas. otherwise nothing of note happened	
	27		Fine day. Aerial activity & usual harassing fire on back areas	
	28		Fine day. Nothing of importance happened during the day.	
	29		Very fine day. Enemy artillery more active, on support lines and near CALVERLEY COPSE	
	30		Fine day. Batt. relieved by 23rd Royal Fusiliers. Very quiet relief, which was complete by 8-50 p.m	

A5834 Wt. W4973/M687 750,000 8/16 D. D. & L. Ltd. Forms/C.2118/13.

Instructions regarding War Diaries and Intelligence Summaries are contained in F. S. Regs., Part II. and the Staff Manual respectively. Title pages will be prepared in manuscript.

WAR DIARY
or
INTELLIGENCE SUMMARY.
(Erase heading not required.)

Army Form C. 2118.

Sheet No. 427.

Place	Date	Hour	Summary of Events and Information	Remarks and references to Appendices
BRIGADE RESERVE NEAR MONCHY	JULY 31		Fine day. Men cleaning up. Nothing of importance happened	
			Effective Strength 1. 7. 18 35 Officers 948 Other Ranks	
			Ration Strength 1. 7. 18 20 Officers 714 Other Ranks	
			Effective Strength 31. 7. 18 38 Officers 922 Other Ranks	
			Ration Strength 31. 7. 18 27 Officers 699 Other Ranks	
			Casualties for month	
			Officers. 1 Killed 1 Wounded 0 Missing	
			Other Ranks. 4 Killed 42 Wounded 0 Missing.	
			E W Powell Lieut. Colonel Comndg 1st Bn Berks Regt	

A5834 Wt. W4973/M687 750,000 8/16 D. D. & L. Ltd. Forms/C.2118/13.

Instructions regarding War Diaries and Intelligence Summaries are contained in F. S. Regs., Part II. and the Staff Manual respectively. Title pages will be prepared in manuscript.

CONFIDENTIAL

WAR DIARY
or
~~INTELLIGENCE SUMMARY~~.
(Erase heading not required.)

Army Form C. 2118.

Sheet No 428

99

2/1 R. Berks Regt.
KERTILLERS
1/20 000.

Place	Date	Hour	Summary of Events and Information	Remarks and references to Appendices
MONCHY.	1/8/18		Weather fine. A and B Companies bathed at MONCHY.	
"	2/8/18		Very dull and showery. Battalion HQ, C and D Companies bathed at MONCHY.	MLL
"	3/8/18		Showery. Vicinity of QUESNOY FARM shelled during the morning. Casualties 1 O.R. killed 2 ORs wounded.	MLL
"	4/8/18		Battalion relieved 1st K.R.R.C in left sub-sector: C Company taking over the whole front. B Coy in support A and D Coys in reserve. Relief complete at 9.20 pm	MLL
Front line near AYETTE.	5/8/18		Day very dull and wet. Orders were received for the whole Bde. front to be taken over by the Battalion: accordingly 23rd R. Fus. were relieved in R. sub-sector. Bn HQ remained at F.9.B. A Company right front, C Company left front, D Company right support B Company left support. Relief complete 6 PM.	MLL
"	6/8/18		Weather wet. Day very quiet. 2/Lt CUMMING and 2/Lt MEADE joined the Battalion.	MLL
"	7/8/18		Day very quiet.	MLL
"	8/8/18		Day quiet. A and C Companies were relieved by D and B Companies respectively: relief complete at 7.35 PM.	MLL
"	9/8/18.		Day quiet.	MLL

A5834 Wt. W4973/M687 750,000 8/16 D. D. & L. Ltd. Forms/C.2118/13.

Sheet No 429

Army Form C. 2118.

Instructions regarding War Diaries and Intelligence Summaries are contained in F. S. Regs., Part II. and the Staff Manual respectively. Title pages will be prepared in manuscript.

WAR DIARY

or

~~INTELLIGENCE SUMMARY.~~

(Erase heading not required.)

Place	Date	Hour	Summary of Events and Information	Remarks and references to Appendices
Front line near AYETTE	10/8/18		Weather fine. Day very quiet. MCC	
"	11/8/18		Nothing of importance happened during the day. Hostile aircraft were active over our lines during the evening. MCC	
	12/8/18		Day very quiet. Lt HUMBLEY rejoined from Hospital. In the evening the Battn. was relieved by 1/K.R.R.C. and moved into Support positions, Bn HQ remained in the old position. MCC	
Support Positions behind DOUCHY.	13/8/18		About 150 rounds of Gas Shell fell in the vicinity of QUESNOY FARM at 9.45 PM – otherwise very quiet. MCC	
	14/8/18		At 2.30am 1/KRRC and 1/KINGS raided enemy posts in front of AYETTE At 1.30pm a wire was received stating that our patrols were entering PUISIEUX and that the enemy was shelling SERRE. Patrols were sent forward by 1/K.R.R.C. and found that the enemy were still holding MOYBLAIN Trench. A and C Companies which had been ordered to move to CALVERLEY and CARUSO Copses, returned to their old positions at about 12 midnight. Everything normal during the night. MCC	
"	15/8/18		Day very quiet. Weather fine. MCC	
"	16/8/18		The Battalion was relieved by 2/S. STAFFS 6th Inf. Bde and marched back to billets in ST AMAND. Relief was completed by 12 midnight and the Battalion arrived at billets at about 2.30AM 17/8/18. MCC	
ST AMAND	17/8/18		'A' Company bathed at HUMBERCAMP in the morning. All Officers and N.C.Os attended a lecture at LA BEZEQUE at 5PM on "Co-operation between Tanks and Infantry." MCC	

A5834 Wt. W4973/M687 750,000 8/16 D. D. & L. Ltd. Forms/C.2118/13.

Sheet No 430

Army Form C. 2118.

Ref. Map ERVILLERS 1/20'000.

Instructions regarding War Diaries and Intelligence Summaries are contained in F. S. Regs., Part II. and the Staff Manual respectively. Title pages will be prepared in manuscript.

WAR DIARY
~~or~~
INTELLIGENCE ~~SUMMARY.~~

(*Erase heading not required.*)

Place	Date	Hour	Summary of Events and Information	Remarks and references to Appendices
ST AMAND	18/8/18		Orders (attached marked 'A') were received that the Brigade would attack on the morning of the 21st inst. with the 1st R. BERKS and 23rd R. Fus in front and the 1/K.R.R.C in support. During the morning the Battalion took part in a tactical exercise in cooperation with Tanks. B C and D Companies bathed at HUMERCAMP in the afternoon. In the evening the 37th Divisional Theatre was reserved for the Battalion for a special performance.	MU
"	19/8/18		From 2pm to 7pm the Brigade carried out practice attacks with Tanks at LA BEZEQUE Wood. Preparations were continued for the forthcoming operations.	MU
"	20/8/18		The day was spent in final preparations for the attack. At 8.15pm the Battalion left St AMAND in lorries going via POMMIER to MONCHY where it debussed and marched to the jumping-off positions in front of the AYETTE - BUCQUOY Road.	MU
Near AYETTE	21/8/18		The Battalion was in position by 1.30AM. B and D Companies were to capture the 1st Objective. A and C Companies to pass through them and capture and consolidate the 2nd Objective. Six Tanks (Mark IV) to assist in the attack. At 4.55AM the attack commenced in conjunction with troops on the right and left. The morning was very misty and it was difficult to keep direction. The Tanks especially were soon in trouble and were of little assistance to the Battalion. However all objectives were captured up to time with little resistance except from isolated M Gs. and the 3rd Division passed through to capture COURCELLES and the railway beyond. Battn H.Q. were established at F18A 9.0. and at 7AM	

A5834 Wt. W4973/M687 750,000 8/16 D. D. & L. Ltd. Forms/C.2118/13.

Sheet Nº 431.

Army Form C. 2118.

Instructions regarding War Diaries and Intelligence Summaries are contained in F. S. Regs., Part II. and the Staff Manual respectively. Title pages will be prepared in manuscript.

WAR DIARY

~~or~~

~~INTELLIGENCE SUMMARY.~~

(*Erase heading not required.*)

Place	Date	Hour	Summary of Events and Information	Remarks and references to Appendices
(continued)	21/8/18		communication was open with Brigade H.Q via the old Battalion H.Q at F.16 b 8.0. At 7pm orders were received that the Bde was to be relieved by 76th Inf. Bde and would move to QUESNOY FARM and the PURPLE LINE.	(initials)
QUESNOY FARM.	22/8/18		The relief was finally completed at 6.40AM and Bn HQ and D Company reached QUESNOY FARM by 8.30AM. The men slept and rested during the day and orders were given for salvaging to be carried out in the evening. However at about 7PM the B.G.C. arrived at Bn HQ and stated that the Battalion was to come under the orders of 6th Inf. Bde. and be prepared to carry out an attack on ERVILLERS the next morning. At 9.15PM 6th Inf. Bde. Order Nº 382 was received and later G1, BMS.10 and BMS.11 (marked "B" and attached). Verbal instructions and later M.P. 598 were issued to Companies (marked "C" and attached).	(initials)
QUESNOY FARM	23/8/18		The Battalion moved off from QUESNOY FARM at 5AM by platoons to the AYETTE-BUCQUOY Road. At 7AM the road was crossed, and companies moved into position in A.7.D. Here final details for the attack on ERVILLERS were settled, and at 10AM the Battn. moved to the assembly positions in A 22 A arriving there 15 minutes before Zero. During the halt the enemy commenced shelling the assembly positions and by 11AM, when the attack commenced, a heavy barrage was down on A 16, 17, 22 and 23 squares. This barrage was shortened as the advance continued and the Battn. had some casualties including Rev. C.K BELL C.F. and Lt HUMBLEY, who were both killed. All objectives of the Brigade were captured without serious opposition from the enemy infantry, who surrendered freely as our men came near.	

A5834 Wt. W4973/M687 750,000 8/16 D. D. & L. Ltd. Forms/C.2118/13.

Sheet No 432

Army Form C. 2118.

WAR DIARY

~~or~~

~~INTELLIGENCE SUMMARY.~~

(*Erase heading not required.*)

Instructions regarding War Diaries and Intelligence Summaries are contained in F. S. Regs., Part II. and the Staff Manual respectively. Title pages will be prepared in manuscript.

Place	Date	Hour	Summary of Events and Information	Remarks and references to Appendices
	23/8/18 (continued)		The 5th Inf. Bde. on the Right failed to capture BEHAGNIES and throughout the day Field Gun and M.G. fire from the ridge N.E of BEHAGNIES was very troublesome. The final dispositions of the Battn. were:- A Company in sunken road in A 24 D. C and D Companies in ERVILLERS – BEE WOOD Trench in B.19. The 2nd S. STAFFS were holding the E. edge of the village and B Company were withdrawn to Battn. HQ. which had been established in the bank at A. 23 B 5.8. Rations and water were brought up by the Transport to Bn HQ during the night and carried to the companies by B. Company: tools and wire were carried up to the 2nd S. STAFFS.	M.K.a.
ERVILLERS	24/8/18		Dispositions the same as during the night 23/24. At 10 AM B.G.C. 99th Inf. Bde came to Bn HQ and gave orders for the Battn to get ready to attack and capture the high ground N. of MORY and get into line with the Guards Division, who were reported to be holding MORY SWITCH as far south as B.9.D 5.5. 1/K.R.R.C. to be in support and 10 Tanks (Mark V) to assist. A barrage of smoke and heavies to be placed on the high ground N.E of BEHAGNIES, which was not going to be attacked. Cavalry to follow up, and, if the opportunity occurred, to go through the Battn and turn S. - E of MORY. At the same time an attack was to be made S. of SAPIGNIES. Zero to be at 12.30 PM if possible. BM 244 and BM 245 (attached marked "D") – the latter fixing Zero for 3.30 pm – were then received. The Companies were withdrawn from their positions and the Battn assembled in the valley at Bn HQ. where orders for the attack were given verbally to Company commanders.	

A5834 Wt. W4973/M687 750,000 8/16 D. D. & L. Ltd. Forms/C.2118/13.

Sheet No 433

Army Form C. 2118.

Instructions regarding War Diaries and Intelligence Summaries are contained in F. S. Regs., Part II. and the Staff Manual respectively. Title pages will be prepared in manuscript.

WAR DIARY
~~or~~
~~INTELLIGENCE SUMMARY.~~

(Erase heading not required.)

Place	Date	Hour	Summary of Events and Information	Remarks and references to Appendices
	20/8/18 (continued)		At 2.45 PM the Battalion moved forward by platoons at 100 yards interval (keeping at the bottom of the valley N. of ERVILLERS) to the jumping off positions B. 8. c. 4.0. At 3.30 PM the barrage descended on the line B 15. A 25 – B 20 D 68 where it remained for 12 minutes, then moving forward 300 yards every 3 minutes. The Battalion came under heavy M.G fire as soon as it entered B. 15 square and was held up on the left by guns firing from the trenches in B. 15 D. Tanks and Infantry worked up on the right, and the whole line was then able to resume the advance, finishing up on the line of the sunken-road B 15 D 95.00 – MORY COPSE inclusive – MORY SWITCH: touch being obtained with the Guards in B. 9 D. Until dark M.G. fire was very heavy from the ridge N.E. of BEHAGNIES and from B 10 c and D. A large number of prisoners were captured – representing 5 different Regiments, and considerable casualties were inflicted on the enemy by Tanks and Infantry. No Officers became casualties, but 60 – 80 O.Rs. were hit: a very large percentage of these by M.G. fire. Directly our troops were on their objectives cavalry began to move up the valley in B 15 A but were unable to get through owing to the intense M. G. fire. Battalion HQ were established at B. 14 A 94, and visual communication with 99th Inf. Bde. (A 17 central) opened at 5 PM. At 8 PM a message was received that the Brigade would be relieved by a Battn. of the 187th Inf. Bde. At am the relief was completed and the Battn. assembled at Bn HQ and marched by companies to A. 17. central where a 15 minute halt was made and water issued from the 2 Battalion water-carts, which had moved forward to that point.	

A5834 Wt. W4973/M687 750,000 8/16 D. D. & L. Ltd. Forms/C. 2118/13.

Sheet No 434

Army Form C. 2118.

Instructions regarding War Diaries and Intelligence Summaries are contained in F. S. Regs., Part II. and the Staff Manual respectively. Title pages will be prepared in manuscript.

WAR DIARY

~~or~~

~~INTELLIGENCE SUMMARY.~~

(Erase heading not required.)

Place	Date	Hour	Summary of Events and Information	Remarks and references to Appendices
	24/8/18 (continued)		Orders were there received that the Battalion was to bivouac in F.12 c.: the Battn arrived there at about 5 AM 25/8/18.	
			Through the operations August 21st - 24th the weather was very hot with little wind. Supply arrangements worked very smoothly and the men were never really short of SAA, food or water. Large numbers of prisoners were captured, together with M.Gs, Rifles and countless other stores. Owing to the pace at which the operations were carried out, no attempt could be made to make even a rough list of the captured material.	
			The total casualties for the 4 days were:-	
			OFFICERS Killed. LIEUT W.L. HUMBLEY	
			Rev: C.H. BELL MC C.F.	
			Wounded CAPT LORD MC. MM., LIEUT BADWIN, 2/LIEUT BUSH, 2/LIEUT CUMMING, 2/LIEUT THORBY.	
			Other Ranks: Killed 24.	
			Wounded 196	
			Missing 7.	
			To Hospital N.Y.D. Gas. 35.	

A5834 Wt. W4973/M687 750,000 8/16 D. D. & L. Ltd. Forms/C.2118/13.

Sheet No. 435.

Army Form C. 2118.

Instructions regarding War Diaries and Intelligence Summaries are contained in F. S. Regs., Part II. and the Staff Manual respectively. Title pages will be prepared in manuscript.

WAR DIARY

~~or~~

~~INTELLIGENCE SUMMARY.~~

(*Erase heading not required.*)

Place	Date	Hour	Summary of Events and Information	Remarks and references to Appendices
Near AYETTE	25/8/18.		Battalion slept and rested during the day. In the evening the Battn. moved to the vicinity of CALVERLEY COPSE, occupying the old trenches and shelters there.	M.A.
CALVERLEY COPSE.	26/8/18 } 27/8/18 }		Battalion rested and refitted with short parades in the mornings. 2/Lts ALLSON, LANE, SAVILLE, EVANS, TOMEY and BRAYBROOKE joined.	M.A.
Near AYETTE	28/8/18			
"	29/8/18.		Companies carried out attack practices in the morning.	M.A.
"	30/8/18		The Battalion carried out an attack practice from 9.30 am – 12.30 pm.	M.A.
"	31/8/18.		Company training in the morning. Companies bathed at AYETTE during the afternoon.	M.A.

E. W. Powell Lt. Col.,
Comm^dg 1st Royal Berkshire Regt.

A5834 Wt. W4973/M687 750,000 8/16 D. D. & L. Ltd. Forms/C.2118/13.

Instructions regarding War Diaries and Intelligence Summaries are contained in F. S. Regs., Part II. and the Staff Manual respectively. Title pages will be prepared in manuscript.

CONFIDENTIAL

WAR DIARY
~~or~~
~~INTELLIGENCE SUMMARY.~~
(Erase heading not required.)

SHEET No 436.

Army Form C. 2118.

Map reference Sheet 57c N.E. 57B N.W. 1/20,000.

1 R Berks Regt

VOL 47

Place	Date	Hour	Summary of Events and Information	Remarks and references to Appendices
CALVERLEY COPSE Near AYETTE	1/9/18.		The Battalion paraded for Divine Service at 10 AM. At 11 AM a demonstration was given with Tracer ammunition. 2/Lt BRAYBROOKE and 110 other ranks joined the Battalion. In the evening orders were received that the Battalion was to be ready to move at 1 hours notice from 6 30 am 2/9/18. (initials)	
"	2/9/18		The Battalion, with Echelon A, left CALVERLEY COPSE at 11.45 am and arrived at B 29 A between MORY and VAULX at 5 PM. dinners were eaten on the march E. of COURCELLES. Battalion H.Q. were established at B. 29. A D 6. At 5.30 PM verbal instructions were issued by the B.G.C. that 1/K.R.R.C and 23rd R Fus would attack at about 5 AM 3/9/18 and capture the high ground between MORCHIES and LAGNICOURT: the Battalion to be in Reserve and remain in B. 29 A. Transport lines were fixed at A. 24 A 36. Weather showery. (initials)	
Near MORY.	3/9/18.		At 5.20 am 23rd R Fus and 1/K.R.R.C attacked and captured all objectives with very slight opposition, and patrols were sent forward. 6th Inf Bde then passed through to follow up the enemy who were retiring. BM 285 (attached marked 'A') was received at 8.10 am, and the Battalion moved at 8.45 am in fours with 100 yards between platoons. Verbal orders were issued at VAUX WOOD at about 9.30 am by the Divisional Comdr and B.G.C. that 99th Inf. Bde would be in Reserve the Battalion to bivouac in the valley in C.28 A and D. The Battalion arrived there by 10.15 AM. Bn HQ were established at C 29 c 06. BM 290, containing instructions for the concentration which had already taken place, was received at 1.10 PM. Echelon A moved to C 28 D 80 and Echelon B with Rear Brigade HQ to B.29 A. BM 292 (attached marked 'B') was received at 2.20 PM.	

A5834 Wt W4973/M687 750,000 8/16 D. D. & L. Ltd. Forms/C.2118/13.

SHEET No 437

Army Form C. 2118.

Instructions regarding War Diaries and Intelligence Summaries are contained in F. S. Regs., Part II. and the Staff Manual respectively. Title pages will be prepared in manuscript.

WAR DIARY

~~or~~

~~INTELLIGENCE SUMMARY.~~

(Erase heading not required.)

Place	Date	Hour	Summary of Events and Information	Remarks and references to Appendices
	3/9/18 (continued)		At 9.15 PM B.G.C. arrived at Battalion H.Q with the new Brigade Commander Brig: Gen: A.E. Mc NAMARA CMG DSO and gave orders that the Battalion was to be ready to move forward a short distance at 7 AM 4/9/18. At 11.30 PM orders were received that the Battalion was to be in position in J.15 B and D by 7 AM, and to remain there in readiness. At 11.40 PM BM 298 was received altering the positions to J.14 B and D. A101 (attached marked 'D') was issued at 11.45 PM.	
Near LAGNICOURT	4/9/18		At 5.15 AM the Battalion moved by platoons, arriving in J.14 B and D by 6.45 AM. Battalion HQ J.8.c.2.3. A, B and C Companies in trench J 15 c 0 3 to J 8 c 8 0. D Company in sunken road J 14 A 2 5 to J.14.A.2.9. Echelon B moved forward to C 28 D during the morning. At 10.15 AM verbal instructions were received that 99th Inf. Bde. would relieve 6th Inf. Bde. during the night. The Battalion to move forward to E. of DOIGNIES in the afternoon. At 12.15 PM a Conference was held at Battalion HQ and at 2 PM the Commanding Officer, Adjutant and the four Company Commanders rode up to reconnoitre the line to be taken over. At 8.45 PM the Battalion moved forward to J.17c where it remained whilst 1st Kings Regt: carried out a local attack to reach the Canal in K 20 and K 26. Then:- D Company relieved a company of 2/S. Staffs holding main line of resistance on the high ground between HERMIES and DEMICOURT: relief complete 11.25 PM. A Company relieved a company of 2/S. Staffs with one platoon in K 25 A and one platoon and Coy. H.Q. immediately W. of HERMIES: relief complete 6.10 AM.	

A5834 Wt. W4973/M687 750,000 8/16 D. D. & L. Ltd. Forms/C.2118/13.

SHEET No 438

Army Form C. 2118.

Instructions regarding War Diaries and Intelligence Summaries are contained in F. S. Regs., Part II. and the Staff Manual respectively. Title pages will be prepared in manuscript.

WAR DIARY

~~or~~

~~INTELLIGENCE SUMMARY.~~

(Erase heading not required.)

Place	Date	Hour	Summary of Events and Information	Remarks and references to Appendices
	4/9/18 (continued)		C Company relieved a company of 1/Kings holding trench K 20 c 1 0 to K 14 c 2.7. relief complete 6.50 AM B Company relieved a company of 1/Kings holding the high ground in K. 26 A up to the Canal: relief complete 11 AM. Battalion HQ J. 18 D 4 8. The Battalion was in touch with 37th Division on the Right at SQUARE COPSE and 1/KRRC on the Left. [initials]	
In the line DEMICOURT - HERMIES.	5/9/18		At about 8 AM the enemy commenced to shell the SPOIL HEAP K 20 central. A patrol of C Company under 2/LT EVANS was sent out and posts were established N. and S. of the SPOIL HEAP: these were later withdrawn, the ground being covered by Vickers and Lewis Guns. It was afterwards decided to hold the Canal Bank with posts from the SPOIL HEAP to K. 14 D 9 7, and accordingly C Company sent parties forward after dark. The enemy, however, was found to be holding SLAG AVENUE and it was decided in consultation with the Brigade, to occupy the posts at dawn should the enemy have evacuated them. [initials]	
"	6/9/18		At 6.30 AM patrols were sent forward to see whether the enemy had again evacuated SLAG AVENUE, but heavy M.G fire from the N.E. prevented any information being gained. Later in the morning patrols located an enemy post at K. 20. c. 7.8. In the evening A Coy. relieved C Coy in the left front sub-sector: C Coy. moving to the R. Support positions on relief. Hostile Artillery and Trench Mortars were very active throughout the day and night. [initials]	
"	7/9/18		Enemy shelling continued to be heavy, especially in the early morning. At 5.30 AM parties from A and B Companies under 2/LT ALLSON and 2/LT KIRBY moved forward up GONG Trench and the S. end of SLAG AVENUE with the object of establishing	

A5834 Wt. W4973/M687 750,000 8/16 D. D. & L. Ltd. Forms/C.2118/13.

SHEET No 439

Army Form C. 2118.

Instructions regarding War Diaries and Intelligence Summaries are contained in F. S. Regs., Part II. and the Staff Manual respectively. Title pages will be prepared in manuscript.

WAR DIARY

~~or~~

~~INTELLIGENCE SUMMARY.~~

(Erase heading not required.)

Place	Date	Hour	Summary of Events and Information	Remarks and references to Appendices
	7/9/18 (continued)		posts on the W. bank of the Canal from the SPOIL HEAP to K 14 D 65.10. The operation was completely successful and posts were established at K. 20 B 23, K. 20 B 46, K 14 D 65.10, and one in SLAG AVENUE at about K. 14 D 55. 9 prisoners and 1 M.G were captured: our casualties were:- 2/Lt KIRBY wounded, 1 OR killed and 3 ORs wounded. At 10 AM about 50 of the enemy counter-attacked the post at K. 14 D 65.10. over the top from FAGAN SUPPORT: after a short fight they were driven back with loss: our posts remained intact. At 3 PM D Coy: moved into O.B.L. Avenue to support A Coy. and established Coy. HQ with A Coy. C Coy: moved Coy: HQ and the platoon from behind HERMIES into the positions vacated by D Coy. At about 4 PM under cover of a heavy artillery and trench-mortar barrage which had been going on for an hour the enemy in considerable strength again counter-attacked and succeeded in regaining the posts on the Canal Bank and the post in SLAG AVENUE: we established blocks in GONG TRENCH and the S. end of SLAG AVENUE near it's junction with O.B.L. AVENUE. Our casualties during the whole day were 2/Lt KIRBY and 2/Lt ALLSON wounded. 5 ORs killed 19 ORs wounded and 15 ORs missing. The night was comparatively quiet. [initials]	
	8/9/18		Hostile artillery considerably less active. the situation remained unchanged. At 8.30 PM the Battalion was relieved by 2nd H.L.I. and the Brigade came into Support. On relief the Battalion moved to J 8 A and C with Bn HQ in the sunken road at J. 8. c. 0 6 Relief complete 1.15 AM 9/9/18 [initials]	

A5834 Wt. W4973/M687 750,000 8/16 D. D. & L. Ltd. Forms/C.2118/13.

SHEET No 440

Army Form C. 2118.

Instructions regarding War Diaries and Intelligence Summaries are contained in F. S. Regs., Part II. and the Staff Manual respectively. Title pages will be prepared in manuscript.

WAR DIARY
~~or~~
~~INTELLIGENCE SUMMARY~~.
(Erase heading not required.)

Place	Date	Hour	Summary of Events and Information	Remarks and references to Appendices
Near BEAUMETZ	9/9/18		Battalion rested during the day and improved bivouacs and shelters. [initials]	
"	10/9/18		Nothing of importance occurred. Rain fell at intervals throughout the day and the weather became considerably colder. [initials]	
"	11/9/18		Weather again wet. Lt C.C. HEDGES joined the Battalion. [initials]	
"	12/9/18		Companies bathed at MORCHIES in the afternoon. [initials]	
"	13/9/18		Weather showery. Company training 8-30 - 12-30. Brigadier watched Companies at work L.P.	
	14.9.18.		Company training in the morning. Arms inspected by Brigade Armourer Sgt L.P.P.	
	15.9.18		2/Lt Murray admitted to hospital. Nothing of interest happened L.P	
RESERVE MORY	16.9.18		Batt moved into Corps reserve in MORY area. Batt H.Q C & D Coys in vicinity of sunken road B27a 90 A & B Coys in sunken Road running due N. from MORY (B15 & 16). Capt Pugh returned from leave. Capt Stokes & Dempsey proceeded on French leave.	

A5834 Wt. W4973/M687 750,000 8/16 D. D. & L. Ltd. Forms/C.2118/13.

SHEET No 441

Army Form C. 2118.

Instructions regarding War Diaries and Intelligence Summaries are contained in F. S. Regs., Part II. and the Staff Manual respectively. Title pages will be prepared in manuscript.

WAR DIARY
or
INTELLIGENCE SUMMARY.
(Erase heading not required.)

Place	Date	Hour	Summary of Events and Information	Remarks and references to Appendices
RESERVE near MORY	17.9.18		Batt. H.Q C & D Coys move to new area about 200 yards from previous positions. Day very wet. 2/Lt Young, Harris & Frost joined for duty. Companies Training	
	18.9.18		Training by Companies. Day very windy, & occasional showers Reinforcement of 10 O.R. joined for duty	
	19.9.18		Battalion did practise attack with Tanks. Brigadier was present & held a conference when points of the attack were criticised.	
	20.9.18		Training under Company arrangements. Day very wet & Route March previously arranged had to be cancelled. Reinforcement of 14 O.R joined for duty.	

A5834 Wt. W4973/M687 750,000 8/16 D. D. & L. Ltd. Forms/C.2118/13.

SHEET No 442

Army Form C. 2118.

Instructions regarding War Diaries and Intelligence Summaries are contained in F. S. Regs., Part II. and the Staff Manual respectively. Title pages will be prepared in manuscript.

WAR DIARY
or
INTELLIGENCE SUMMARY.
(Erase heading not required.)

Place	Date	Hour	Summary of Events and Information	Remarks and references to Appendices
RESERVE near MORY	21.9.18		Commanding officer left for England in order to attend Old Comrades Association meeting. Maj. Anderson M.C. assumed Command. Capt Boshell left for England on 6 months tour of duty & was struck off strength. Battalion Route march & attacks by Companies. C.O & Adjutant attended conference at Bde H.Q.	
	22.9.18		Capt Nugent transferred to 2nd Batt. Church parade service held. Day very wet & windy	
	23.9.18		Fine day. Company training. Battalion went through Gas Chamber. ~~Gen~~ Coy practised throwing German bombs	
	24.9.18		Battalion practised moving over the open in artillery formation. Day fine & bright. Capt Allfrey returned from Paris leave	

A5834 Wt. W4973/M687 750,000 8/16 D. D. & L. Ltd. Forms/C.2118/13.

SHEET No 443

Army Form C. 2118.

Instructions regarding War Diaries and Intelligence Summaries are contained in F. S. Regs., Part II. and the Staff Manual respectively. Title pages will be prepared in manuscript.

WAR DIARY
or
INTELLIGENCE SUMMARY.

(Erase heading not required.)

Place	Date	Hour	Summary of Events and Information	Remarks and references to Appendices
RESERVE near MORY	24.9.18		Brigade instruction No1 marked "A" received. 2/Lt BOULD & DEAN join	
	25.9.18		Company Training. Fine day. Capt Talbot granted leave to England. Brigade instruction No2 marked "C" and Brigade Operation Order No256 received. marked B 2nd Div (marked "D") and 99th Brigade (marked E) administrative orders received	
	26.9.18		Fine day but very windy. Batt moved in Evening to BEAUMETZ area. O.O. 185 attached marked "G". 1 officer & 44 O.R left for Divisional Reception Camp. Addition to 2nd Division Administrative Orders received marked D. 11a.m. R. Berks administrative orders issued marked "H". Brigade Order No 257 Received marked "J" followed by Bm/S585/19 giving the time of Zero as 5-20 a.m on the 27th. Bm 466 received marked "K" giving details of the first two probable moves, on receipt of this, orders were issued to Coys who were told to be ready to move at short notice after 6 a.m on the 27th. Very wet & cold night	
	27.9.18		Hazy morning & roads very sticky. At 6-58 a.m orders were	

A5834 Wt. W4973/M687 750,000 8/16 D. D. & L. Ltd. Forms/C.2118/13.

Army Form C. 2118.

Instructions regarding War Diaries and Intelligence Summaries are contained in F. S. Regs., Part II. and the Staff Manual respectively. Title pages will be prepared in manuscript.

WAR DIARY
or
INTELLIGENCE SUMMARY.
(*Erase heading not required.*)

Place	Date	Hour	Summary of Events and Information	Remarks and references to Appendices
BEAUMETZ	27.9.18		received to move to trenches in J 10 c & d vacated by 1st Kings Regt. Battalion moved in Artillery formation. Observers reconnoitred the route & guided Companies to their positions. The weather had now improved & there was every prospect of a fine day.	
Trenches in J10 c & d			The trenches were reached at 8-8 a.m. 2/Lt Gould (who was attached to Battalion H.Q as Communication officer) went to Brigade which was situated on the HERMIES – DEMICOURT Road, to report arrival in new area & location of Battalion H.Q. Lt Col Powell rejoined the Battalion here from leave to England. At 10.50 a.m 2/Lt Gould returned with orders for the Battalion to move to area K 8 c.	
W of CANAL DU NORD in TRENCHES in K 8 c			Battalion moved in Artillery formation & arrived at 12-20 p.m. 2/Lt Gould left for Brigade to report position. Col Powell went to Brigade & was told that he must not go into action with the Battalion. Col Powell left the Battalion & proceeded to the Transport lines. At 12.55 p.m 2/Lt Gould returned with orders that we were to move to area K 9 b East of Canal. At this time the Canal was being rather heavily shelled by the enemy.	
E of CANAL in K 9 b			Battalion advanced in Artillery formation & arrived at new area at 2.25 p.m. At 2-35 p.m the C.O went to Brigade for a conference on his return Company Commanders were sent for & were told that RIBECOURT had been taken but that GRAINCOURT was in	

SHEET No 445

Army Form C. 2118.

Instructions regarding War Diaries and Intelligence Summaries are contained in F. S. Regs., Part II. and the Staff Manual respectively. Title pages will be prepared in manuscript.

WAR DIARY
or
INTELLIGENCE SUMMARY.

(Erase heading not required.)

Place	Date	Hour	Summary of Events and Information	Remarks and references to Appendices
E of CANAL in K9b			enemy hands. Our left flank had to be protected. To do this an outpost line was established. C & D Coys were in front line 'B' Coy in Support and 'A' Coy in Reserve. Battalion H.Q was established in a dugout previously occupied by MINENWERFER Personnell. While here we were worried by an enemy M.G. Post which, though surrounded still held out. At 3-30 p.m the enemy M.G Post was reduced by the Guards & about 100 prisoners including a Battalion Commander were captured. At 4.55 B.M. 10 marked 'L' was received ~~sent~~ & the C.O sent	
TRENCHES in K17 b & d			for Company Commanders & explained the situation to them. At 5-30 p.m Battalion moved in Artillery formation to trenches in K17 b & d arriving at 7 p.m. Very poor accomodation & very cold. Battalion was told to remain here & await orders. At 9-30 p.m all Commanding Officers were sent for by the Brigadier. At 11-30 p.m the C.O returned & all Company Commanders were sent for. The C.O had received verbal instructions from Brigade that the Battalion was to attack at 5 a.m on the 28th. The situation was discussed & the C.O issued verbal orders to Company Commanders	

A5834 Wt. W4973/M687 750,000 8/16 D. D. & L. Ltd. Forms/C.2118/13.

SHEET No 446.

Army Form C. 2118.

Instructions regarding War Diaries and Intelligence Summaries are contained in F. S. Regs., Part II. and the Staff Manual respectively. Title pages will be prepared in manuscript.

WAR DIARY
or
INTELLIGENCE SUMMARY.
(Erase heading not required.)

Place	Date	Hour	Summary of Events and Information	Remarks and references to Appendices
TRENCHES in K17b o d	28th		At 12-30 a.m B.M 13 (marked 'M') was received giving orders for the attack & Battalion Order (marked 'O') was issued to Companies at 1-45 a.m B.M 14 (marked 'N') received giving particulars of barrage & modification of operation orders, the contents of this message was conveyed verbally by the Commanding Officer to the Company Commanders. The Battalion left for the assembly positions at 2 a.m arriving at 3-15 a.m. Everyone was very pleased to get there as owing to the dark & the mass of debris in FLESQUIERES it was no easy matter to find ones way. At 4.45 a.m the Battalion attacked 'A' Company on Right Front 'B' Coy left front 'D' Coy Right support & 'C' Coy left support. At 5.30 a.m the first objective was (GRAINCOURT TRENCH) was captured with very little opposition. Information took a long time to reach Battalion H.Q but at 9-15 to the relief of all concerned messages arrived which reported that the Battalion was holding the W. bank of the Canal de St QUENTIN. Previous to the receipt of above messages Battalion H.Q had moved forward to a trench in L 15 d. 2. 8. At 10 a.m the C.O. left Batt H.Q towards	

A5834 Wt. W4973/M687 750,000 8/16 D. D. & L. Ltd. Forms/C.2118/13.

SHEET No 447

Army Form C. 2118.

Instructions regarding War Diaries and Intelligence Summaries are contained in F. S. Regs., Part II. and the Staff Manual respectively. Title pages will be prepared in manuscript.

WAR DIARY
or
INTELLIGENCE SUMMARY.

(*Erase heading not required.*)

Place	Date	Hour	Summary of Events and Information	Remarks and references to Appendices
NOYELLES	28th		companies: Weather very wet. Battalion H.Q moved to NOYELLES at 11 a.m. The Brigadier called at Batt H.Q at 12.15 pm to get the exact situation. He was very pleased & asked that Companies be told that he appreciated very much the good work done by them. Every thing was now fairly normal except that a Boche aeroplane was dropping bombs & firing tracer bullets into NOYELLES. ~~At~~ The weather remained very wet. At 5.15 p.m Battalion H.Q moved into a dugout in NOYELLES & the Battalion line was reorganised & held in depth. A & B Coys in the front line & C & D in support in dugouts in NOYELLES at this time the shelling was very heavy. At 7 p.m the 17th Royal Fusiliers forced their way across the canal. At 8-45 p.m Bm 28 (marked "P") received containing orders to attack & cross the canal at 5 a.m on the 29th on receipt of this a Battalion Order (marked "R") was issued to Companies. At 11.15 p.m Bm 30 (marked "S") was received giving further details & modification of attack. During the	

A5834 Wt. W4973/M687 750,000 8/16 D. D. & L. Ltd. Forms/C.2118/13.

SHEET No 448

Army Form C. 2118.

Instructions regarding War Diaries and Intelligence Summaries are contained in F. S. Regs., Part II. and the Staff Manual respectively. Title pages will be prepared in manuscript.

WAR DIARY
or
INTELLIGENCE SUMMARY.
(Erase heading not required.)

Place	Date	Hour	Summary of Events and Information	Remarks and references to Appendices
NOYELLES	28th		night all sorts of rumours were afloat the most persistent one being that the 17th Royal Fusiliers had been driven back across the canal. The atmosphere was cleared however at 4-30 a.m. when a message was	
	29.9.18		received which said that the 17th Royal Fusiliers had been counterattacked during the night but still held their positions East of the Canal. At 5 a.m. the attack on the canal was launched "A" Coy carrying out the first phase. Two platoons crossed when the only bridge left standing on our front was destroyed by enemy fire. One platoon of "D" Coy also crossed by a Southern bridge in the area of the K.R.R. & these men temporarily attached themselves to the 1/60th Rifles. The men who crossed the Canal were fighting hard & "D" Coy was ordered to reinforce "A" Company. "B" Company held the W. bank of the Canal & by skillful use of platoon weapons kept up superiority of fire and generally were of great assistance to the attacking troops. "C" Company were in dugouts in NOYELLES and remained in Battalion Reserve. Owing to the bridges being destroyed the battalion was unable to cross the bridge until later in the day. At 12 noon the Brigadier arrived at	

A5834 Wt. W4973/M687 750,000 8/16 D. D. & L. Ltd. Forms/C.2118/13.

SHEET No 449

Army Form C. 2118.

Instructions regarding War Diaries and Intelligence Summaries are contained in F. S. Regs., Part II. and the Staff Manual respectively. Title pages will be prepared in manuscript.

WAR DIARY
or
INTELLIGENCE SUMMARY.
(Erase heading not required.)

Place	Date	Hour	Summary of Events and Information	Remarks and references to Appendices
NOYELLES	29.9.18		Batt H.Q and it was arranged that 'C' Company were to relieve a company of the 1st K.R.R.C. who had crossed the canal & were in conjunction with the K.R.R's to attack & capture the dotted green line. At 1-30 p.m. 'C' Company left to relieve 1st K.R.R.C with orders to attack RANGE WOOD at 2-30 p.m. As the C.O was under the impression that British patrols had already entered RANGE WOOD 2/Lt Gould was sent to reconnoitre the position. He returned at 2.25 p.m and reported that RANGE WOOD was held by us and our troops were well in advance of it, it was however too late to modify the attack or stop the barrage. At 2-30 p.m the attack on the green dotted line was launched and all objectives secured. Nothing of unusual interest occurred until 5 p.m when orders were issued by the C.O (see B22 marked 'O' issued to Coys) that the Battalion was to be organised in depth. The C.O went forward to visit Companies & establish forward Batt. H.Q. Adjt remained behind to await instructions before moving forward. Between six and eight o'clock rumours	

A5834 Wt. W4973/M687 750,000 8/16 D. D. & L. Ltd. Forms/C.2118/13.

SHEET No 450

Army Form C. 2118.

Instructions regarding War Diaries and Intelligence Summaries are contained in F. S. Regs., Part II. and the Staff Manual respectively. Title pages will be prepared in manuscript.

WAR DIARY
or
INTELLIGENCE SUMMARY.

(*Erase heading not required.*)

Place	Date	Hour	Summary of Events and Information	Remarks and references to Appendices
MARCOING SUPPORT EAST of CANAL DE ST QUENTIN	29.9.18		of enemy massing on our front were very prevalent. All wires to companies were cut & the enemy were shelling heavily. At 8 p.m a message from the C.O arrived which stated that all Companies were in position & that there was no sign of enemy massing. He thought the enemy fire was probably brought on by our own troops moving across ~~the Canal~~ the open & by the Cavalry who at this time shewed a few signs of getting into action. Forward Batt H.Q was established in dugout ~~at~~ G1d36 At 10.15 p.m. rear Batt H.Q arrived at the new Headquarters bringing with them the ration limbers. The night was very wet indeed. In the meantime at 9-20 p.m 99th Brigade Order M12 (marked 'V') was received on receipt of which the C.O issued verbal instructions to O.C. 'D' Coy to take over the posts of the 17th Royal Fusiliers mentioned in Brigade Order M.12. 'D' Coy then proceeded to take over the posts & were established in their new positions at 11-45 p.m	
	30.9.18		At ~~?~~ 1 p.m. 'D' Coy were withdrawn from the posts to take up position	

SHEET No 451

Army Form C. 2118.

WAR DIARY
or
INTELLIGENCE SUMMARY.

(Erase heading not required.)

Instructions regarding War Diaries and Intelligence Summaries are contained in F. S. Regs., Part II. and the Staff Manual respectively. Title pages will be prepared in manuscript.

Place	Date	Hour	Summary of Events and Information	Remarks and references to Appendices
POSITIONS EAST of CANAL DE ST QUENTIN	30.9.18		to cover the right flank of the Battalion. About this time the General visited us & explained the situation which was still a little obscure. The night was very quiet & nothing of unusual importance occurred. The following day was very quiet & we had orders to push forward if enemy retreated. The air was full of rumours but nothing of special interest occurred. At 7 p.m B.M 46 (marked 'W') was received giving details of relief of the Battalion by the 2ND H.L.I, this confirmed a phone message previously sent by the General. G.B 6 (marked X) was then issued to Companies giving details of relief. Relief was carried out without casualties and was complete at about 1.15 a.m Battalion proceeded to trenches behind line wood in L 9 c & d with Batt H.Q at L 9 c 22, & was settled in at 3 a.m.	

A5834 Wt. W4973/M687 750,000 8/16 D. D. & L. Ltd. Forms/C.2118/13.

SHEET No 452

Army Form C. 2118.

Instructions regarding War Diaries and Intelligence Summaries are contained in F. S. Regs., Part II. and the Staff Manual respectively. Title pages will be prepared in manuscript.

WAR DIARY
or
INTELLIGENCE SUMMARY.

(Erase heading not required.)

Place	Date	Hour	Summary of Events and Information	Remarks and references to Appendices
			The following decorations have been granted for the operations which took place between the 21st & 24th August	
			Distinguished Service Order	
			Lt Col. D. W. Powell	
			Second bar to the Military Cross	
			Capt V. G. Stokes M.C.	
			Military Cross	
			2/Lt Titley	
			2/Lt Jacob	
			Distinguished Conduct Medal	
			No a/C.S.M Jones	
			No Pte	
			Bar to the Military Medal	
			No 8630 L/Sgt Byles MM; No 10126 L/C J. Piper M.M.; 201726 Sgt C. W. Cheney M.M.	
			220311 L/Sgt W. J. Day M.M.; 9788 Sgt G. Funnell M.M	
			Military Medal	
			44093 L/C Gilbert; 13713 L/C Polston; 9830 Sgt Walters DCM; 41728 Cpl Herbert	
			39078 L/C Clacey; 220626 Pte Bellwood; 50744 Pte Foster; 58660 Pte Robbins	
			37624 Sgt N. Taft; 11728 Cpl Marjoram; 229030 Pte Susall; 9161 L/C Hayden	
			8339 Sgt Illsley; 50718 Pte Stirrich; 9810 Pte Shephard	

A7092 Wt. W128 9/M1293. 750,000. 1/17. D. D & L. Ltd. Forms/C2118/14.

SHEET No 453

Army Form C. 2118.

Instructions regarding War Diaries and Intelligence Summaries are contained in F. S. Regs., Part II. and the Staff Manual respectively. Title pages will be prepared in manuscript.

WAR DIARY
or
INTELLIGENCE SUMMARY.

(Erase heading not required.)

Place	Date	Hour	Summary of Events and Information	Remarks and references to Appendices

During the operations from the 27th to the 30th Sept the Battalion suffered casualties as under

	Officers	O.R
Killed	–	17
Wounded	3	83
Missing	–	18

The captures by the Battalion during this period include

~~The following decorations have been granted for the operations which took place between the 21st & 24th August~~

Prisoners	217	
Guns	10	(including one 8" one 5.9" & three 4.2")
Trench Mortars	5	
Machine Guns	35	
Horses	3	

[illegible] Lt.-Colonel
Commdg 1st Royal Berks Regt.

A5834 Wt. W4973/M687 750,000 8/16 D. D. & L. Ltd. Forms/C.2118/13.

WAR DIARY. Sept 1918.

		OFFICERS	OTHER RANKS.
RATION STRENGTH	1-9-18 —	26.	541.
EFFECTIVE STRENGTH	do: —	37.	707.
RATION STRENGTH	30-9-18 —	26	618.
EFFECTIVE STRENGTH	do: —	37	781.

	KILLED.	WOUNDED	MISSING
OFFICERS	NIL	5	NIL.
OTHER RANKS	25	130	20.

RB 1/50

To Headquarters 99th Inf Bde

Herewith narrative of events from 1/9/18 to 9/9/18 in accordance with your BM 403.

15/9/18.

R W Powell Lt-Col.

Capt & Major for Lt-Col

Commdg 1st R'y'l Berks Regt.

"A" Form
MESSAGES AND SIGNALS.

Army Form C. 2121.
(In pads of 100.)

No. of Message ....

Prefix .... Code .... m. Office of Origin and Service Instructions.	Words.	Charge.	This message is on a/c of: ....Service (Signature of "Franking Officer.")	Recd. at ....m. Date .... From .... By ....
	Sent At ....m. To .... By			

TO { 2: DW.

Sender's Number.	Day of Month.	In reply to Number.	AAA
* BM 423	18/9		

Herewith 1st R. Berks "Narrative" for period 1–9 Sept

Narratives of 23rd R Fus and 1/KRRC will be forwarded when received.

Farquharson Capt
for A.G.C.
99 Inf Bde

2nd DIVISION
GENERAL STAFF
No. GA 1730
Date 18.9.18

From
Place
Time

The above may be forwarded as now corrected. (Z)

.... Censor. Signature of Addressor or person authorised to telegraph in his name.

* This line should be erased if not required.

(6661) Wt. W. 492/M1647 of 10.4.17.—65 M Pads.—W.M., Ltd., Cardiff [E 1187]

99th Brigade.

2nd Division.

1st BATTALION

ROYAL BERKSHIRE REGIMENT

APRIL 1918.

CONFIDENTIAL

Instructions regarding War Diaries and Intelligence Summaries are contained in F. S. Regs., Part II. and the Staff Manual respectively. Title pages will be prepared in manuscript.

WAR DIARY
or
INTELLIGENCE SUMMARY.
(Erase heading not required.)

Army Form C. 2118.

1ST BATTN ROYAL BERKSHIRE REGT.

SHEET No 393

Place	Date	Hour	Summary of Events and Information	Remarks and references to Appendices
ENGELBELMER & HEDAUVILLE	APRIL 1		A Quiet day. The Battalion at ENGELBELMER. the men being in bivouac shelters on the outskirts of the Village which was being occasionally heavily shelled. At night the Brigade was relieved by units of 6th Brigade and the Battn moved back to billets at HEDAUVILLE, which was reached about 9pm. Casualties NIL. The night was quiet. Still at 1 hours notice to move	
" March route to BEAUVAL	2.		At 4am orders ~~were received~~ to proceed by march route to AMPLIER area were received (attached). Moved off at 10.15 am by route FORCEVILLE - ACHEUX - LOUVENCOURT - VAUCHELLES-LES-AUTHIE - MARIEUX. Here orders were received diverting the Battn to BEAUVAL, as there was no accomodation at AMPLIER. Dinners were eaten outside MARIEUX, and the Battn moved off again at 2.30 pm via BEAUQUESNE to BEAUVAL, arriving there at 5pm. Billets good but very far apart. Only 1 man fell out on march	
BEAUVAL to HOUVIN HOUVIGNEUL	3.		The morning was spent resting, cleaning up and inspections. It was decided to keep the 2 Company organization for the present. No 1 Coy under command of Capt M.P. PUGH and No 2 under command of Capt E.D.D'O. ASTLEY - but care was taken to retain the 4 Company administrative arrangements active. During the morning a warning order for move to FREVENT area was received. Dinners at noon and Transport moved off at 1pm. No further orders were received, but the Battn was embussed at 4pm, reached FREVENT - (via DOULLENS) at 6pm - debussed and marched to HOUVIN-HOUVIGNEUL, arriving at 7.30 pm. Billets scattered but quite good.	
HOUVIN HOUVIGNEUL			An easy day. Companies at disposal of Company Commanders for inspection and re-organization. Passes granted daily to 10% strength from 2pm to Tattoo.	

A7092). Wt. W12839/M1293 750,000. 1/17. D. D & L., Ltd. Forms/C2118/14.

CONFIDENTIAL

Instructions regarding War Diaries and Intelligence Summaries are contained in F. S. Regs., Part II. and the Staff Manual respectively. Title pages will be prepared in manuscript.

WAR DIARY
or
INTELLIGENCE SUMMARY.
(Erase heading not required.)

Army Form C. 2118.

SHEET No 394

Place	Date	Hour	Summary of Events and Information	Remarks and references to Appendices
HOUVIN-HOUVIGNEUL	APRIL 5.		Morning very rainy. Training carried on under Company arrangements - and special classes of Instruction for Lewis Gunners commenced.	
"	6.		Training continued, but interfered with by the rain. A large reinforcement of 282 O.R (almost entirely transfers from HERTFORDSHIRE YEOMANRY) joined and posted to Companies. 2/Lieut A.B. FEATHERSTONE reported for duty and posted to A Company. Brig Genl Ironside dined in the Officers Mess.	
"	7		Sunday. A Parade Service was held behind Officers Mess at 9.30 am. A Reinforcement of OR joined and posted to Companies. Lieut ARNOLD and Sgt Woods attached to the Battn as special Musketry Instructors	
"	8.		C & D Companies on the Rifle Range, but shooting abandoned owing to the rain. At midnight orders were received to move to IVERGNY. (attached).	
IVERGNY	9.		A wet morning but fine in afternoon. After dinners the Battn marched to IVERGNY (Bn Order attached). Billets poor and far apart. 57 OR Reinforcement joined here - also 2 Sergeant Instructors in Lewis Gun from 3rd Army School attached to the Battn to help in training.	
"	10		The morning was taken up by Commanding Officers Inspection of Companies organization. Lewis Guns and rifles were inspected by Brigade Armourer Sergeant. Major G.A. POCOCK. M.C (formerly in the Battn) with 2 Sergeant Instructors in Lewis & Machine Guns from G.H.Q. School LE TOUQUET - also a Staff Sergeant A.G.S. were attached to the Battn to assist in training	

A7092. Wt. W128,39/M1293 750,000. 1/17. D. D & L., Ltd. Forms/C2118/14.

CONFIDENTIAL

Instructions regarding War Diaries and Intelligence Summaries are contained in F. S. Regs., Part II. and the Staff Manual respectively. Title pages will be prepared in manuscript.

WAR DIARY
or
INTELLIGENCE SUMMARY.
(Erase heading not required.)

SHEET No 395.

Army Form C. 2118.

Place	Date	Hour	Summary of Events and Information	Remarks and references to Appendices
IVERGNY to SOMBRIN	11		Commanding Officer's Drill Parade at 10.30 am. At 11. Warning Order received, and later Bde O.O No 231. for move to SOMBRIN were received. These orders with Battn Orders are attached. SOMBRIN was reached at 5.30pm. Billets very fair. 2/Lieuts JOHNSTON & HERRING to Hospital sick.	
"	12		Under orders received from Brigade the Commanding Officer and Coy Commanders proceeded by lorry to reconnoitre the front line N of ADINFER WOOD. held by the Guards Divn. During their absence Order (attached) received for move to LAHERLIÈRE area. "1st Reinforcement" of 104 O.R. sent back to 2nd Division Depot Battn. 3 O.R. Joined from the Depot Battn. After dinner the Battn moved to LAHERLIERE under attached Order, arriving at 3.30pm. but billets being occupied by labour units, men were not settled down until 6 pm. Billets poor and scattered.	
LAHERLIERE				
"	13		A quiet day. Commanding Officer and O.C. Coys reconnoitred "purple line" under B.M.(S).1859 attached. Warning that we should go into the line next night received.	
"	14		A dull and very cold day. Box respirators inspected by Brigade Gas Officer. Church Service at 9am. In the evening the Battn relieved the 3rd Battn Grenadier Guards in the LEFT sub-sector (Bde O.O. attached). Relief complete 12 M.N. Casualties NIL. The line was organized in depth – 2 Companies holding the front series of posts, a Company in support and a Company in reserve. DISPOSITION MAP attached.	
FRONT LINE BOIRY-ST MARTIN "	15		Night and day quiet. The front line was isolated during daylight, being on a forward slope without any communication trenches. A prisoner surrendered to one of our patrols in the early morning. Slight shelling of our lines in early evening.	

A7092. Wt. W12839/M1293 750,000. 1/17. D. D & L., Ltd. Forms/C2118/14.

CONFIDENTIAL

Instructions regarding War Diaries and Intelligence Summaries are contained in F. S. Regs., Part II. and the Staff Manual respectively. Title pages will be prepared in manuscript.

WAR DIARY
or
INTELLIGENCE SUMMARY.
(Erase heading not required.)

SHEET No 396

Army Form C. 2118.

Place	Date	Hour	Summary of Events and Information	Remarks and references to Appendices
FRONT LINE BOIRY-ST-MARTIN	16.		Weather still cold. An uneventful day. Work only possible at night and confined to improvement of the posts and wiring. Inter-Company relief. A Co relieving D Co on R front – C relieving B Co on L front – B coming to SUPPORT and D to RESERVE. Relief complete at M.N – casualties NIL. (Order annexed). Defence Scheme (R.B.28) attached.	
"	17		Warmer and some rain. A dull day and uneventful. RESERVE Coy occupied with collecting salvage. 1 O.R. wounded by shell splinter.	
"	18		Warm and misty. Relieved at night by 1/K.R.R.C. – relief complete 10.30 pm. Casualties 1 OR wounded. Bde and Battn Orders annexed. The following officers reported for duty this day and were posted to Companies as follows:– Capt R. Talbot. M.C. to command C Coy; Lieut J.G.L. Dawson and Lieut Banner to A Company. 2/Lieuts Ayres and White to B Company. 2/Lieut Brown to C Company. Lieut F. Lawson to D Company.	
TO RESERVE BLAIREVILLE				
"	19		Dispositions in Brigade Reserve. Bn HQ in hutments on BLAIREVILLE – HENDECOURT road. B. Coy in Purple Reserve Line on RANSART – ADINFER road. A. C. and D Companies in Purple Line N and E of ADINFER. During the day all Companies bathed at BERLES-AU-BOIS. Commdg Officer's conference with all officers at Battn H.Q. A severe bombardment of the vicinity of Bn H.Q. was experienced from 5-5.30 pm. and at intervals afterwards, but no casualties resulted. A very cold day with frequent snow storms.	
"	20		A fine day and warmer, but cold at night. Usual enemy harassing fire in back areas. At night we relieved 23/R.F. in RIGHT sub sector (Bn O.O. attached). Relief complete 10.20 pm. Casualties NIL. A fine moonlit night and warm.	

A7092). Wt. W12839/M1293 750,000. 1/17. D. D & L., Ltd. Forms/C2118/14.

CONFIDENTIAL

Instructions regarding War Diaries and Intelligence Summaries are contained in F. S. Regs., Part II. and the Staff Manual respectively. Title pages will be prepared in manuscript.

WAR DIARY
or
INTELLIGENCE SUMMARY.
(Erase heading not required.)

SHEET No 397.

Army Form C. 2118.

Place	Date	Hour	Summary of Events and Information	Remarks and references to Appendices
FRONT LINE (RIGHT) BOIRY-ST-MARTIN	21.		A fine bright day. Dispositions as per statement and plan attached. We found a complete length of line. all posts having been connected up. but the greater part was still shallow and narrow. and connection was as yet incomplete with the LEFT sub-sector. These defects were remedied during our tour. A great advantage was the fact that the line could be reached and passed along by day. and the Support Company & Coy HQ. of Coys in the line were all on the Reverse slope and out of enemy view. Bn HQ. in an old burnt-out German dug-out. but it afforded ample accomodation. although a dangerous shelter. most of the supporting timbers having been removed. Enemy artillery was active registering all day – otherwise it was quiet. 3 OR (1 since died of wounds) were wounded by a shell at SUGAR FACTORY. Good work accomplished during the night improving the trenches and wiring.	
"	22		Weather still warm and fine. and uneventful. Major ANDERSON M.C. (11th Bn Middlesex Regt attd 5th Royal Berkshire Regt). joined the Battn. as temporary 2nd in Command.	
"	23		Still fine but misty. allowing considerable freedom of movement. of which full use was made. collecting salvage and improving the trenches. A quiet day. At night inter-Company relief took place under attached order. Relief complete at 11.30 pm. casualties NIL.	
"	24.		Still fine and misty. An uneventful day. From midnight to 2 am. a gas bombardment of the COJEUL valley took place. The wind carried the gas back & at Bn H.Q. masks had to be worn for a short time. but none of the Companies were affected.	

A7092. Wt. W12839/M1293 750,000. 1/17. D. D & L., Ltd. Forms/C2118/14.

CONFIDENTIAL

Instructions regarding War Diaries and Intelligence Summaries are contained in F. S. Regs., Part II. and the Staff Manual respectively. Title pages will be prepared in manuscript.

WAR DIARY
or
INTELLIGENCE SUMMARY.
(*Erase heading not required.*)

SHEET No 398

Army Form C. 2118.

Place	Date	Hour	Summary of Events and Information	Remarks and references to Appendices
FRONT LINE (RIGHT) BOIRY-St. MARTIN	25		Still foggy, but clearer by noon. The enemy shelled our front line heavily for the first time, especially on the LEFT, but no casualties were caused. One "blind" 5.9" shell fell right into the trench where men were sleeping. 1 O.R. reported sick next day, suffering from "shell-shock". 2/Lieut MANNING, who was wounded in CAMBRIN sector last summer, rejoined this day and posted to A Coy. Lieut DAWSON coming to Bn HQ. as Assistant Adjutant.	
" BRIGADE RESERVE. PURPLE LINE.	26.		A quiet day - still misty and very warm. Relieved at night by 1 K.R.R.C. (Bn O.O. attached). A quick relief, complete by 10.30 pm. and no casualties. Special wire report and Work Report for the tour are attached. The Battn moved back into Bde Reserve, the Companies being disposed as on 19th instant. Battn HQ. in old Brigade HQ. in BLAIREVILLE.	
"	27		A Co and ½ B Coy bathed at BERLES-AU-BOIS. C Company provided a working party of 100 O.R. digging the PURPLE LINE. EAST of ADINFER, from 5 to 9 pm. No casualties, although enemy shelled the vicinity at intervals.	
"	28.		The remainder of the Battn bathed. Commanding Officer's Conference. A quiet day.	
" FRONT LINE (LEFT) BOIRY-ST-MARTIN	29		1 Officer per Company to 1st Line Transport for 3 days rest. Major Anderson to "Brigade Rest Camp" to be in charge of troops left out of the line by units of the Brigade, including 1 platoon from each of our Companies. At night the Battn relieved 23/R.F. in LEFT sub-sector. (Bn O.O annexed) Relief complete. 11pm. Casualties NIL.	

CONFIDENTIAL

Instructions regarding War Diaries and Intelligence Summaries are contained in F. S. Regs., Part II. and the Staff Manual respectively. Title pages will be prepared in manuscript.

WAR DIARY
or
INTELLIGENCE SUMMARY.
(Erase heading not required.)

Army Form C. 2118.

SHEET No 399

Place	Date	Hour	Summary of Events and Information	Remarks and references to Appendices
FRONT LINE (LEFT) BOIRY ST MARTIN	30		A very wet and miserable day. Enemy Trench Mortars and "Granatenwerfer" very active all day. Casualties 2 OR wounded	
			Casualties during the month. Officers. NIL. killed 1 wounded (Lieut Shipton)	
			O.R. NIL. " 10 "	
			Effective Strength 30/4/18. 30 officers and 1186 OR - TOTAL 1216.	
			Ration Strength 30/4/18 28 officers and 749 O.R - TOTAL. 777	
			April was not an exhilarating month for the Battn. At its commencement scarcely 200 of the "old" hands were left to us. and though in subsequent weeks we received large parties of reinforcements, transferred from other units, they were all absolutely without experience and very young. These drafts were thrust on us while we were in the throes of moving from one sector to another - we were without our "nucleus" - & we were scarcely given time to post them to Companies & get platoons nominally organized before we were again put into the line, and expected to live up to our old reputation for good work & smart appearance. This entailed very hard work on the officers and N.C.O's. and good progress was made, and some training effected with the help of the 2nd Divnl Depot Battn - but it was lucky we were in a "peace" sector. The end of the month found us, as at the beginning, hoping for a few weeks out of the line for training & organization.	

M Bostie Lieut - Col: ~~Cmdg~~ 1/Royal Berkshire Regiment.

A7092). Wt. W12839/M1293 750,000. 1/17. D. D & L., Ltd. Forms/C2118/14.

1st Bn Royal Berkshire Regt.

Narrative of Events 1/9/18., to 9/9/18.

CALVERLEY COPSE 1/9/18.

The Battalion paraded for Divine Service at 10 am. At 11 am a demonstration was given with Tracer ammunition. 2/Lieut BRAYBROOKE and 110 other ranks joined the Battalion. In the evening orders were received that the Battalion was to be ready to move at 1 hours notice from 6-30 am 2/9/18.

CALVERLEY COPSE. 2/9/18.

The Battalion with Echelon A, left CALVERLEY COPSE at 11-45 am and arrived at B. 29. A between MORY and VAULX at 5 pm, dinners were eaten on the march East of COURCELLES. Battalion H. Qrs were established at B. 29. A. 0. 6. At 5.30 pm verbal instructions were issued by the B. G. C that 1/K.R.R.C and 23rd Royal Fusiliers would attack at about 5 am 3/9/18 and capture the high ground between MORCHIES and LAGNICOURT, the Battalion to be in reserve and remain in B. 29. A Transport Lines were fixed at A. 24. A. 36. Weather showery.

Near MORY 3/9/18.

At 5.20 am 23rd Royal Fusiliers and 1/K.R.R.C attacked and captured all objectives with very slight opposition, and patrols were sent forward. 6th Inf Bde then passed through to follow up the enemy who were retiring. B.M. 285 was received at 8.10 am and the Battalion moved at 8.45 am in fours with 100 yards between platoons. Verbal orders were issued at VAUX WOOD at about 9.30 am by the Divisional Commander and B.G.C that 99th Inf Bde would be in Reserve, the battalion to bivouac in the valley in C. 28. A & D. ~~29. C. 0. 6~~ The battalion arrived there by 10.15 am. Battn H. Qrs were established at C. 29. C. 0. 6. B.M. 290 containing instructions for the concentration which had already taken place was received at 1.10 pm. Echelon A moved to C. 28. D. 80 and Echelon B with Rear Brigade H.Qrs to B. 29. A. B.M. 292 was received at 2.20 pm. At 9.15 pm B.G.C arrived at Bn H. Qrs with the new Brigade Commander, Brig-Gen. A.E. McNAMARA. C.M.G. D.S.O and gave orders that the Battalion was to be

3/9/18 Continued .. to be..

ready to move forward a short distance at 4 am 4/9/18. At 11.30 pm orders were received that the Battalion was to be in position in J. 15. B. & D by 4 am, and to remain there in readiness. At 11.40 pm B.M. 298 was received altering the positions to J. 14. B. & D. A. 101 was issued at 11.45 pm.

near LAGNICOURT 4/9/18.

At 5.15 am the Battalion moved by platoons, arriving in J. 14. B&D. by 6.45 am. Battn. H. Qrs J. 8. c. 23. "A" "B" & "C" Companies in trench J. 15. c. 03 to J. 8. c. 80. "D" Coy in Sunken Road J. 14. A. 25. to J. 14. A. 29. Echelon B moved forward to C. 28. D during the morning. At 10.15 am verbal instructions were received that 99th Inf. Bde. would relieve 6th Inf Bde. during the night, the Battalion to move forward to East of DOIGNIES in the afternoon. At 12.15 pm a Conference was held at Battn. H. Qrs and at 2 pm the Commanding Officer, Adjutant, and the four Company Commanders rode up to reconnoitre the line to be taken over. At 8.45 pm the Battalion moved forward to J. 17. c. where it remained whilst 1st Kings Regt carried out a local attack to reach the canal in K. 20 and K. 26. Then:-
"D" Coy relieved a company of 2/S. Staffs holding main line of resistance on the high ground between HERMIES and DEMICOURT: Relief complete 11.25 pm.
"A" Coy relieved a company of 2/S. Staffs with one platoon in K. 25. A, and one platoon and Coy. H. Qrs immediately West of HERMIES: Relief complete 6.10 am.
"C" Coy relieved a company of 1/Kings holding trench K. 20. c. 10. to K. 14. c. 2.7: Relief complete 6.50 am.
"B" Coy relieved a company of 1/Kings holding the high ground in K. 26. A up to the Canal. Relief complete 11 am. Battn. H. Qrs J. 18. D. 4. 8.
The Battalion was in touch with 34th Division on the Right at SQUARE ~~WOOD~~ COPSE and 1/K.R.R.C on the Left.

In the line DEMICOURT - HERMIES. 5/9/18.

At about 8 am the enemy commenced to shell the SPOIL HEAP. K. 20. Central. A patrol of "C" Company under 2/Lieut. EVANS was sent out and posts were established N and S of the SPOIL HEAP: these were

5/9/18 Continued .... these were

later withdrawn, the ground being covered by Vickers, and Lewis Guns. It was afterwards decided to hold the Canal Bank with posts; from the SPOIL HEAP to K.14.D 97. and accordingly 'C' Coy sent parties forward after dark. The enemy however was found to be holding SLAG AVENUE and it was decided in consultation with the Brigade, to occupy the posts at dawn should the enemy have evacuated them.

In the Line.
DEMICOURT- HERMIES.
6. 9. 18.

At 6-30 am patrols were sent forward to see whether the enemy had again evacuated SLAG AVENUE, but heavy M.G. fire from the N.E prevented any information being gained. Later in the morning patrols located an enemy post at K.20. C. 7.8. In the evening 'A' Coy relieved 'C' Coy in the Left front Sub. Sector: 'C' Coy moving to the Right Support positions on relief. Hostile Artillery & Trench Mortars were very active throughout the ~~night~~ day and night.

- do -
7/9/18

Enemy shelling continued to be heavy, especially in the early morning. At 5.30 am parties from 'A' & 'B' Companies under 2/Lieut. ALLSOPP and 2/Lieut KIRBY moved forward up GONG Trench and the S end of SLAG AVENUE with the object of establishing posts on the W bank of the CANAL from the SPOIL HEAP to K.14.D. 65. 10. The operation was completely successful and posts were established at K. 20. B. 23., K. 20. B. 46., K.14. D. 65. 10., and one in SLAG AVENUE at about K.14. D. 55., 9 prisoners and 1 M.G were captured: our casualties were: 2/Lieut KIRBY wounded, 1. O.R killed and 3. O.Rs wounded.

At 10 am about 50 of the enemy counter-attacked the post at K. 14. D. 65. 10, over the top from FAGAN Support: after a short fight they were driven back with loss, our posts remained intact. At 3 pm 'D' Coy moved into O.B.L Avenue to support 'A' Coy, and established Coy. H.Qrs with 'A' Coy. 'C' Coy moved Coy. H.Qrs and the platoon from behind HERMIES into the positions vacated by 'D' Coy. At about 4 pm under cover of a heavy artillery and Trench Mortar barrage which had been going on for an hour the enemy in considerable strength again counter-attacked and succeeded in regaining the posts on the Canal Bank and the post in SLAG AVENUE: we established blocks in GONG Trench and the S end of SLAG AVENUE near its junction with O.B.L AVENUE. Our casualties during the whole day were 2/Lieut KIRBY and

7/9/18 Continued - (and)

and 2/Lieut ALLSON wounded. 5. Other Ranks killed, 19 other ranks wounded, missing 15 other ranks. The night was comparatively quiet.

In the Line. DEMICOURT. HERMIES. 8. 9. 18.

Hostile artillery considerably less active, the situation remained unchanged. At 8.30 pm the Battalion was relieved by 2nd H.L.I., and the Brigade came into Support. On relief the Battalion moved to J. 8. A & C with Battn. H.Qrs in the Sunken Road at J. 8. c. 06. Relief complete 1.15 am 9/9/18.

Since being relieved 9/9/18 the Battalion has taken no further part in the operations.

15/9/18.

[signature] Lieut. Colonel.
Commdg 1st Bn Royal Berks Regt.

CONFIDENTIAL

Sheet No 454.

Army Form C. 2

Vol 1st R Berks

Instructions regarding War Diaries and Intelligence Summaries are contained in F. S. Regs., Part II. and the Staff Manual respectively. Title pages will be prepared in manuscript.

WAR DIARY
~~or~~
~~INTELLIGENCE SUMMARY.~~
(Erase heading not required.)

Place	Date	Hour	Summary of Events and Information	Remarks and references to Appendices
W of NINE WOOD	1/10/18		The Battalion rested and cleaned up during the day. Weather fine but cold.	
	2/10		Weather cold with some rain.	
"	3/10		Fine. 2 hours training in the morning. At 6 PM the Battalion was ordered to be ready to move forward at short notice on account of the successful operations carried out by the Fourth Army. This was cancelled later. During the morning a few H.V. shells fell in the vicinity of the Battalion. Casualties 1 OR Killed.	
	4/10		No training was carried out as the Battalion expected to move forward during the day. Weather cold. Major G.B Anderson M.C. left the Battalion to proceed to the Senior Officers School at ALDERSHOT. Captain M P PUGH. DSO. M.C. taking over the duties of Second in Command.	
"	5/10		Companies carried out 2 hours training and ½ hour Salvaging in the morning. Weather still cold.	
	6/10		Summer Time ended at 1 AM when watches were put back one hour. At 11 am the Commanding Officer attended a conference at Brigade HQ where preliminary instructions for an attack to be made on Oct 8th were issued verbally.	
	7/10		During the day the men rested and everything was got ready for the move up to the jumping off positions in the night. Brigade Orders and Instructions are attached (marked 'A'). Battalion Order (attached marked 'B') was issued at 2 PM. At 11.40 pm the Battalion moved off as laid down in the above order, and were in position ready to attack by 2.50 AM 8/10/18. There were no casualties during the move up.	

(A7092). Wt. W12839/M1293. 750,000. 1/17. D. D. & L., Ltd. Forms/C.2118/14.

CONFIDENTIAL

Instructions regarding War Diaries and Intelligence Summaries are contained in F. S. Regs., Part II. and the Staff Manual respectively. Title pages will be prepared in manuscript.

WAR DIARY

or

~~INTELLIGENCE~~ SUMMARY.

(Erase heading not required.)

Sheet No 455 Army Form C. 2118.

Place	Date	Hour	Summary of Events and Information	Remarks and references to Appendices
Near RUMILLY	8/10		At 4.30 am the attack commenced and the Battalion moved forward behind the 23rd R Fus and 1/K.R.R.C. When approaching the sunken road in G 17 B and D C Company came under M.G. fire from some of the enemy who had surrendered to the 23rd R Fus and then decided to fight again: these men were soon put out of action.	
			On arrival at the 1st Objective (RED LINE) which had been captured by the 23rd R. Fus. and 1/KRRC it was found that the 3rd Division had lost direction and come a long way too far to the left. When the Battalion moved through to attack the 2nd Objective there were no troops on the right flank, and B Company (in touch with the 1/KRRC) were about 500 yards to the left of C Company. Consequently on approaching FORENVILLE C and D Companies came under intense M.G. fire from both flanks and were unable to get further than the main road. At about 8.15 AM. 5 enemy tanks drove back the 63rd Division and 1 enemy tank drove back the 3rd Division to the RED LINE. These Tanks commenced to work along the RED LINE, but heavy Lewis Gun and Rifle fire was opened on the tank moving N. from SERANVILLERS and it finally turned and withdrew: the Tanks operating in the vicinity of NIERGNIES appeared to be put out of action.	
			At 8.30AM. an order was sent to C and D Coys. to withdraw to the RED LINE, and under heavy M.G. fire from both flanks and their left rear these two companies (about 80 strong) managed to regain the main line. The Battalion was then reorganised, A and B Companies holding the RED LINE, with C and D Companies 500 yards behind in G 18a	

(A7092). Wt. W12839/M1293. 750,000. 1/17. D. D. & L., Ltd. Forms/C.2118/14.

CONFIDENTIAL

SHEET No456 Army Form C. 2118.

WAR DIARY ~~or~~ ~~INTELLIGENCE SUMMARY.~~

(Erase heading not required.)

Instructions regarding War Diaries and Intelligence Summaries are contained in F. S. Regs., Part II. and the Staff Manual respectively. Title pages will be prepared in manuscript.

Place	Date	Hour	Summary of Events and Information	Remarks and references to Appendices
Near RUMILLY	8/10		At 1 p.m. instructions were issued verbally by the B.G.C. that the attack on FORENVILLE was to be carried out at 4.30 p.m. with 1 Company of 1/KRRC on the left, 2 Companies of 1/R.BERKS on the right with 2 Platoons of 23/R.FUS. The 3rd Division were to be asked to capture SERANVILLERS at the same time. ZERO hour was afterwards put forward to 3 P.M. as the 3rd DIVISION had already attacked SERANVILLERS at 1 P.M. Accordingly A and B Coys attacked at 3 P.M. (Order marked C attached).	
			The attack again met heavy M.G. fire from the right flank as the 3rd Division had failed to capture SERANVILLERS and little progress was made.	
			At 6 P.M. the 17th R.FUS. passed through and attacked FORENVILLE in conjunction with the 3rd Division on the right, and as SERANVILLERS and LA TARGETTE were captured the attack was successful and FORENVILLE taken.	
	9/10		At 1 A.M. S.C. 138 (attached marked 'D') was received stating that the Division would be automatically relieved as the Guards Division passed through to continue the attack. The Battalion was to concentrate W. of NINE WOOD and then march to bivouacs N. of FLESQUIERES	
			Casualties during the operations were as follows:—	
			Officers. KILLED:— LIEUT. C.C. Hedges M.C.; 2/LT. L.E. Saville. Died of Wounds:— 2/LT. W. Toomey. Wounded:— 2/LT. C.H. Banner; 2/LT. K.B. ~~Coldpole~~ Catchpole	
			Other Ranks: Killed 16; Wounded 86; Missing 12; N.Y.D. Gas 4.	

(A7092). Wt. W12839/M1293. 75,000. 1/17. D. D. & L., Ltd. Forms/C.2118/14.

CONFIDENTIAL

Instructions regarding War Diaries and Intelligence Summaries are contained in F. S. Regs., Part II. and the Staff Manual respectively. Title pages will be prepared in manuscript.

WAR DIARY
or
~~INTELLIGENCE SUMMARY.~~
(Erase heading not required.)

SHEET 457

Army Form C. 2118.

Place	Date	Hour	Summary of Events and Information	Remarks and references to Appendices
FLESQUIERES	9/10 (con.)		The Battalion arrived at 11 AM. Day fine. 2/LT. H.E. Hale joined the Battalion, Lt. C. Lapworth also joined the Battalion as Quartermaster.	
	10/10		Capt. E.L. Jerwood M.C. joined the Battn. The day was spent in cleaning up.	
	11/10		Battalion reorganised. 54 OR. joined the Battn. (34 from Divisional Wing)	
	12/10		C.O. inspected the Battalion on parade at 10 AM. B.G.C. addressed the Battalion at 10.45 AM.	
WAMBAIX	13/10		The Battalion moved to WAMBAIX in accordance with Bde. Order No 259 (attached marked "E") Battn. arrived at WAMBAIX at 12 NOON. Billets were very dirty and full of débris, but after being cleared out were made very comfortable, a large percentage of the men having beds. Weather dull but no rain.	
	14/10		Training was carried out in the morning and Companies bathed during the afternoon. Day fine. Excellent ground for training all around the village.	
	15/10		Company training and musketry on the Range 8.30 AM to 12.30 PM. LT. COL. D.W. Powell DSO relinquished command of the Battn. on proceeding to England for a 6 months' tour of duty.	
	16/10		Weather wet. Company Training from 8.30 AM. to 12.30 PM. LT. COL. J.A. Southey assumed command of the Battn. Platoon Football Competition in the afternoon.	

(A7092). Wt. W12839/M1293. 750,000. 1/17. D. D. & L., Ltd. Forms/C.2118/14.

CONFIDENTIAL

WAR DIARY or ~~INTELLIGENCE SUMMARY.~~

SHEET 458

Army Form C. 2118.

Instructions regarding War Diaries and Intelligence Summaries are contained in F. S. Regs., Part II. and the Staff Manual respectively. Title pages will be prepared in manuscript.

(Erase heading not required.)

Place	Date	Hour	Summary of Events and Information	Remarks and references to Appendices
WAMBAIX	17/10		Company Training 9 AM. to 1 PM. Football in the afternoon. 30 Reinforcements joined the Battalion.	
	18/10		B.G.C. inspected the Transport at 10.30 AM. Company training 9 AM. to 1 PM. Brigade Boxing, and Platoon Football Competition in the afternoon. Battalion won 3 events out of 4 in the Boxing Competition	
	19/10		Battalion Attack Practice 9 AM – 1 PM. In the afternoon Battalion Football Team played Divisional H.Q. Result 1–3. Divisional Concert Party in the evening.	
WAMBAIX – CARNIERES	20/10		At 10 AM. Battalion moved to CARNIERES in accordance with Bde Order No 260. Battn arrived in billets at 12.15 PM. Billets very comfortable. Weather dull, with some rain.	(attached marked 'F')
	21/10		Battalion spent the day resting. Platoon Football Competition in the afternoon	
CARNIERES – ST. HILAIRE	22/10		At 5 PM. Battalion moved to ST. HILAIRE. Whole Battalion billetted in factory. Arrived there by 7.15 PM. Placed on 2 hours' notice from 9 AM. Weather wet	
FACTORY ST. HILAIRE	23/10		At 11.30 AM orders were received to be prepared to move at 1.0 PM; shortly afterwards the orders were confirmed and the Battn moved off by Platoons at 100 yards interval to the area immediately E of ST. PYTHON. Cookers and Lewis Gun Limbers came with the Battalion	

(A7092). Wt. W12839/M1293. 750,000. 1/17. D. D. & L., Ltd. Forms/C.2118/14.

CONFIDENTIAL

Instructions regarding War Diaries and Intelligence Summaries are contained in F. S. Regs., Part II. and the Staff Manual respectively. Title pages will be prepared in manuscript.

WAR DIARY

or

~~INTELLIGENCE SUMMARY.~~

(*Erase heading not required.*)

SHEET 459

Army Form C. 2118.

Place	Date	Hour	Summary of Events and Information	Remarks and references to Appendices
ST. PYTHON	23/10		The Battn arrived at Cross Roads V30d6.8. at 2.45 P.M. where it halted for 20 minutes. Verbal orders were here issued by B.G.C. for the Battn. to move at once W. of VERTAIN. Whilst on the move orders were received for the Battn. to halt near the road in W20b. The C.O. then proceeded to Bde H.Q. in VERTAIN where orders (attached marked 'G') were issued for the Battn. to move forward and relieve 2/H.L.I. at once and to attack early the next morning. Rations for the next day were issued to the men and a hot meal served. At 8.15 p.m. the Battn. moved off by Platoons and met guides at the Cross Roads W3b6.4.	Refce Map 51A 1/40000 and 51A SE 1/20000
			The Battn. was to attack at 4 AM with 23/R.Fus. on Right and 9th Northumberland Fus. on Left and capture the line of the Road R7d5.1 – R7a5.2. Companies formed up in their assembly positions by 11.45 P.M. as follows:–	
			A Coy. Right front Q29d2.0. to Q28d.5.6	
			C Coy. Left front Q28d5.6. to Q28a7.1.	
			B Coy Support in Q34a.	
			D Coy. Reserve Q34c.	
			Battn. H.Q in Sunken Road at W3b6.0.	
Near BERMERAIN	24/10		At 4 AM the attack commenced behind a creeping barrage (Barrage Table attached marked H).	
			The ECAILLON River was found to be deeper than was expected and most of the men went in up to their waists	

(A7092). Wt. W12839/M1293. 750,000. 1/17. D. D. & L., Ltd. Forms/C.2118/14.

CONFIDENTIAL

WAR DIARY or INTELLIGENCE ~~SUMMARY~~.

(Erase heading not required.)

Sheet 460

Army Form C. 2118.

Instructions regarding War Diaries and Intelligence Summaries are contained in F. S. Regs., Part II. and the Staff Manual respectively. Title pages will be prepared in manuscript.

Place	Date	Hour	Summary of Events and Information	Remarks and references to Appendices
Near RUESNES	24/10 (con)		On topping the rise in Q24 heavy M.G. fire was encountered from the direction of PARQUIAUX, but the line continued to advance and the objective was captured and consolidated, a total advance of 4000 yards over difficult country and two rivers. On the final objective the Battn. was in touch on the Right with 23/R Fus. but the 9th Northumberland Fusiliers on the Left were driven back to the line LA FOLIE – LARBLIN leaving the Left flank exposed for a depth of 2500 yards. Accordingly C and D Coys formed a defensive flank facing N.W. from K7a 5.2 to Q18c 5.9 with A and B Coys. holding the Road in K7a and d. 1/KRRC. continued the defensive flank in a S.W. direction to LA FOLIE.	
			Battn. H.Q.rs were established in a ravine at Q28 b 9.9 in communication with Bde H.Q.rs at RSCARMAIN and later by telephone with the Coys.	
			About 300 prisoners and 10 machine guns were captured during the advance.	
			At about 1.45 pm. the enemy attempted to counter attack, but the attack failed to make any progress and the line remained intact. During the evening the 4/Oxfords (61st Divn.) attacked and occupied the high ground in Q11 and Q12 and touch was obtained with them in Q12.c and d by 3 AM on 25/10/18.	
	25/10		At 1 AM a patrol was sent forward to the Railway and found that the enemy were holding posts in K7 b and K8a with machine guns.	
			At 9.30 AM. B Coy. were ordered to put posts on the Railway line as the 3rd Division were reported to be holding BELLEVUE FARM in R15 b. By 12 noon the posts were established and in touch on both flanks and later they were pushed forward	

(A7092). Wt. W12839/M1293. 750,000. 1/17. D. D. & L., Ltd. Forms/C.2118/14.

CONFIDENTIAL

SHEET 461

Army Form C. 2118.

Instructions regarding War Diaries and Intelligence Summaries are contained in F. S. Regs., Part II. and the Staff Manual respectively. Title pages will be prepared in manuscript.

WAR DIARY
or
~~INTELLIGENCE~~ SUMMARY.

(*Erase heading not required.*)

Place	Date	Hour	Summary of Events and Information	Remarks and references to Appendices
Near ROESNES	25/10 (contd)		to the River in R12c, A patrol of A Coy going as far as VILLERS POL without being fired on by machine guns or Rifles.	
			By 6 PM a line of posts was established on the Road in R2 b and the remainder of A and B Coys moved forward E of the railway. C and D Coys moving forward to the Road in R7 a and b. Two platoons of 1/KRRC in Q24a were placed at the disposal of the Battn.	
			Hostile artillery was active throughout the day and the area R7 and R8 was heavily shelled at intervals.	
	26/10		At 3.30 AM 2 coys of 7/K.S.L.I relieved A and B Coys in front of the Railway and 1 Coy of 1/KRRC relieved C and D Coys behind the Railway, the Battn moving into the E end of BERMERAIN. The relief was completed by 6.30 AM.	
			The Casualties during the operations were —	
			Officers — Wounded: Capt. E.L. Jerwood M.C, 2/Lt H.J. Odell, 2/Lt H. Street, 2/Lt J. Gould D.C.M.	
			Other Ranks — Killed 10, Wounded 66, Missing 7.	

(A7092). Wt. W12839/M1293. 750,000. 1/17. D. D. & L., Ltd. Forms/C.2118/14.

CONFIDENTIAL

Instructions regarding War Diaries and Intelligence Summaries are contained in F. S. Regs., Part II. and the Staff Manual respectively. Title pages will be prepared in manuscript.

WAR DIARY

or

~~INTELLIGENCE SUMMARY.~~

(Erase heading not required.)

Sheet 462. Army Form C. 2118.

Place	Date	Hour	Summary of Events and Information	Remarks and references to Appendices
BERMERAIN	26/10		The Battn. rested and reorganised during the day. LT. W. C. Hanney M.C., LT F. Cooper, 2/LTS G. Bysh, A. W. Owen, and G. H. Whistance joined the Battn. Weather fine.	
	27/10		At 7.30 P.M. the Battn. was relieved by two Companies of the 2nd Gordons and marched to SOLESMES arriving there at 9.45 P.M. Billets good. 2/LT J. E. Dye joined the Battn.	
SOLESMES	28/10		The morning was spent in cleaning up. In the afternoon the Divisional Band played in the Town and there was a concert in the evening. Weather fine. A few shells from a H.V. Gun fell in the Town during the day and two civilians were killed. At 11.30 P.M. orders were received that the Battn. would probably move to ESCARMAIN at 10AM on the 29th. Definite orders to this effect were received 2 hours late.	
	29/10		At 9.50AM the Battn. marched to ESCARMAIN arriving there at 11.30AM. Billets good, but some shells fell in the village during the day and night. Orders (attached marked 5) were received placing the Battn. on 1 hours notice from 7AM to 9AM daily	
ESCARMAIN	30/10		Day spent in scrubbing equipment and general cleaning. Weather fine	
	31/10		The village was lightly shelled during the afternoon and 2 ORs were wounded. 2/LT. J. G. Fawcus and 2/LT F. Clemetson joined the Battn.	

Instructions regarding War Diaries and Intelligence Summaries are contained in F. S. Regs., Part II. and the Staff Manual respectively. Title pages will be prepared in manuscript.

WAR DIARY

~~or~~

~~INTELLIGENCE SUMMARY.~~

(Erase heading not required.)

Army Form C. 2118.

SHEET No 463

Place	Date	Hour	Summary of Events and Information	Remarks and references to Appendices
			Effective Strength 1/10/18 36 Officers 781. O Ranks	
			Ration Strength 1/10/18 26 Officers 618. O Ranks	
			Effective Strength 31/10/18 38 Officers 606 O Ranks	
			Ration Strength 31/10/18 32 Officers 490. O Ranks	
			<u>Casualties for month</u>:-	
			Officers KILLED. 2 WOUNDED 10 MISSING NIL	
			O Ranks. KILLED 46 WOUNDED 268 MISSING. 16.	
			[illegible] Major	
			Comndg [illegible] Regt.	

(A7092). Wt. W12839/M1293. 750,000. 1/17. D. D. & L., Ltd. Forms/C.2118/14.

CONFIDENTIAL

Instructions regarding War Diaries and Intelligence Summaries are contained in F. S. Regs., Part II. and the Staff Manual respectively. Title pages will be prepared in manuscript.

WAR DIARY

~~or~~

~~INTELLIGENCE SUMMARY.~~

(Erase heading not required.)

Army Form C. 2118

VR 49

SHEET Nº 464

1st ROYAL BERKS REGT.

Place	Date	Hour	Summary of Events and Information	Remarks and references to Appendices
ESCARMAIN	1/11/18		Weather fine. Warning orders were received that the 2nd Div would be relieved by the Guards and 62nd Div. on night of 2nd/3rd. Company training was carried out in the morning and Salvaging in the afternoon.	
			2/LTS J.H. Edgar, H. Kemp, N.J. Dell, and R.A. Wenn, joined the Battalion.	
			Battalion Hdqrs were shelled during the night. Casualties 1 OR Killed. 1 OR wounded.	
			LT COL J.A. Southey admitted to Hospital.	
	2/11/18		Weather wet. At 1430 the Battalion moved to St. HILAIRE in accordance with Bde orders Nº 265 (attached marked A'). The Battn arrived there at 1730 and was billeted in the factory.	
ST. HILAIRE	3/11/18		Orders and instructions received for forthcoming operations. Day wet. Church Parade at 1000.	
			2nd Lt G.R. Turner joined the Battalion.	
			The Battalion placed on two hours notice to move, from 0900 4/11/18.	
	4/11/18		The Battn was put on 2 hours notice to move from 0900 hrs. Later in the day this was cancelled and the Battn was to be on 1 hours notice 0600 hours 5/11/18.	
			LT, COL R J. Brett assumed command of the Battn. Weather fine.	
	5/11/18		At 0800 hours the Battn. was taken off 1 hours notice and was to be ready to move at 2 or 3 hours notice. At 1130 hours orders were received that the Battn would not move during the day. It was later stated that a move would probably not be made for 2 or 3 days. Rain fell throughout the day.	
			87 ORs reinforcements joined the Battalion.	
	6/11/18		The Commanding Officer inspected companies in organisation during the morning. Weather very wet.	

(A7092). Wt. W12839/M1293. 750,000. 1/17. D. D. & L., Ltd. Forms/C.2118/14.

CONFIDENTIAL

Instructions regarding War Diaries and Intelligence Summaries are contained in F. S. Regs., Part II. and the Staff Manual respectively. Title pages will be prepared in manuscript.

WAR DIARY

~~or~~

~~INTELLIGENCE SUMMARY.~~

(Erase heading not required.)

Army Form C. 2118.

SHEET Nº 465

Place	Date	Hour	Summary of Events and Information	Remarks and references to Appendices
ST. HILAIRE	7/11/18		Weather misty but no rain. At 0900 hours the Battn went for a Route march via BOUSSIERES – BEVILLERS – QUIEVY returning by 1200. A short tactical exercise was done en route. At 1730 hrs a concert was given in the factory by the 1/RRRC concert party and band. At about 1800 hrs orders were received that the Battn would move to ESCARMAIN on the 9th probably starting at 0900 hrs.	
	8/11/18		At 0945 hours the Battalion marched to ESCARMAIN arriving there at about 1300 hours. The roads were very full of transport and the Battalion was frequently compelled to halt owing to blocks in the traffic. Weather wet. Billets good.	
ESCARMAIN	9/11/18		Company training in the morning. Football in the afternoon.	
	10/11/18		Church parade at 0930 hrs. The final of the platoon competitions was played at 1400 hrs. Result:– Nº 7 PLATOON 2. D Coy HDQRS 1.	
	11/11/18		All ranks under 35 years of age went for a four mile cross-country run at 0900 hrs. Hostilities ceased at 11.00. The Battalion played 6th Field Ambulance at Football in the afternoon and lost 0–1.	
	12/11/18		Weather fine. The day was spent in cleaning up the area and collecting salvage.	
	13/11/18		Weather fine. Cleaning up.	
	14/11/18		Weather fine. 140 ORs on working parties salvaging and road mending from 0900 to 1230 hours. Companies bathed in the afternoon and were medically inspected as to their fitness to march, in the evening.	

CONFIDENTIAL

Instructions regarding War Diaries and Intelligence Summaries are contained in F. S. Regs., Part II. and the Staff Manual respectively. Title pages will be prepared in manuscript.

WAR DIARY
~~or~~
~~INTELLIGENCE SUMMARY.~~

(Erase heading not required.)

Army Form C. 2118.

SHEET Nº 466.

Place	Date	Hour	Summary of Events and Information	Remarks and references to Appendices
ESCARMAIN	15/11/18		The Brig-Gen inspected billets in the morning. The remainder of the day was spent in preparation for the forthcoming marches. 57 O.R.s proceeded to the Divisional Reception Camp as being unlikely to complete the march to the Rhine	
	16/11/18		Weather fine and cold. At 11-06 hrs the Battn left ESCARMAIN and marched via CAPELLE - BEAUDIGNIES - LE QUESNOY to VILLERSPOL arriving there at 1400 hrs. The Battn was complimented by the B.G.C. on its excellent turn out. Casualties on the march - NIL	
VILLERS POL	17/11/18		11-00 hours Battalion Parade. The remainder of the day was spent in cleaning up. There was a voluntary C of E service at 17.30 hours	
	18/11		Weather dull with a little snow and rain. At 11-10 the Battalion left VILLERS POL and marched via GOMEGNIES - AMFROIPRET - BERMERIES - BAVAY to LA LONGUEVILLE arriving there at 16.25 hrs. Casualties on the march - NIL.	
LA LONGUEVILLE	19/11		The Battn rested during the day	
	20/11		Weather dull. At 0810 hrs the Battalion left LA LONGUEVILLE and marched via DOUZIES - MAUBEUGE - BERSILLIES to VILLERS - SIRE - NICOLE arriving there at 1205 hours. Casualties on the march - NIL. Capt W. J. GREEN M.C rejoined the Battalion from 6 months tour of duty at home	

CONFIDENTIAL

Instructions regarding War Diaries and Intelligence Summaries are contained in F. S. Regs., Part II. and the Staff Manual respectively. Title pages will be prepared in manuscript.

WAR DIARY
or
~~INTELLIGENCE SUMMARY.~~
(Erase heading not required.)

Army Form C. 2118.

SHEET No 467

Place	Date	Hour	Summary of Events and Information	Remarks and references to Appendices
VILLERS-SIRE-NICOLE.	21/11/18		2 Officers and 100-ORS were employed on cleaning roads during the morning. Weather fine	
	22/11		1 Off and ~~50 O.R.s~~ 50 other ranks were employed on cleaning roads during the morning. Weather fine	
	23/11		1 Lewis Coy drill during the morning. Football in the afternoon.	
	24/11		At 0810 hrs the Battn. left VILLERS-SIRE-NICOLE and marched via MONTIGNIES-ESTINNE AU MONT to BINCHE arriving there at 11.45 hours. Billets were good	
BINCHE	25/11		At 0955 hrs the Battalion left BINCHE and marched via ANDERLUES-FONTAINE L'EVEQUE to MARCHIENNE AU PONT arriving there at 1345 hrs. Weather dull with some rain. The Battalion was again complimented on its excellent turn-out. Billets were good.	
MARCHIENNE AU PONT	26/11		The Battalion rested and cleaned up during the day.	
	27/11		The Battn bathed during the morning and in the afternoon beat the M.G. Battn at football 3-2.	
	28/11		At 0945 hrs the Battn left MARCHIENNE AU PONT and marched via CHARLEROI-TRIEUX to CHATELET arriving there at 1250 hrs. Weather wet. In the afternoon the Battn was photographed by companies.	

CONFIDENTIAL

Instructions regarding War Diaries and Intelligence Summaries are contained in F. S. Regs., Part II. and the Staff Manual respectively. Title pages will be prepared in manuscript.

WAR DIARY
or
~~INTELLIGENCE SUMMARY.~~

(Erase heading not required.)

Army Form C. 2118.

SHEET No 468.

Place	Date	Hour	Summary of Events and Information	Remarks and references to Appendices
CHATELET	29/11/18		At 0902 hrs the Battalion left CHATELET and marched via PRESLES–VITRIVAL to FOSSE arriving there at 1200 hrs. Weather dull.	
FOSSE	30/11		0900 Battalion Parade. At 1030 hrs the Divisional Commander inspected the billets.	

R. J. Brett. Lt. Col.
Cmdg. 1st Royal Berks Regt.

(A7092). Wt. W12839/M1293. 75,000. 1/17. D. D. & L., Ltd. Forms/C.2118/14.

Instructions regarding War Diaries and Intelligence Summaries are contained in F. S. Regs., Part II. and the Staff Manual respectively. Title pages will be prepared in manuscript.

WAR DIARY

~~or~~

~~INTELLIGENCE SUMMARY.~~

(*Erase heading not required.*)

Army Form C. 2118.

SHEET No 469.

Place	Date	Hour	Summary of Events and Information	Remarks and references to Appendices
			Effective Strength 1/11/18 38 Officers -and 606 Other Ranks.	
			Ration " 1/11/18 32 " " 490 " "	
			Effective Strength 30/11/18 40 " " 730 " "	
			Ration " 30/11/18. 27 " " 555 " "	
			Battle. Casualties:-	
			Officers — NIL —	
			Other Ranks. Killed 1. Wounded 1.	
			3/12/18. R. J. Brett. Lieut. Colonel Commdg 1st Roy. Berkshire Regt	

(A7092). Wt. W12839/M1293. 750,000. 1/17. D. D. & L., Ltd. Forms/C.2118/14.

CONFIDENTIAL

Instructions regarding War Diaries and Intelligence Summaries are contained in F. S. Regs., Part II. and the Staff Manual respectively. Title pages will be prepared in manuscript.

WAR DIARY
or
INTELLIGENCE SUMMARY.
(Erase heading not required.)

Army Form C. 2118.

1 R Berks R

1850

Place	Date	Hour	Summary of Events and Information	Remarks and references to Appendices
FOSSE.	1/12/18		Weather cold + fine. Church parade at 11.15 hours	
"	2/12/18		The Battalion bathed and cleaned up during the morning + in the afternoon lost to the 2nd MG Battalion at football. 1 to 4. Weather cold + fine.	
"	3/12/18		Weather dull. At 10.00 hours the Battalion went for a short route march via ARSIMONT – AISEMONT returning to Billets about 12.30 hours.	
FOSSE BEEZ	4/12/18		At 08.45 hours the Battalion left FOSSE and marched via SART ST LAURENT – BUZET – GROS BUISSON – LA PLANTE – NAMUR – to BEEZ arriving there at 14.45 hours. Weather wet. 1 other rank fell out on the march.	
BEEZ " ANDENNE.	5/12/18		At 09.50 hours the Battalion left BEEZ and marched via MARCHE-LES-DAMES — MANECHE — FORESSE — SCLAYN to ANDENNE arriving there at 13.15 hours. Weather fine.	
ANDENNE. VIERSET BARSE	6/12/18		At 08.57 hours the Battalion left ANDENNE and marched via BEN AHIN – HUY — HTE SARTE to VIERSET BARSE arriving there at 14.15 hours. Weather fine.	
VIERSET BARSE COMBLAIN LA TOUR	7/12/18		At 08.17 hours the Battalion left VIERSET BARSE and marched via STREE – SENY – OUFFET – COMBLAIN FAIRON. to COMBLAIN LA TOUR arriving there at 14.50 hours. There was a halt for one hour at OUFFET where the Battalion had tea.	

(A7092). Wt. W12839/M1293 750,000 1/17. D. D. & L., Ltd. Forms/C.2118/14.

CONFIDENTIAL

Instructions regarding War Diaries and Intelligence Summaries are contained in F. S. Regs., Part II. and the Staff Manual respectively. Title pages will be prepared in manuscript.

WAR DIARY
or
INTELLIGENCE SUMMARY.

(*Erase heading not required.*)

Army Form C. 2118.

Place	Date	Hour	Summary of Events and Information	Remarks and references to Appendices
COMBLAIN LA TOUR	8/12/18		The Battalion rested during the day.	
BASSE DESNIE	9/12/18		At 09.18 hours the Battalion left COMBLAIN LA TOUR and marched via AWAN - AYWAILLE - BELLEVAUX - to BASSE DESNIE arriving there at 15.40 hours. There was a halt for 50 minutes East of AYWAILLE where the Battalion had tea. Weather very wet.	
	10/12/18.		The Battalion rested during the day.	
BURNENVILLE	11/12/18		At 09.20 hours the Battalion left BASSE DESNIE and marched via SPA - FRANCORCHAMPS to BURNENVILLE arriving there at 14.15 hours. There was a halt for 30 minutes at MALCHAMPS. where the Battalion had tea. The frontier was crossed at 13.30 hours. Weather very wet. B.C. & D Companies were billetted in METZ.	
LAGER ELSENBORN	12/12/18		At 08.50 hours the Battalion left BURNENVILLE and marched via MALMEDY. - XHOFFRAIX - SOURBRODT to LAGER ELSENBORN arriving there at 15.20 hours. There was a halt for 30 minutes at LONGFAYE where the Battalion had tea. Weather very wet - rain falling almost continuously throughout the day.	

(A7092). Wt. W12839/M1293. 750,000. 1/17. D. D. & L., Ltd. Forms/C.2118/14.

CONFIDENTIAL

Instructions regarding War Diaries and Intelligence Summaries are contained in F. S. Regs., Part II. and the Staff Manual respectively. Title pages will be prepared in manuscript.

WAR DIARY
or
INTELLIGENCE SUMMARY.

(Erase heading not required.)

Army Form C. 2118.

Place	Date	Hour	Summary of Events and Information	Remarks and references to Appendices
LAGER ELSENBORN	13/12/18		At 09.00 hours the Battalion left LAGER ELSENBORN and marched via ELSENBORN – MONTJOIE to IMGENBROICH arriving there at 13.50 hours. Rain again fell continuously during the march.	
IMGENBROICH	14/12/18		At 08.00 hours the Battalion left IMGENBROICH and marched via SIMMERATH – SCHMIDT to NIDEGGEN arriving there at 13.40 hours. 5 other ranks fell out on the march owing to new Boots having to be issued. Weather dull & showery.	
NIDEGGEN	15/12/18		Sunday. Weather fine – there was a voluntary Church of England service at 11.00 hours.	
	16/12/18		The Battalion rested during the day.	
	17/12/18		The Battalion rested. Physical training 09.00 – 10.00 hours. Weather showery. Lt L E PARSONS rejoined Battalion.	
	18/12/18		Weather Dull & Stormy – Battalion resting & cleaning up.	
	19/12/18		At 7.15 hours the Battalion left NIDEGGEN and marched via DROVE – NIEDRAU and DUREN to ARNOLDSWEILER arriving at 11.35 hours. Weather threatening but only slight showers. Draft of 1 Officer. Lt. R FROST and 258 O.R. joined nearly all from the 3rd Battalion Oxf. and Bucks Lt Infantry	

(A7092). Wt. W12839/M1293. 750,000. 1/17. D. D. & L., Ltd. Forms/C.2118/14.

Confidential

Instructions regarding War Diaries and Intelligence Summaries are contained in F. S. Regs., Part II. and the Staff Manual respectively. Title pages will be prepared in manuscript.

WAR DIARY
or
INTELLIGENCE SUMMARY.

(Erase heading not required.)

Army Form C. 2118.

Place	Date	Hour	Summary of Events and Information	Remarks and references to Appendices
ARNOLDS WEILER.	20/12/18		Weather Showery. Battalion cleaning up equipment. New draft paraded for inspection by Commanding Officer + Medical Officer. General turn-out good! fitting of equipment showed lack of training. average service 6 months. Area reconnoitred for football grounds. Information received that Battalion will probably not move to final area until after Christmas.	
	21/12/18		Sgt Major's "B" Drill Parade. – on the whole good. Officers interviewed with a view to filling up AF Z15. Period for leave reduced to 3 months. Rain.	
	22nd.	–	Church Parade 1 officer + 30 OR per Company. 11.00 hours.	
	23rd		Coys at disposal of Company Commanders. Battalion marched to DUREN for Baths. On arrival at 2nd Army Reception Camp – baths were not in working order + no trace of Baths Officer or staff could be found.	
	24th.		Coys preparing for Christmas.	
	25th.		Christmas Day. Holy Communion 07.45. 08.15. + 11.30 hours Parade Service. (1 officer 40 OR's per Coy) at 11.00 hours. Dinners were a great success. + the men unanimously declared this to be their best Christmas overseas. Dull cold + showery. – a little snow.	

(A7092). Wt. W12839/M1293. 750,000. 1/17. D. D. & L., Ltd. Forms/C.2118/14.

CONFIDENTIAL

Instructions regarding War Diaries and Intelligence Summaries are contained in F. S. Regs., Part II. and the Staff Manual respectively. Title pages will be prepared in manuscript.

WAR DIARY
or
INTELLIGENCE SUMMARY.

(Erase heading not required.)

Army Form C. 2118.

Place	Date	Hour	Summary of Events and Information	Remarks and references to Appendices
ARNOLDSWEILER	26th		Fine and frosty. Coys at disposal of Coy Commanders. Orders received to dispatch 26 coalminers to England for demobilisation.	
	27th		Moved to STEENSTRATH and LICH. distance 8 miles arriving at 12.15 hours. Weather cold & frosty – rain later. 2nd Lieut Cassidy 1 long-service man. + 26 miners sent to England.	
	28th		Moved to NETTESHEIM area. Distance about 14 miles – arriving about 14.30 hours. A very wet day. 2nd Lt Letley MC. 1 long service man and 19 miners sent to England.	
	29th		Sunday. Voluntary service at 18.00 hours. 6 officers. + 62 OR's joined Bn from Divl. Wing.	
	30th		Major General Inspected C Coys billets. 1 officer + 50 OR. cleaning up roads. 4 OR's sent to COLOGNE	
	31st		Coys at disposal of Coy Commanders. 7 OR's sent to England under "Watford" allotment.	

R. J. Brett Lieut. Col.
Comdg 1/R. Berkshire Regt.
1/1/19.

(A7092). Wt. W12839/M1293. 750,000. 1/17. D. D. & L., Ltd. Forms/C.2118/14.

www.ingramcontent.com/pod-product-compliance
Lightning Source LLC
Chambersburg PA
CBHW080830010526
44112CB00015B/2484
* 9 7 8 1 4 7 4 5 0 3 8 4 6 *